TALES
Of
WONDER

WRITTEN AND COLLECTED
BY
MATTHEW GREGORY LEWIS

IN TWO VOLUMES

A NEW CRITICAL EDITION
EDITED & ANNOTATED
BY
BRETT RUTHERFORD

VOLUME II

YOGH &
THORN
BOOKS

PITTSBURGH, PENNSYLVANIA

Yogh & Thorn Edition March 2012
Rev 1.3
Second Printing May 2017

Originally Published in Two Volumes in 1801
Notes and Annotations Copyright 2012 by Brett Rutherford

Yogh & Thorn Books are published by
THE POET'S PRESS
2209 Murray Avenue #3/ Pittsburgh, PA 15217
www.poetspress.org

This is the 197th book from The Poet's Press

ISBN 0-922558-62-0 (paperback)
ISBN 0-922558-64-7 (hardcover)

CONTENTS

Introduction to Volume I   ix
Introduction to Volume II   xii
Annotations and Notes   xvii

TALES OF WONDER, VOL. II
XXXIII   Tam O'Shanter   *Robert Burns*   19
            Robert Burns Relates Three Supernatural
                Tales 33
XXXIV   The Witches' Song   *Ben Jonson*   36
XXXV   Admiral Hosier's Ghost   *Richard Glover*   41
            Admiral Hosier's Expedition
                Tobias Smollett   46
XXXVI   Margaret's Ghost   *David Mallet*   47
XXXVII   The Hermit   *Thomas Parnell*   50
XXXVIII   Edwin of the Green   *Thomas Parnell*   60
XXXIX   Theodore and Honoria   *John Dryden*   69
            Nastagio degli Onesti   *Giovanni Boccaccio*   83
XL   Dreams   *John Dryden (after Chaucer)*   87
XLI   History of Porsenna, King of Russia
                Thomas Lisle   93
XLII   The Fatal Sisters   *Thomas Gray*
                (Icelandic)   122
            Walter Scott on the Original Oral Tradition   126
            Supernatural Tidings from the Battle of
                Clontarf   *George Webb Dasent*   127
XLIII   The Descent of Odin   *Thomas Gray*
                (Icelandic)   132
XLIV   The Witch of Wokey   *Henry Harrington*   138
XLV   The Marriage of Sir Gawaine
                Thomas Percy   142
XLVI   King Arthur's Death   *Thomas Percy, ed.*   154
XLVII   Fair Margaret and Sweet William
                Thomas Percy, ed.   163
XLVIII   Sweet William's Ghost   *Thomas Percy, ed.*   166
XLIX   The Boy and the Mantle   *M.G. Lewis, ed.*   169
            The Boy and the Mantle   *Thomas Percy, ed.*   177

L   Saint Patrick's Purgatory   *Robert Southey*   184
Saint Patrick's Purgatory (Revised)
    Robert Southey   192
A.D. 1153 — Saint Patrick's Purgatory
    Roger of Wendower   199
The Destruction of St. Patrick's Purgatory   210
LI   The Cinder King   *Anon.*   217
LII   The Bleeding Nun   *Anon.*   219
LIII   The Maid of the Moor, or, The Water Fiends
    George Colman, Jr.   224
LIV   The Laidley Worm of Spindlestone Heughs
    Robert Lambe   230
LV   Mary's Dream   *John Lowe*   238
LVI   Clerk Colvin   *Scottish Ballad*   240
LVII   Willy's Lady   *M.G. Lewis,*
    from a Scottish Ballad   244
LVIII   Courteous King Jamie
    M.G. Lewis, from a Scottish Ballad   248
LVIX   Tam Lin   *M.G. Lewis,*
    from a Scottish Ballad   252
Tam Lin   *Robert Burns, ed.*
    (Scottish Ballad)   261
LX   Lenora   *William Taylor of Norwich,*
    after Gottfried August Bürger   268

BIBLIOGRAPHY   282
ABOUT THIS BOOK   293

INTRODUCTION
TO VOLUME 1

Tales of Wonder is a landmark work in the history of Gothic literature, and a milestone in Romantic poetry. Percy Shelley owned the book as a young man, and drew ghosts and monsters in its margins; indeed, a cluster of Shelley's juvenile poems are imitations of the supernatural ballads collected here. Sir Walter Scott allowed himself to be tutored by its author and compiler, and both Scott and Robert Southey provided Gothic poems and ballads for the collection, originally to be titled *Tales of Terror*.

When the promised anthology failed to appear in due course, Scott pulled together the poems he had in hand and privately printed a sampler, titled *An Apology for Tales of Terror*. Only five copies of this 1799 book survive, and its mere existence has led some to believe, erroneously, that the *Apology* is the first edition of the present work.

Tales of Wonder was published in 1801 in two volumes in London, printed by W. Bulmer and Co., and sold by J. Bell. A second edition was issued later that year, in one volume, with Robert Southey's poems removed.[1] The single-volume second edition was the bookseller's response to complaints about the price of the two-volume set, and the inclusion, in the second volume, of many poems readily available to readers. The first Dublin printing in 1801 was the one-volume version. The two-volume version did not lack for buyers, however: an 1805 printing in Dublin, "printed for P. Wogan," is based on the two-volume original, and includes Southey's poems once again.[2]

Another book, confusingly titled *Tales of Terror*, appeared later in 1801, and as the bookseller suggested it as a suitable companion for Lewis's *Tales of Wonder*, it was mistakenly assumed by many to be Lewis's own work. The authorship of the spurious *Tales of Terror* has never been determined. The anthology contains a number of inflated parodies of supernatural ballads, alongside some that seem to be in the Lewis vein. Aside from an interesting verse Apologia for the Gothic that reflects contemporaneous debates about horror and The Sublime, it is otherwise a sophomoric production, perhaps intended to ridicule Lewis. Lewis seems to have ignored it, or to have quietly enjoyed the further notoriety it produced. It cost someone a good deal of money to produce, so it is

---

[1] "There is a sort of Imbroglio about Southey's ballads, which must be settled," Lewis wrote to Walter Scott (Peck 119).

[2] Louis Peck notes an 1817 edition in London with 32 poems, an 1836 edition with only 23, and a 1925 "catchpenny" edition with only eight poems (133).

not beyond the realm of possibility that Lewis himself participated in some way.

More than two decades ago, I came into possession of a dog-eared copy of Henry Morley's 1887 compilation, titled *Tales of Terror and Wonder*. Morley cobbled together the Lewis original with the spurious *Tales of Terror*, and, where pages were missing from his copies of the two books, he simply omitted those poems. Morley's introductory essay has so many rabbit holes of error that it is best not to read it, nor to torment others by citing it.

My original intent, when embarking on this project, was simply to find Lewis's first edition and to make it available once again.

At first glance, many of these poems seem to be works of pure imagination. Many occupy a Gothic realm of knights, libidinous monks, devils and witches, ravished damsels and haunted woods. Once I had determined to annotate the poems, however — intending to limit myself to defining arcane words for today's students or general readers — I discovered that many of these poems have a deep history, rooted not only in their literary sources but also in specific times and places. My intertextual detective work has sought out alternate tellings of the narrative in these poems, in some cases finding the actual source, one dating back to 300 BCE.

The research into these poems also introduced me to the work of several generations of scholars who collected Runic poetry and English and Scottish ballads. These eccentrics — some clerics and some gentlemen with the income and inclination to explore monastery libraries or transcribe Runic stone carvings — were at work in a serious intellectual project: to ground Britain in an alternate pre-history that was neither Biblical nor Greco-Roman. This pagan yearning for Icelandic and Danish and Saxon literary and historical roots, is celebrated in some of the poems in this book. Although there are no dour Druids here, the lore of Wotan/Odin and the sombre epics of the North figure large.

The annotations in this new edition document the origins of the poems Lewis translated or selected. In some cases, I have inserted alternate translations or originals; in others I am content to point interested readers to the sources. The great mother lode of English and Scottish ballads can be found in Bishop Percy's *Reliques of Ancient English Poetry*, LeGrand's *Fabliaux*, and Evans' *A Collection of Old Ballads*. Child's *English and Scottish Popular Ballads*, although published later in the century (starting in 1868), is also cited frequently in the notes, since the Child ballad collection is comprehensive and the numbering of the ballads therein has become a standard cataloging reference.

It should not be forgotten that the literary ballad, where it is not a complete invention, is fossil evidence of a work intended to be sung, and accompanied by some kind of instrument. Some supernatural ballads were also transmitted in broadsheets and printed collections, often with musical notation. Ballad-singing was a tea-time entertainment, and sophisticated settings of such ballads by Haydn and Beethoven kept the text of the ballad in the public eye as song lyrics. The leap from folk-lyric to literary ballad set a higher standard for the ballad-as-text, and Lewis and his peers made it their business to add metric regularity and poetic diction into the sometimes rougher-hewn originals. Sometimes the texts are Anglicised or modernized; other times a new-fangled poem is cast in archaic language, either for atmosphere or as an outright literary hoax.

These editors, who collected ballads from oral transmission, also stood on the shoulders of monks and chroniclers who passed along, in Latin, wonderful tall tales such as "The Old Woman of Berkeley." One approaches these ballad compilations with awe and caution commingled: some of the poets in this collection were involved in the creation of mock ballads that passed back into the literature.

Now that this first of two volumes is in hand, it is possible to step back and look at the remarkable range of work Lewis has assembled, skewed as the first volume is with the compiler's eagerness to put his own work forward. Here we are treated to a ghost/vampire tale first penned around 300 BCE; a Runic funeral song from the tenth century CE; a meeting between the Saxon invader of England and a Roman ghost; a Nordic warrior woman's incantation to raise her father from the dead; Goethe's blood-curdling multi-voiced "Erl-King" and fatal water nymphs; the monk and nun who try (unsuccessfully) to save their witch mother from the Devil; a proud painter's encounters with Satan; a doomed romance set in the horrific landscape of the War of the Spanish Succession; and the endless forest ride of "The Wild Huntsmen." (In the second volume, the reader will encounter work by Burns, Dryden, Jonson, Gray, and Bürger, as well as items from the Percy and Evans collections of old ballads.)

One caveat for the reader weaned on modern poetry is that even the "Romantic" poets featured here employ forms, meters and language from an era earlier than their own, even sometimes to the extent of perpetrating a literary hoax à la Ossian. The Gothic esthetic by its nature is backward-looking. It takes some adjustment for today's reader to enjoy these poems for what they are, and read them in the context of their own time. Against the stifling moral and correct tone of most 18th century verse, this is pretty strong stuff, a bracing counter-esthetic.

We need also remember that Lewis — whose Gothic plays shocked and appalled London audiences, and whose lurid novel, *The Monk*, mixed sex and demon possession — invested much in this book. Far more than just self-promotion of his own Gothic verses, the range of material selected demonstrates the unbroken interest in the weird and wonderful stretching back to antiquity.

A certain degree of macabre relish, what I call "the smile behind the skull," is also evident throughout. The poems here are unlikely to frighten anyone other than the superstitious, or very small children; instead, they delight those of a Gothic predilection who enjoy the sublime frisson of danger and supernatural awe. The tone of this book sets the mode for erudition, arcane allusion, atmosphere and devastation — with a dose of *Grand Guignol* humor for the initiate — that we will see later in Edgar Allan Poe and H.P. Lovecraft. Lovecraft would have recognized Lewis and the antiquarian eccentrics whose work anticipates Gothic poetry, as brothers.

I would like to acknowledge Lance Arney, who many years ago undertook the task of typing the 1887 *Tales of Terror and Wonder* into a computer. He raised the question of whether some of the poems in that edition were so absurd as to be parodies, and, as it turned out, he was correct.

In one of those delightful (or dismaying) coincidences of publishing, my first edition of Volume I of *Tales of Wonder* was published in October 2010, and Broadview Editions issued its own *Tales of Wonder*, edited by Douglass H. Thomson, the same month. I had not been familiar with any of Dr. Thomson's remarkable work except his research, published online, into the Walter Scott *Apology for Tales of Terror*, to which I had referred readers. Thomson's masterful introduction and notes go into great depth about the place of Lewis's work in the development of Gothic romanticism, and he devotes many pages to the problem of parody in the supernatural poems Lewis wrote and chose. Although he limits himself to Volume I and selections from Volume II, and a few selections from the spurious *Tales of Terror*, Thomson's edition is indispensable for scholars.

My somewhat different focus requires the republication and annotation of both volumes, as Lewis presented them in 1801, illuminated by a study of the textual and narrative sources of the poems, and such information about the poets as will shed light on the interpretation of the text. I am also undaunted by the "tales of plunder" accusation against Lewis for using already-familiar poems and ballads, since most of the texts presented here will be new to today's reader. My aim in this two-volume edition is to serve the educated general reader (whose existence I still believe in) as well as the scholar. Happily, since this project is published in print and in ebook format with today's "on demand" technology, I can continue to revise *Tales of Wonder* as new information comes to hand.

I hope that this new edition of the real *Tales of Wonder* will help restore Matthew Gregory Lewis to his rightful place in the history of Gothic literature and of Romanticism. Although biographers of Mary Shelley have made note of "Monk" Lewis's visit to the Villa Deodati in 1816, and the sharing of ghost stories among Lewis, Lord Byron, Dr. Polidori, and Percy and Mary Shelley, none seem to have realized who among them had the most to say about the writing of a ghost story.

I am delighted that *Tales of Wonder* is finally coming into its own.

—Brett Rutherford
University of Rhode Island
October 10, 2010/ February 4, 2012

INTRODUCTION
TO VOLUME II

Although Volume II of *Tales of Wonder* has little original writing by Matthew Gregory Lewis, it nonetheless completes his project of assembling poems in a Norse-Germanic-English thread, all containing some element of the supernatural. Lewis's change of heart about the anthology's title, from the intended *Tales of Terror*, to *Tales of Wonder*, is made clear by the inclusion of long poems like Parnell's "The Hermit," Southey's "Saint Patrick's Purgatory," and Lisle's "Porsenna, King of Russia," where the marvelous elements are subordinated to other ends. Lewis had written to Scott in 1798 with a somewhat more restricted agenda: "The plan I had proposed to myself is to collect all the *marvellous* ballads which I can lay hands upon. Ancient as well as modern will be comprised in my design . . . [A] ghost or a witch is a *sine qua non* ingredient in all the dishes of which I mean to compose my hobgoblin repast."

Lewis was pilloried for including poems in his second volume that were already familiar to readers, so much so that the collection was nicknamed "Tales of Plunder." This criticism falls short for modern readers, few of whom will have seen any but the real warhorses in this volume, such as Burns "Tam O' Shanter" and Bürger's "Lenore." I have chosen to edit and annotate all 60 poems that were in Lewis's 1801 first edition, and to treat them to the same degree of exploration of sources and points of interest about the poets and translators.

The reader seeking more Gothic thrills in the Lewis mode will not be disappointed, as this volume is full of hair-raising chase scenes with witches, demons and ghosts, fairy abductions, ghostly brides and bridegrooms, Valkyries and prophetesses, a dragon, the Lady of the Lake, and the description of the torments of Purgatory that influenced Dante as he commenced his *Divine Comedy*.

The poets and translators featured in this volume range from the stellar to the unknown, the stars including Robert Burns, Thomas Gray, John Dryden, Robert Southey, Ben Jonson, Thomas Parnell, Bishop Thomas Percy, and William Taylor of Norwich. The sources range from the Icelandic Eddas to Scottish ballads, Latin chronicles, Chaucer and Boccaccio.

The mix of serious poems with others that subvert the genre of the Gothic and even hold the genre to scorn continues in this volume. As in Volume I, Lewis shows a willingness to publish mock-ballads, the most extreme being Colman's "The Maid of the Moor," rather clearly intended to ridicule Lewis's own Gothic productions. After living with these texts and their sources for so long — and having spent a lifetime as a producer of my own Gothic poetry — I am not really that baffled by Lewis's willingness to entertain mockery, or even to participate in its creation. I would not be surprised, either, if Lewis, or a circle of his immediate friends, produced the nearly parodic *Tales of Terror* volume. Bunbury, one of the poets in Volume I of *Tales of Wonder*, illustrated *Tales of Terror*, and both books have the same publisher.

First, it seems apparent that the interest in the supernatural among most of these writers is historical and antiquarian. They are not occult practitioners nor are they, for the most part, presenting the supernatural in order to come around, via a final moral, to preach conventional mythology (religion). Even when poets such as Southey and Lewis do so, the moral seems tongue-in-cheek, or a preventive against the censor. My point is that almost none of these poems are presented as though the poets believed in the supernatural, and only the extremely superstitious would be frightened by reading them. Horror, to its practitioners and its smarter audience, has always been the literary equivalent of a fine chocolate truffle.

The other reason I see Lewis as amenable to parody, and even able to participate in self-parody, is by placing him in context as a gay writer. Lewis was overtly homosexual, yet socially situated and well-behaved enough to avoid being arrested or prosecuted. His writing occupies a special discourse, that would ultimately be identified with the word "camp." Although "camp" is implicitly connected to gay writing and pop culture in the 20th century, I see no reason why the concept cannot be applied to cultural productions of Lewis's time. "Camp" encompasses an ironic manner and self-mockery. It also relies on "over the top" exaggeration, something Lewis shows himself, again and again, willing and able to indulge in, adding lurid details to the already-gruesome fare he dishes out.

Lewis's apparent misogyny, which becomes even more evident in this volume, takes on a different cast if the poet is seen as a gay man entering into the psyches of the threatened females in these poems as alter egos: subjects, not objects. If the damsel-as-dragon who must be kissed in "The Laidley Worm" is the poet in drag (so to speak), we begin to see these Gothic productions as subversive theatrics. Lewis's put-upon damsels are self-projections. He does not so much make women suffer, as he makes himself suffer as he imagines women do. His dramatic sense is true as well: a man threatened by a monster is not nearly so *interesting* as a woman so threatened; she has more to lose.

Lewis's outsider persona is inseparable from his own writing, and, I would hazard to say, even from his work as editor of *Tales of Wonder*. Lockhart, Scott's biographer, describes Lewis as a "good-natured fopling, the pet and plaything of certain fashionable circles."[3] Scott wrote some notes to an edition of Byron's diary that give a first-person impression:

> [H]ow few friends one has whose faults are only ridiculous. ...He did much good by stealth, and was a most generous creature . . . Lewis was fonder of great people than he ought to have been, either as a man of talent or as a man of fashion. You would have sworn he had been a *parvenu* of yesterday, yet he lived all his life in good society. . . . Mat had queerish eyes — they projected like those of some insects, and were flattish on the orbit. His person was extremely small and boyish — he was indeed the least man I ever saw, to be strictly well and neatly made. I remember a picture of him by Saunders being handed round at Dalkeith House. The artist had ingeniously flung a dark folding-mantle around the form, under which was half-hid a dagger, a dark lantern, or some such cut-throat appurtenance; with all this the features were pre-served and ennobled. It passed from hand to hand into that of Henry, Duke of Buccleuch, who, hearing the general office affirm that it was very like, said aloud, "Like Mat Lewis! Why that pic-ture's like a MAN!" He looked, and, lo! Mat Lewis's head was at his elbow. This boyishness went through life with him. He was a child, and a spoiled child, but a child of high imagination; and so he wasted himself on ghost-stories and German romances. He had the finest ear for rhythm I ever met with — finer than Byron's."[4]

Other Lewis biographies have noted that Lewis was well-received in certain social circles, and intensely disliked in others. Lord Byron swore never to go to Lewis's house for dinner again after finding the "Monk" entertaining a room full of handsome ensigns, and not a lady in sight. Since Lewis's sexual orientation was unprintable, the reader was left from scant anecdotes to believe that Lewis was disapproved of for his manners at table, and for conversational gaffs. Until John Berryman "outed" Lewis in his 1953 introduction to *The Monk*, scholars had shied away from this aspect of Lewis's life and character.

From the description above, one can picture Lewis as the Truman Capote of his time: the harmless gay writer invited to parties for his droll stories, but as likely to offend as to please. As a creature of the theater, staging his Gothic plays, Lewis was also enmeshed in theater gossip and the politics of competing actresses seeking to be immolated

---

[3] Lockhart, 7.
[4] Lockhart, 10-11.

in his next play, and he heaped lavish praise on his "male favorites" among the actors.

Lewis's role as a social outsider shows itself not only in his choice of genre, the Gothic, but also in his taste as an editor. He did not hesitate to choose poems by out-of-favor poets, such as David Mallet, a notorious atheist, or to include the long and curious poem, "Porsenna, King of Russia," a mythological melange full of thinly-disguised same-sex affections written by a poet who fled England for decades after a scandal involving "blasphemy and other vile practices." So far as I can tell, no one has ever explored this once-popular poem and connected it to the facts of its author's life. It turns out to have a lot to do with Lisle's long exile from England after a sex scandal.

Let us return, however, to Lewis's main intent, and ours, in sharing and annotating this book: the "goblin repast" of 28 poems contained herein. It is fitting that Volume II is book-ended with two of the most famous supernatural poems in the literature: Robert Burns' "Tam O'Shanter" and William Taylor's adaptation of Bürger's "Lenore." Both are set on horseback, and indeed the whole book is replete with flying horses, and demonic chases, evidence that everyone from the god Odin to the Devil kept a stable. There are fewer graveyards than one might expect here, but grottoes, caves and forests abound.

Damsels are threatened, pursued, captured, turned to dragons, murdered, or return as ghosts or as "the Bleeding Nun." We are shipwrecked in Panama, torn to bits by demon hounds in an Italian forest, and then seized by Father Time after a 300-year-long love feast in the Land of Felicity. Then, after some meetings with Norse gods, Scottish ghosts, "lothly ladies" and a dragon, we are plunged into Purgatory from a cave in Northern Island.

In the poem, "Saint Patrick's Purgatory," we brush against a real horror, as we learn that the fantasies of Purgatory that later inspired Dante were the result of penitents' confinement in a pitch-dark cave after a week of fasting, an abuse almost certain to produce hallucinations if not death by fright. Once I came to know it was a real place, I felt compelled to research its history and to relate, via historical documents, the story of the "cave" that induced this nightmare thread in literature.

By holding Bürger's "Lenore" for last, in William Taylor of Norwich's English adaptation as "Lenora," Lewis caps *Tales of Wonder* with the work that joined English and German Romanticism, all the more fitting since the German poem itself comes from an English source, the ballad "Sweet William's Ghost."

Bringing this work to a conclusion is a happy occasion, but only a milestone. Lewis reached just the cusp of the 19th century with his anthology, so I have in prepared a sequel in two volumes, *Tales of Terror: The Supernatural Poem Since 1800*. Although there have been, and will be, other anthologies of supernatural poetry, I hope to add to the heap with some lesser-known gems of British and American poetry in the genre, as well as the warhorses — commencing with Coleridge, Shelley, Byron, and Poe — that one would expect to find in such a collection.

—Brett Rutherford
University of Rhode Island
February 21, 2012/
Pittsburgh, PA
May 17, 2017

ANNOTATIONS AND NOTES

All of the unattributed annotations in this book are my own. The original footnotes by Lewis are marked as "—MGL," and I have availed myself of Sir Walter Scott's 1833 annotations to his own poetry, marking those "—WS." Some notes by Thomas Gray or his posthumous editor (—TG) are interspersed in "The Fatal Sisters" and "The Descent of Odin." In several of the poems in Volume II, I use the poet's initials to indicate that certain footnotes were provided by the poet, not Lewis or myself.

Reattribution of authorship of certain poems is indicated in square brackets; likewise, insertions of missing or surpressed lines.

In "Tam O'Shanter," I started with Robert Burns' own explanatory notes and expanded upon them, mostly adding more explanations of Scottish words and place-names culled from other editions of Burns (and online). With Burns, I have only initialed footnotes containing additional research or speculation.

Elsewhere, I have added my initials to annotations only on those occasions where mine are interspersed with those of others, or where I wanted to make clear that a certain note was *not* by Lewis or one of the poets. I welcome correspondence from readers and scholars, and would be pleased to correct or elaborate on any of the notes should new information come to light. As the great Cuvier said: "An error corrected is new knowledge."

The items identified in the Table of Contents with Roman numerals correspond to the items originally published in Volume II of the 1801 London edition of *Tales of Wonder*. The indented items in the Table of Contents comprise the source documents, alternate texts and additional notes. None of these source materials were in Lewis's 1801 edition, nor in any subsequent edition.

Both volumes in this series contain the same Bibliography.

Tam O'Shanter

ROBERT BURNS

[A Tale.

> "Of Brownyis and of Bogillis full is this Buke."
> — Gawin Douglas][a]

When chapman billies[1] leave the street,
And drouthy[2] neebors,[3] neebors meet,
As market-days are wearing late,
An'[4] folk begin to tak the gate;[5]
While we sit bousing[6] at the nappy,
An' getting fou[7] and unco[8] happy,
We think na[9] on the lang Scots miles,[10]
The mosses, waters, slaps, and styles,[11]
That lie between us and our hame,[12]
Whare[13] sits our sulky sullen dame,
Gathering her brows like gathering storm,
Nursing her wrath to keep it warm.

[a] The subtitle "A Tale" and the Epigraph appear in Burns' Collected Poems, but did not appear in the Lewis volume.
1. *Chapman billies*. Peddler boys.
2. *Drouthy*. Thirsty.
3. *Neebors*. Neighbours.
4. *An'*. And.
5. *Tak the gate*. Return home.
6. *Bousing*. Drinking.
7. *Fou*. Drunk.
8. *Unco*. Very.
9. *Na*. Not.
10. *Lang Scots miles*. Long Scots miles. Scotland had its own mile, based on the distance from the castle to Holyrood Abbey in Edinburgh. Scotland did not adopt English miles until 1824.
11. *Mosses, waters, slaps and styles*. Bogs, waters, pools, and styles. Styles are openings or breaches in fences or stone walls.
12. *Hame*. Home.
13. *Whar*. Where.

<19>

This truth fand[14] honest Tam O'Shanter,
As he frae'[15] Ayr ae[16] night did canter,
(Auld[17] Ayr wham[18] ne'er a town surpasses,
For honest men and bonny[19] lasses.

O Tam! had'st thou but been sae[20] wise,
As ta'en thy ain[21] wife Kate's advice!
She tauld[22] thee weel?[23] thou was a skellum,[24]
A blethering,[25] blustering, drunken blellum;[26]
That frae November till October,
Ae market-day thou was nae[27] sober;
That ilka melder,[28] wi' the miller,
Thou sat as lang as thou had siller;[29]
That every naig was ca'd a shoe on,[30]
The smith and thee gat roaring fou on;
That at the L——d's house,[31] even on Sunday,
Thou drank wi' Kirkton Jean till Monday.
She prophesy'd that, late or soon,
Thou would be found deep drown'd in Doon;[32]
Or catch'd wi' warlocks in the mirk,[33]
By Alloway's auld haunted kirk.'[34]

---

14. *Fand.* Found.
15. *Frae.* From.
16. *Ae.* One.
17. *Auld.* Old.
18. *Wham.* Whom.
19. *Bonny, or bonnie.* Handsome.
20. *Sae.* So.
21. *Ain.* Own.
22. *Tauld.* Told.
23. *Weel.* Well.
24. *Skellum.* A rogue.
25. *Blethering.* Talking idly, chattering.
26. *Blellum.* A babbler.
27. *Nae.* Never.
28. *Ilka melder.* Each installment of grain, i.e., Tam gets drunk while waiting for the miller to grind his grain into flour.
29. *Siller.* Money, from silver.
30. *That every naig was ca'd a shoe on.* Every time a horse had a shoe nailed on.
31. *L——d's house.* Lord's House. An act of self-censorship on the part of Lewis's printer. Burns spells it out in his text. Printers in England were wary of blasphemy charges —BR.

<20>

Ah, gentle dames! it gars me greet[35]
To think how mony[36] counsels sweet,
How mony lengthen'd sage advices,
The husband frae the wife despises!

But to our tale: Ae market night,
Tam had got planted unco right;
Fast by an ingle,[37] bleezing[38] finely,
Wi' reaming swats,[39] that drank divinely;
And at his elbow, Souter[40] Johnny,
His ancient, trusty, drouthy crony;[41]
Tarn lo'ed him like a vera brither;[42]
They had been fou for weeks thegither.[43]
The night drave[44] on wi' sangs and clatter;[45]
And ay the ale was growing better:
The landlady and Tam grew gracious,
Wi' favours, secret, sweet, and precious:
The souter tauld his queerest stories;
The landlord's laugh was ready chorus:
The storm without might rair'[46] and rustle,
Tam did na mind the storm a whistle.

---

32. *Doon*. The River Doon.
33. *Mirk*. Dark.
34. *Alloway Kirk*. The roofless church of Alloway, two miles south of the town of Ayr, abandoned in 1756.
35. *Gars me greet*. Makes me weep.
36. *Mony*. Many.
37. *Ingle*. Fire.
38. *Bleezing*. Burning.
39. *Reaming swats*. Foaming ale.
40. *Souter*. A shoemaker.
41. *Crony, or cronie*. An old acquaintance.
42. *Vera brither*. Very brother.
43. *Thegither*. Together.
44. *Drave*. Passed.
45. *Sangs and clatter*. Songs and discourse.
46. *Rair*. Roar.

<21>

Care, mad to see a man sae happy,
E'en drown'd himself amang the nappy,[47]
As bees flee hame wi' lades[48] o' treasure,
The minutes wing'd their way wi' pleasure:
Kings may be bless'd, but Tam was glorious,
O'er a'[49] the hills o' life victorious!

But pleasures are like poppies spread,
You seize the flower, its bloom is shed;
Or like the snow falls in the river,
A moment white — then melts for ever;
Or like the borealis race,
That flit ere you can point their place;
Or like the rainbow's lovely form,
Evanishing amid the storm. —

Nae man can tether[50] time or tide;
The hour approaches Tam maun[51] ride;
That hour, o' night's black arch the key-stane,
That dreary hour he mounts his beast in;
And sic[52] a night he tacks[53] the road in,
As ne'er poor sinner was abroad in.

    The wind blew as 'twad blawn[54] its last;
The rattling showers rose on the blast;
The speedy gleams the darkness swallow'd;
Loud, deep, and lang, the thunder bellow'd:
That night a child might understand,
The deil[55] had business on his hand.

---

47. *Amang the nappy*. Among the ales.
48. *Lades*. Loads.
49. *A'*. All.
50. *Tether*. Tie.
51. *Maun*, Must.
52. *Sic*. Such.
53. *Tacks*. Takes.
54. *As 'twad blawn*. As if it would have blown.
55. *Deil*. The Devil.

<22>

Weel[56] mounted on his grey mare, Meg,
A better never lifted leg,
Tam skelpit[57] on through dub and mire,[58]
Despising wind, and rain, and fire;
Whiles[59] holding fast his gude[60] blue bonnet;
Whiles crooning[61] o'er some auld Scots sonnet;
Whiles glow'ring'[62] round wi' prudent cares,
Lest bogles[63] catch him unawares:
Kirk-Alloway was drawing nigh,
Whare ghaists and houlets[64] nightly cry. —

---

56. *Weel*. Well.
57. *Skelpit*. Galloped.
58. *Dub and mire*. Pools of water, and mud.
59. *Whiles*. Sometimes.
60. *Gude*. Good.
61. *Crooning*. Humming or singing.
62. *Glow'ring*. Staring.
63. *Bogles*. Bad spirits.
64. *Ghaists and houlets*. Ghosts and owlettes.

<23>

By this time he was cross the ford,[65]
Whare in the snaw[66] the chapman smoor'd;[67]
And past the birks[68] and meikle staine,[69]
Whare drunken Charlie brak's neck-bane;[70]
And thro' the whins,[71] and by the cairn,[72]
Whare hunters fand[73] the murder'd bairn;[74]
And near the thorn, aboon[75] the well,
Where Mungo's mither[76] hang'd hersel. —

Before him Doon pours all his floods;
The doubling storm roars thro' the woods;
The lightnings flash from pole to pole;
Near and more near the thunders roll:
When, glimmering thro' the groaning trees,
Kirk-Alloway seem'd in a bleeze;[77]
Thro' ilka bore[78] the beams were glancing;
And loud resounded mirth and dancing. —

---

65. Tam crosses a stream called the Slaphouse Burn. Since this stream had bridges and no known local ford, this detail is considered to be imaginative.
66. *Snaw*. Snow.
67. *The chapman smoor'd*. The peddler smothered.
68. *Birks*. Birch trees.
69. *Meikle stane*. A large stone.
70. *Brak's neck-bane*. Broke his neck-bone.
71. *Whins*. Gorse plants.
72. *Cairn*. A heap of stones, often a prehistoric burial site. The cairn still stands, on the Campusdoon estate in Ayr.
73. *Fand*. Found.
74. *Bairn*. A child.
75. *Aboon*. Above.
76. *Mungo's Mither*. Mungo's Mother. St. Mungo's Well, located just west of Alloway Church. The suicide is imaginary, as St. Mungo is associated with Glasgow. The Alloway Church had been dedicated to St. Mungo, since Glasgow Cathedral had owned the land. Mungo here might simply refer to a person born in Glasgow, St. Mungo's See. Doubtless the idea of a saint's mother being a suicide verges on the blasphemous. St. Mungo's mother was herself canonized as St. Thanew (Harvey 64) —BR.
77. *Bleeze*. Blaze.
78. *Ilka bore*. Every crevice.

<24>

Inspiring bold John Barleycorn![79]
What dangers thou canst make us scorn!
Wi' tippeny,[80] we fear nae evil;
Wi' usquebae[81] we'll face the devil! —

The swats[82] sea ream'd in Tammie's noddle,[83]
Fair play, he car'd na[84] deils a boddle;[85]
But Maggie stood right sair[86] astonish'd,
Till, by the heel and hand admonish'd,
She ventured forward on the light;
And, vow! Tam saw an unco[87] sight!
Warlocks and witches in a dance;
Nae cotillion brent new frae France,[88]
But hornpipes, jigs, strathspeys,[89] and reels,
Put life and mettle in their heels.
A winnock-bunker[90] in the east,
There sat auld Nick,[91] in shape o' beast;
A towzie-tyke,[92] black, grim, and large,
To gie[93] them music was his charge:

---

79. *John Barleycorn*. The personification of the spirit of ale.
80. *Tippeny*. A weak ale, sold for two pennies a pint.
81. *Usquabae*. Whisky.
82. *Swats*. Fumes.
83. *Noddle*. Head.
84. *Car'd na*. Minded not.
85. *Bodle*. A farthing, a coin worth one quarter of a penny.
86. *Sair*. Sore, seriously.
87. *Unco*. Strange.
88. *Cotillion brent new frae France*. Cotillion brought new from France. The French cotillion, a variety of contredanse, became popular in England in the 1700s. Placing dancers in square formation, it encouraged flirtation, and is the ancestor of the American rural square dance —BR.
89. *Strathspey*. A slow and stately Scottish dance in 4/4 time, slower than a jig or reel. The melody for a strathspey often contains many "snaps," short notes followed by dotted notes. Strathspeys were composed and arranged both for fiddles and for bagpipes —BR.
90. *Winnock-bunker*. Window seat.
91. *Auld Nick*. Old Nick, the Devil.
92. *Towzie-tyke*. A shaggy dog. Mephistopheles first appears in Goethe's *Faust* in the form of a black dog — BR.
93. *To gie*. Give.

<25>

He screw'd the pipes and gart[94] them skirl,[95]
Till roof and rafters a'[96] did dirl.[97] —
Coffins stood round, like open presses,[98]
That shaw'd[99] the dead in their last dresses;
And by some devilish cantrip[100] slight,
Each in its cauld[101] hand held a light. —

By which heroic Tam was able
To note upon the haly table,[102]
A murderer's banes'[103] in gibbet airns;[104]
Twa span-lang,[105] wee,[106] unchristen'd bairns;
A thief, new-cutted frae a rape,[107]
Wi' his last gasp his gab'[108] did gape;
Five tomahawks, wi blude[109] red-rusted,
Five scymitars',[110] wi' murder crusted;

---

94. *Gart*. Made.
95. *Skirl*. Squeal.
96. *A'*. All.
97. *Dirl*. Rattle, shake.
98. *Presses*. Linen closets or wardrobes.
99. *Shaw'd*. Showed.
100. *Cantrip*. A charm or spell.
101. *Cauld*. Cold.
102. *Haly table*. Holy table, the church altar.
103. *Banes*. Bones.
104. *Airns*. Irons.
105. *Twa span-long*. Two spans in length. A span is the width of the hand from the end of the thumb to the end of the little finger, with the fingers fully-extended. The span was used in the absence of measuring tapes or rulers as a rude unit of measure —BR.
106. *Wee*. Little.
107. *New-cutted frea a rape*. New cut from a rope.
108. *Gab*. Mouth.
109. *Blude*. Blood.
110. *Tomahawks . . . scymitars*. Massive emigration from Scotland began around 1725 and accelerated after English repression of Scots culture after the Battle of Culloden in 1745. Tens of thousands, dispossessed by land "clearances" that resembled "ethnic cleansing," fled to America. Scots were also prominent in the British armed forces, placing them in the campaigns such as the Seven Years' War (French and Indian War in America), and Scots figured prominently on both sides of the American Revolution. Revolutionary soldiers in America received tomahawks as part of their kit. Burns here reminds his reader that Scots were dying in faraway places, killed by Indians, Colonials, or Turks, and that their ghosts would nonetheless return to Scotland —BR.

<26>

A garter, which a babe had strangled,
A knife, a father's throat had mangled,
Whom his ain[111] son o' life bereft,
The grey hairs yet stack[112] to the heft;[113]
   [Three lawyers' tongues, turn'd inside out,
   W' lies seam'd like a beggar's clout;[114]
   Three priests' hearts, rotten black as much,[115]
   Lay stinking, vile in every neuk.[116]][117]
Wi' mair[118] o' horrible and awefu',
Which ev'n to name wad be unlawfu'.[119]

As Tammie glowr'd, amaz'd, and curious,
The mirth and fun grew fast and furious:
The piper loud and louder blew;
The dancers quick and quicker flew;
They reel'd, they set, they cross'd, they cleekit,[120]
Till ilka carlin[121] swat[122] and reekit,[123]
And coost her duddies[124] to the wark,[125]
And linket[126] at it in her sark![127]

---

111. *Ain.* own.
112. *Stack.* Stuck.
113. *Heft.* Haft, handle.
114. *Clout.* A patch in a cloth.
115. *Much.* Muck. Excrement, manure or other rotting organic matter. "Much" appears to be an idiosyncratic Burns spelling, as this does not appear in *OED* —BR.
116 *Neuk.* Nook, small corner or recess.
117. *Three lawyers . . . / . . . every neuk.* Burns suppressed these four lines at the behest of a jurist friend and replaced them with the two lines following. They did not appear in Lewis's edition, or in Grose's *Antiquities of Scotland* —BR.
118. *Mair.* More.
119. *Unlawfu'.* Unlawful. A nod to the censorship laws that clamped down on English publishing after the French Revolution —BR.
120. *Cleekit.* Linked together.
121. *Carlin.* A stout old woman.
122. *Swat.* Sweated.
123. *Reekit.* Smoked, steamed.
124. *Coost her duddies.* Cast off her clothes.
125. *Wark.* Work.
126. *Linkit.* Danced.
127. *Sark.* A shirt or shift, an undergarment.

<27>

Now Tam, O Tam! had thae[128] been queans,[129]
A' plump and strapping in their teens,
Their sarks, instead o' creeshie flannen,[130]
Been snaw-white'[131] seventeen hunder linnen![132]
Thir breeks[133] o' mine, my only pair,
That ance[134] were plush, o' gude blue hair,
I wad hae gi'en them off my hurdies, [135]
For ae blink[136] o' the bonnie burdies![137]

But wither'd beldams, auld and droll,
Rigwoodie[138] hags wad spean[139] a foal,
Lowping[140] an' flinging on a crummock,[141]
I wonder didna[142] turn thy stomach.

---

128. *Thae*. These.
129. *Queans*. Young women.
130. *Cretshie flannen*. Greasy flannel. Flannel, orginally made from wool, was manufactured in Wales starting in the 17th century —BR.
131. *Snaw-white*. Snow-white.
132. *Seventeen hunder linnen*. Fine linen, 1700-thread gauge. Huguenots settling in Ulster, Ireland after 1695 established the linen-making industry there, and the use of linen expanded rapidly after 1700 —BR.
133. *Thir breeks*. These breeches. Men's trousers, extending just below the knee. Would be considered an undergarment, as it is the first item one would put on, and the last one would take off —BR.
134. *Ance*. Once.
135. *Hurdies*. Buttocks, hips — *OED*.
136. *Ae blink*. One look.
137. *Bonnie burdies*. Pretty creatures.
138. *Rigwoodie*. Dried-up and wrinkled, resembling twisted twigs, straw or rushes.
139. *Wad spean*. Lewis footnotes this as "would wean." Weaning foals seems a rather benign activity for ghosts and witches. Spean also means "to abort," and "foal" is also used to describe a pregnant mare *(OED)*. This is almost certainly what Burns would have wished to express, since witches were accused of causing stillbirths among humans and animals. The euphemism of weaning for abortion is certainly ironic – abortion being premature weaning! Local "wise women" were midwives and many knew the secrets of abortifacients. Scotland had been swept with witch mania in the 1600s, so this lore would be familiar to Burns' readers —BR.
140. *Lowping*. Jumping.
141. *Crummock*. A crutch.
142. *Didna*. Did not.

<28>

But Tam kend[143] what was what fu' brawlie,[144]
There was ae winsome[145] wench and wawlie,[146]
That night enlisted in the core,[147]
(Lang after kend on Carrick[148] shore;
For mony a beast to dead[149] she shot,
And perish'd mony a bonnie boat,
And shook baith[150] meikle corn and bear,[151]
And kept the country-side in fear),
Her cutty sark,[152] o' Paisley harn,[153]
That while a lassie[154] she had worn,
In longitude tho' sorely scanty,
It was her best, and she was vauntie. — [155]
Ah! little kend thy reverend grannie,
That sark she coft[156] for her wee Nannie,
Wi' twa pund Scots,[157] ('twas a' her riches),
Wad ever grace a dance of witches!

143. *Kend*. Knew.
144. *Brawlie*. Very well.
145. *Winsome*. Buxom.
146. *Wawlie*. Comely.
147. *Core*. Corps.
148. *Carrick*. An Ayrshire district, earldom of the famous Bruce family — BR.
149. *To dead*. To death.
150. *Baith*. Both.
151. *Bear*. Barley.
152. *Cutty sark*. A short shift.
153. *Paisley harn*. A cotton woven in a distinctive pattern, made in the town of Paisley in the Scottish lowlands. The town had a reputation for radical politics and free-thinking, so the wearing of Paisley probably had a caché of radicalism about it — BR.
154. *Lassie*. Little girl.
155. *Vauntie*. Proud.
156. *Coft*. Spun.
157. *Twa pund Scots*. Two pounds in Scottish currency. The Scots pound was worth only about one-twelfth of the British pound sterling during the period of this poem. It took more than two centuries for the two currencies to merge into one.— BR.

<29>

But here my Muse her wing maun cour;[158]
Sic[159] flights are far beyond her pow'r;
To sing how Nannie lap and flang,[160]
(A souple[161] jade[162] she was and strang),[163]

And how Tam stood, like ane[164] bewitch'd,
And thought his very een[165] enrich'd;
Even Satan glowr'd, and fidg'd fu' fain,[166]
And hotch'd and blew wi' might and main;
Till first ae caper, syne anither,[167]
Tam tint[168] his reason a' thegither,[169]
And roars out, "Weel done, Cutty-sark!"
And in an instant all was dark:
And scarcely had he Maggie rallied,
When out the hellish legion sallied.

---

158. *Maun cour*. Must lower.
159. *Sic*. Such.
160. *Lap and flang*. Jumped and flung.
161. *Souple*. Supple.
162. *Jade*. A term of reprobation applied to a woman. Also used playfully, like *hussy* or *minx* — OED.
163. *Strang*. Strong.
164. *Ane*. One.
165. *Een*. Eyes.
166. *Fidg'd fu' fain*. Became very restless.
167. *Syne anither*. Then another.
168. *Tint*. Lost.
169. *A' thegither*. Altogether, entirely.

<30>

As bees bizz[170] out wi' angry fyke,[171]
When plundering herds[172] assail their byke;[173]
As open pussie's[174] mortal foes,
When pop! she starts before their nose;
As eager runs the market-crowd,
When "Catch the thief!" resounds aloud;
So Maggie runs, the witches follow,
Wi' mony an eldritch skreech[175] and hollow.

Ah, Tam! Ah, Tam! thou'll get thy fairin![176]
In hell they'll roast thee like a herrin!
In vain thy Kate awaits thy comin![177]
Kate soon will be a woefu' woman!
Now, do thy speedy utmost, Meg,
And win the key-stane of the brig;[178]

170. *Bizz*. Buzz.
171. *Fyke*. Mood.
172. *Herds*. Shepherds.
173. *Byke*. Bee-hive.
174. *Pussie's*. A hare.
175. *Eldritch screech*. A frightful scream. The term "elrich screik" dates to 1513, in Douglas' *Aeneis*, VII. 108. Eldritch is a word seldom used outside of the small circle of supernatural writers, but the OED does cites its use by Burns, Hawthorne, Lord Lytton and William Dean Howells. It was one of H.P. Lovecraft's favorite adjectives —BR.
176. *Fairin*. A fairing, a present.
177. *Comin*. Coming.
178. *Key-stane of the brig*. Key-stone of the bridge, i.e., the centermost part of a stone bridge. "It is a well-known fact that witches, or any evil spirits, have no power to follow a poor wight any farther than the middle of the next running stream. It may be proper likewise to mention to the benighted traveller, that when he falls in with *bogies*, whatever danger may be in his going forward, there is much more hazard in turning back" — RB.

<31>

There at them thy tail may toss,
A running stream they dare na cross.
But ere the key-stane she could make,
The fient a tail[179] she had to shake!
For Nannie, far before the rest,
Hard upon noble Maggie prest,
And flew at Tam wi' furious ettle;[180]
But little wist she Maggie's mettle —
Ae spring[181] brought off her master hale,[182]
But left behind her ain[183] gray tail:
The carlin claught[184] her by the rump,
And left poor Maggie scarce a stump.

Now, wha[185] this tale o' truth shall read,
Ilk[186] man and mother's son, take heed:
Whene'er to drink you are inclin'd,
Or cutty-sarks run in your mind,
Think, ye may buy the joys o'er dear,[187]
Remember Tam o' Shanter's mare.

---

179. *The fient a tail.* Fient is a petty oath, as, "The devil a tail."
180. *Ettle.* Zeal.
181. *Ae spring.* One jump.
182. *Hale.* Whole.
183. *Ain.* Own .
184. *Claught.* Seized hold on.
185. *Wha.* Who.
186. *Ilk.* Each.
187. *O'er dear.* Too dear.

<32>

ROBERT BURNS RELATES THREE SUPERNATURAL TALES, INCLUDING THE ORIGINAL OF "TAM O'SHANTER."

CLXXIL. — TO MR. FRANCIS GROSE, F.S.A.
DUMFRIES, 1792.

Among the many witch stories I have heard, relating to Alloway Kirk, I distinctly remember only two or three.

Upon a stormy night, amid whistling squalls of wind, and bitter blasts of hail; in short, on such a night as the devil would choose to take the air in; a farmer or farmer's servant was plodding and plashing homeward with his plough-irons on his shoulder, having been getting some repairs on them at a neighbouring smithy. His way lay by the kirk of Alloway, and being rather on the anxious look out in approaching a place so well known to be a favourite haunt of the devil and the devil's friends and emissaries, he was struck aghast by discovering through the horrors of the storm and stormy night, a light, which on his nearer approach plainly showed itself to proceed from the haunted edifice. Whether he had been fortified from above on his devout supplication, as is customary with people when they suspect the immediate presence of Satan; or whether, according to another custom, he got courageously drunk at the smithy, I will not pretend to determine; but so it was that he ventured to go up to, nay, into the very kirk. As luck would have it his temerity came off unpunished.

The members of the infernal junto were all out on some midnight business or other, and he saw nothing but a kind of kettle or caldron,

<33>

depending from the roof, over the fire, simmering some heads of unchristened children, limbs of executed malefactors, etc., for the business of the night. It was in for a penny, in for a pound, with the honest ploughman: so without ceremony he unhooked the caldron from off the fire, and, pouring out the damn'd ingredients, inverted it on his head, and carried it fairly home, where it remained long in the family, a living evidence of the truth of the story.

Another story, which I can prove to be equally authentic, is as follows:

On a market day in the town of Ayr a farmer from Carrick, and consequently whose way lay by the very gate of Alloway kirk-yard, in order to cross the river Doon at the old Bridge, which is about two or three hundred yards farther on than the said gate, had been detained by his business, till by the time he reached Alloway it was the wizard hour, between night and morning.

Though he was terrified with a blaze streaming from the kirk, yet as it is a well-known fact that to turn back on these occasions is running by far the greatest risk of mischief, he prudently advanced on his road. When he had reached the gate of the kirk-yard, he was surprised and entertained, through the ribs and arches of an old gothic window, which still faces the highway, to see a dance of witches merrily footing it round their old sooty blackguard master, who was keeping them all alive with the power of his bagpipe. The farmer stopping his horse to observe them a little, could plainly descry the faces of many old women of his acquaintance and neighbourhood. How the gentleman was dressed tradition does not say; but that the ladies were all in their smocks: and one of them happening unluckily to have a smock which was considerably too short to answer all the purpose of that piece of dress, our farmer was so tickled that he involuntarily burst out with a loud laugh, "Weel luppen, Maggy wi' the short sark!" and recollecting himself, instantly spurred his horse to the top of his speed. I need not mention the universally known fact, that no diabolical power can pursue you beyond the middle of a running stream. Lucky it was for the poor farmer that the river Doon was so near, for, notwithstanding the speed of his horse, which was a good one, against he reached the middle of the arch of the bridge, and consequently the middle of the stream, the pursuing, vengeful hags were so close at his heels, that one of them actually sprung to seize him; but it was too late; nothing was on her side of the stream but the horse's tail, which immediately gave way at her infernal grip, as if blasted by a stroke of lightning; but the farmer was beyond her reach. However, the unsightly, tail-less condition of the vigorous steed was to the last hour of the noble creature's life, an awful warning to the Carrick farmers, not to stay too late in Ayr markets.

<34>

The last relation I shall give, though equally true, is not so well identified as the two former, with regard to the scene; but as the best authorities give it for Alloway, I shall relate it.

On a summer's evening, about the time nature puts on her sables to mourn the expiry of the cheerful day, a shepherd boy, belonging to a farmer in the immediate neighbourhood of Alloway kirk, had just folded his charge, and was returning home. As he passed the kirk, in the adjoining field he fell in with a crew of men and women, who were busy pulling stems of the plant ragwort. He observed that as each person pulled a ragwort, he or she got astride of it, and called out, "Up, horsie!" on which the ragwort flew off, like Pegasus, through the air with its rider. The foolish boy likewise pulled his ragwort, and cried with the rest, "Up, horsie!" and, strange to tell, away he flew with the company. The first stage at which the cavalcade stopt was a merchant's wine-cellar in Bourdeaux, where, without saying "By your leave," they quaffed away at the best the cellar could afford, until the morning, foe to the imps and works of darkness, threatened to throw light on the matter, and frightened them from their carousals.

The poor shepherd lad, being equally a stranger to the scene and the liquor, heedlessly got himself drunk; and when the rest took horse, he fell asleep, and was found so next day by some of the people belonging to the merchant. Somebody that understood Scotch, asking him what he was, he said such a-one's herd in Alloway, and by some means or other getting home again, he lived long to tell the world the wondrous tale.

<35>

The Witches' Song

BEN JONSON

From the *Masque of Queens*, presented at Whitehall, Feb. 2d, 1609[1]

1 WITCH.
I have been all day looking after
A raven feeding upon a quarter;[2]
And, soone as she turn'd her beak to the south,
I snatch'd this morsell out of her mouth.

2 WITCH.
I have beene gathering wolves haires,
The madd dogges foames, and adders eares;
The spurging[3] of a dead man's eyes:
And all since the evening starre[4] did rise.

3 WITCH.
I last night lay all alone
On the ground, to heare the mandrake[5] grone;
And pluck'd him up, though he grew full low:
And, as I had done, the cocke did crow.[6]

---

[1] Lewis found this poem in Percy's *Reliques of Ancient English Poetry*.

[2] *Quarter*. A piece of an animal's carcass, or, more suggestively, a piece of a human body that has been drawn and quartered. Each part of a quartered body contains one limb (arm or leg) and whatever else came detached with it.

[3] *Spurging*. Decaying matter foaming up or being exuded.

[4] *Evening starre*. Venus.

[5] *Mandrake*. The Mandrake plant has a root resembling a human form. Folklore asserted that mandrakes grew spontaneously under gallows, where the sperm of hanged men supposedly fell into the ground and produced mandrakes.

[6] *Cocke did crow*. Witches' activities are often interrupted by the rooster's crow, announcing the coming day. The rising sun dispelled all supernatural activities. Saint-Saens' *Danse Macabre* and Mussorgsky's *Night on Bald Mountain* are 19th-century musical works depicting this sudden interruption of witch frenzy by the coming of day.

<36>

Mandragora fæmina

Mandrake root, from de Bry's *Florilegium Renovatum et Auctum*, 1641.

4 WITCH.

And I ha' beene chusing out this scull
From charnell houses[7] that were full;
From private grots,[8] and publike pits;[9]
And frighted a sexton[10] out of his wits.

5 WITCH.

Under a cradle I did crepe
By day; and, when the childe was a-sleepe
At night, I suck'd the breath;[11] and rose,
And pluck'd the nodding nurse by the nose.

6 WITCH.

I had a dagger: what did I with that?
Killed an infant to have his fat.
A piper it got[12] at a church-ale,[13]
I bade him again blow the wind i' the taile.[14]

---

7. *Charnell houses*. Buildings or vaults used as a repository of bones. Bodies were routinely removed from European churchyards after twenty years' interment to make room for more burials; only the rich and powerful were allotted permanent graves. Bones were either piled up in the open air in a bone-yard, or stored in a charnel house or ossuary. Skulls were readily available for pilfering from such places.
8. *Private grots*. A grotto, cave, or crypt owned by a family and used as a mausoleum.
9. *Publike pits*. Common graves for paupers, potters' fields, or mass graves used for hasty burial of victims of epidemics or warfare.
10. *Sexton*. A church official responsible for buildings and grounds, bell-ringing, and care of the churchyard. A position frequently occupied by an elder, with little by the way of duties and a great temptation for sleep, idleness and drunkenness.
11. *Suck'd the breath*. Witches were accused of smothering infants, often in the shape of a cat. Cats, attracted to the smell of milk on babies' mouths, would occasionally visit an infant's cradle: hence, cats as witches or witches' familiars caught the blame for crib deaths. This folk belief still prevails in the Appalachian region of the United States.
12. *A piper it got*. The witch used the dagger to puncture a bagpipe.
13. *Church-ale*. In the 16th Century, English churches dispensed ale on key festival days such as Easter, Christmas and Whitsuntide.
14. *Wind i' the taile*. Possibly obscene.

<38>

7 WITCH.

A murderer, yonder, was hung in chaines;[15]
The sunne and the wind had shrunke his veines:
I bit off a sinew; I clipp'd his haire;
I brought off his ragges, that danced i' the ayre.

8 WITCH.

The scrich-owles egges and the feathers blacke,
The bloud of the frogge, and the bone in his backe
I have been getting; and made of his skin
A purset, to keep Sir Cranion in.[16]

9 WITCH.

And I ha' beene plucking (plants among)
Hemlock, henbane, adders-tongue, [17]
Night-shade, moone-wort, libbards bane; [18]
And twise by the dogges was like to be tane. [19]

15. *Murderer . . . in chaines*. The bodies of murderers, traitors and other serious offenders were left exposed to the elements, to be picked over by crows. This gruesome display served as a warning to would-be offenders.
16. *Sir Cranion*. Probably the witch's familiar, a demon assuming the form of a small animal.
17. Hemlock, henbane, adders-tongue. Hemlock describes a variety of poisonous plants, the Mediterranean form of which was used to poison Socrates. Henbane is a narcotic and poisonous weed, *Hyoscyamus niger*, believed to kill poultry. Adder's tongue is a fern (*Ophioglossum*) whose structure suggests a snake's tongue and mouth.
18. *Night-shade, moone-wort, libbards bane*. Deadly Nightshade (*Atropa belladonna*) is a poisonous and narcotic plant. Moonwort is a small fern whose fronds have a crescent shape, believed to be a treatment for the bite of a mad dog. Libbards-bane, from Leopard's bane, is a member of the *Aconitum* family to which wolfsbane also belongs, a source of paralyzing strychnine.
19. *Tane*. Taken.

<39>

10 WITCH.

I from the jawes of a gardener's bitch
Did snatch these bones, and then leap'd the ditch:
Yet went I back to the house againe,
Kill'd the blacke cat, and here is the braine.

11 WITCH.

I went to the toad, breedes under the wall,
I charmed him out, and he came at my call;
I scratch'd out the eyes of the owle before;
I tore the batt's wing: what would you have more?

DAME.

Yes: I have brought, to helpe your vows,
Horned poppie, cypresse boughes, [20]
The fig-tree wild, that growes on tombes,
And juice that from the larch-tree comes,[21]
The basiliske's bloud,[22] and the viper's skin:
And now our orgies let's begin.

---

20. *Poppie . . . cypresse.* Poppies are the source of opium. Cypress trees, prominent in cemeteries around the Mediterranean, are associated with death and mourning.

21. *Juice that from the larch-tree comes.* Turpentine from larch trees is used as a base for ointments.

22. *Basilisk.* A mythical flying serpent, whose glance is fatal.

<40>

Admiral Hosier's Ghost

[RICHARD] GLOVER

*This was a Party Song,[1] written by the ingenious author of Leonidas,[2] on
the taking of Porto-Bello from the Spaniards by Admiral Vernon,[3] Nov. 22,
1739. — The case of Hosier, which is here so pathetically represented, was
briefly this: In April, 1726, that commander was sent with a strong fleet
into the Spanish West Indies, to block up the galleons in the ports of that
country, or should they presume to come out, to seize and carry them into
England: he accordingly arrived at the Bastimentos near Porto-Bello;[4] but
being employed rather to overawe than to attack the Spaniards, with whom
it was probably not our interest to go to war, he continued long inactive on
that station, to his own great regret. He afterwards removed to
Carthagena,[5] and remained cruizing in these seas till far the greater part of
his men perished deplorably by the diseases of that unhealthy climate. This
brave man, seeing his best officers and men thus daily swept away, his ships
exposed to inevitable destruction, and himself made the sport of the enemy,
is said to have died of a broken heart. Such is the account of Smollet,[6]
compared with that of other less partial writers. —MGL*

As near Porto-Bello lying,
  On the gently swelling flood,
At midnight, with streamers flying,
  Our triumphant navy rode;

---

[1] *Party-song.* A song associated with a political party or faction, to be sung in
pubs, coffee-houses or political meetings.
[2] *Author of Leonidas.* Richard Glover (1712-1785) was an epic poet, whose 1737
Leonidas concerns the eponymous King of Sparta, who fought the Persians at
Thermopylae. "Admiral Hosier's Ghost" was published in 1740 as a broadsheet
with a hand-colored engraving, indicating that the ballad was to be sung to the
tune of "Come and Listen to My Ditty."
[3] *Admiral Vernon.* Edward "Old Grog" Vernon (1684-1757).
[4] *Porto-Bello.* Present-day Panama. Bastimentos is an island off the Atlantic coast
of Panama.
[5] *Carthagena de Indias*, a city on the north coast of Colombia.
[6] Tobias Smollett (1721-1771), novelist and poet, and author of *A Complete
History of England*, published between 1757 and 1765. Smollett's account is
appended at the end of Glover's poem.

<41>

There, while Vernon sate all glorious
    From the Spaniards' late defeat,
And his crews, with shout victorious,
    Drank success to England's fleet.

On a sudden, shrilly sounding,
    Hideous yells and shrieks were heard;
Then, each heart with fear confounding,
    A sad troop of ghosts appear'd,
All in dreary hammocks shrouded,
    Which for winding sheets they wore,
And with looks, by sorrow clouded,
    Frowning on that hostile shore.

On them gleam'd the moon's wan lustre,
    When the shade of Hosier brave
His pale bands was seen to muster,
    Rising from their watery grave.
O'er the glimmering wave he hied him,
    Where the *Burford*[7] rear'd her sail,
With three thousand ghosts beside him,
    And in groans did Vernon hail.

— "Heed, oh heed, our fatal story,
    I am Hosier's injur'd ghost;
You, who now have purchas'd glory,
    At this place where I was lost!
Though in Porto-Bello's ruin
    You now triumph, free from fears,
When you think on our undoing,
    You will mix your joy with tears.

---

[7] *Burford*. Admiral Hosier's ship.

<42>

July 1740. C. Mosley's Engraving for "Admiral Hosier's Ghost.
(British Museum.)

"See these mournful spectres sweeping
    Ghastly o'er this hated wave,
Whose wan cheeks are stain'd with weeping;
    These were English captains brave.
Mark those numbers, pale and horrid,
    Those were once my sailors bold:
Lo, each hangs his drooping forehead,
    While his dismal tale is told!

<43>

"I, by twenty sail attended
    Did this Spanish town affright;
Nothing then its wealth defended,
    But my orders not to fight.
Oh! that in this rolling ocean
    I had cast them with disdain,
And obey'd my heart's warm motion
    To have quell'd the pride of Spain!

"For resistance I could fear none,
    But with twenty ships had done
What thou, brave and happy Vernon,
    Hast achiev'd with six alone.
Then the Bastimentos never
    Had our foul dishonour seen,
Nor the sea the sad receiver
    Of this gallant train had been.

"Thus, like thee, proud Spain dismaying,
    And her galleons leading home,
Though condemn'd for disobeying,
    I had meet a traitor's doom;
To have fallen, my country crying
    He has play'd an English part,
Had been better far than dying
    Of a griev'd and broken heart.

"Unrepining at thy glory,
    Thy successful arms we hail;
But remember our sad story,
    And let Hosier's wrongs prevail.
Sent in this foul clime to languish.
    Think what thousands fell in vain,
Wasted with disease and anguish,
    Not in glorious battle slain.

<44>

"Hence with all my train attending
　　From their oozy tombs below;
Through the hoary foam ascending,
　　Here I feed my constant woe:
Here, the Bastimentos viewing,
　　We recall our shameful doom,
And, our plaintive cries renewing,
　　Wander through the midnight gloom.

"O'er these waves for ever mourning
　　Shall we roam, deprived of rest,
If, to Britain's shores returning,
　　You neglect my just request;
After this proud foe subduing,
　　When your patriot friends you see,
Think on vengeance for my ruin,
　　And for England shamed in me." —

<45>

ADMIRAL HOSIER'S EXPEDITION

King George, that he might not seem to convert all his attention to the affairs of the North, had equipped two other squadrons, one of which was destined for the West Indies, under the command of admiral Hosier: the other, conducted by Sir John Jennings, having on board a body of land-forces, sailed from St. Helen's on the twentieth day of July, entered the bay of St. Antonio, then visited Lisbon, from whence he directed his course to the bay of Bulls near Cadiz, and cruised off Cape St. Mary's, so as to alarm the coast of Spain, and fill Madrid with consternation. Yet he committed no act of hostility: but was treated with great civility by the Spanish governor of Cadiz, who supplied him with refreshments. Rear-admiral Hosier, with seven ships of war, had sailed in April for the Spanish West Indies, with instructions to block up the galleons in the port of that country; or should they presume to come out, to seize and bring them to England. Before his arrival at the Bastimentos, near Porto Bello, the treasure, consisting of above six millions sterling, had been unloaded, and carried back to Panama, in pursuance of an order sent by an advice-boat, which had the start of Hosier. This admiral lay inactive on that station, until he became the jest of the Spaniards. He returned to Jamaica, where he found means to reinforce his crews; then he stood over to Carthegena. The Spaniards had by this time seized the English South Sea ship at La Vera Cruz, together with all the vessels and effects belonging to that company. Hosier in vain demanded restitution: he took some Spanish ships by way of reprisal, and continued cruising in those seas until the greater part of his men perished deplorably by the diseases of that unhealthy climate, and his ships were totally ruined by the worms. This brave officer restricted by his orders from obeying the dictates of his courage, seeing his best officers and men daily swept off by an outrageous distemper, and his ships exposed to inevitable destruction, is said to have died of a broken heart, while the people of England clamoured against this unfortunate expedition, in which so many lives were thrown away, and so much money expended, without the least advantage to the nation. It seems to have been a mean piratical scheme to rob the court of Spain of its expected treasure, even while a peace subsisted between the two nations.
—Tobias Smollett. *The History of England from the Revolution to the Death of George the Second*, p. 220.

<46>

Margaret's Ghost[1]

[DAVID] MALLET[2]

'Twas at the silent solemn hour,
    When night and morning meet,
In glided Margaret's grimly ghost,
    And stood at William's feet. [3]

Her face was like an April morn,
    Clad in a wintry cloud;
And clay-cold was her lily hand,
    That held her sable shroud.

So shall the fairest face appear,
    When youth and years are flown:
Such is the robe that kings must wear,
    When death has reft their crown.

---

[1] *Mallet.* David Mallet (1705-1765), was originally named David Malloch. This forgotten poet's career is outlined in some detail in Robert Chambers' *A Biographical Dictionary of Eminent Scotsmen.* This poem achieved great notoriety in Mallet's youth, and launched his poetic career. He was also co-author, with James Thomson, of the masque *King Alfred,* from which "Rule, Britannia" is derived. His efforts as a landscape poet in the manner of Thomson, and as a playwright, failed. Although he had aristocratic patrons, he became involved in many literary and political imbroglios. Mallet, as a freethinking social outcast who "became a great declaimer in London coffee-houses, against the Christian religion" (Chambers 572), may have appealed to Lewis on many levels.

[2] This poem is based on an early ballad, "Fair Margaret and Sweet William," found in Volume III of Bishop Percy's *Reliques of Ancient English Poetry* (pp. 120-124). This supernatural poem, cast in "eights and sixes," alternating lines of eight and six syllables, uses a mode familiar in ballads and hymns. Mallet's poem was originally published as "William and Margaret" in *The Plain Dealer* #36 (1723).

[3] For a discussion of variants of the comings and goings of ballad ghosts named Margaret and William, see Lowry Wimberly's *Folklore in English and Scottish Ballads,* pp. 250-253. Mallet's poem is quoted briefly in the comparison. Bishop Percy praises Mallet's poem and adds it at the end of Volume III of his *Reliques of Ancient English Poetry.* Percy asserts that Mallet saw only several verses of the original ballad, quoted in a play by Fletcher, *Knight of the Burning Pestle.* The original ballad is quite hair-raising, and differs considerably in outline and detail from Mallet's treatment, and Lewis includes that poem later in this volume.

<47>

Her bloom was like the springing flower,
    That sips the silver dew;
The rose was budded in her cheek,
    Just opening to the view.

But love had, likc the canker-worm,
    Consumed her early prime:
The rose grew pale, and left her cheek; —
    She died before her time.

— "Awake!" she cried, "thy true love calls,
    Come from her midnight grave;
Now let thy pity hear the maid
    Thy love refused to save.

"This is the dark and dreary hour,
    When injured ghosts complain;
Now yawning graves give up their dead,
    To haunt the faithless swain.

"Bethink thee, William, of thy fault,
    Thy pledge, and broken oath;
And give me back my maiden vow,
    And give me back my troth.

"Why did you promise love to me,
    And not that promise keep?
Why did you swear mine eyes were bright,
    Yet leave those eyes to weep?

"How could you say my face was fair,
    And yet that face forsake?
How could you win my virgin heart,
    Yet leave that heart to break?

<48>

"Why did you say my lip was sweet,
    And made the scarlet pale?
And why did I, young witless maid,
    Believe the flattering tale?

"That face, alas! no more is fair;
    These lips no longer red:
Dark are my eyes, now closed in death,
    And every charm is fled.

"The hungry worm my sister is;
    This winding sheet I wear:
And cold and weary lasts our night,
    Till that last morn appear.

But hark! the cock has warn'd me hence!
    A long and last adieu!
Come see, false man, how low she lies
    Who died for love of you." —

The lark, sung loud, the morning smiled
    With beams of rosy red;
Pale William shook in every limb,
    And raving left his bed.

He hied him to the fatal place,
    Where Margaret's body lay;
And stretch'd him on the grass-green turf,
    That wrapt her breathless clay.

And thrice he call'd on Margaret's name,
    And thrice he wept full sore;
Then laid his cheek to her cold grave,
    And word spake never more.

<49>

The Hermit[1]

[THOMAS] PARNELL[2]

Far in a wild,[3] unknown to public view,
From youth to age a reverend Hermit grew;
The moss his bed, the cave his humble cell,
His food the fruits, his drink the crystal well:
Remote from men, with God he pass'd the days,
Prayer all his business, all his pleasure praise.

A life so sacred, such serene repose,
Seem'd heav'n itself, till one suggestion rose:
That Vice should triumph, Virtue Vice obey,
This sprung some doubt of Providence's sway:
His hopes no more a certain prospect[4] boast,
And all the tenour[5] of his soul is lost;

---

[1] Lewis probably obtained this Thomas Parnell poem from the 1770 reprint of *Poems on Several Occasions*, edited by Alexander Pope. Voltaire told a variant of the same tale in his *Zadig*, and the original of the story has been traced back to Spanish, Hebrew and Koranic text. William Axon reconstructed the narrative's tortured and mysterious history in 1881, and gives several of the originals in full in their earliest known translations. The passage of this tale through three religious traditions into the hands of the skeptical Voltaire and the Gothic Lewis is fascinating. "The Hermit" remained a highly popular poem through the end of the Victorian era. Of "The Hermit," the 1855 biographical and critical note by George Gilfillan says: "In it he tells a tale that had been told in Arabic, French, and English, for the tenth time; and in that tenth edition tells it so well, that the public have thanked him for it as for an original work. Of course, the story not being Parnell's, it is not his fault that it casts no light upon the dread problems of Providence it professed to explain. But the incidents are recorded with ease and liveliness; the characters are rapidly depicted, and strikingly contrasted; and many touches of true poetry occur." (90)

[2] Thomas Parnell (1679-1718), a Dublin-born clergyman and poet, was a member of the circle of Jonathan Swift and Alexander Pope. He is credited with founding the "Graveyard School" of English poetry. He preferred London to his native Ireland, which he excoriated, "abusing his native bogs and his fellow-countrymen in verse" (Gilfillan 87). Of his many poems, only a few were chosen by Dr. Johnson and Oliver Goldsmith as worth passing on to posterity (fewer than those originally chosen by Pope, who included more classical specimens). There is evidence from letters that Pope had high regard for Parnell as a Greek and Latin translator.

[3] *Wild*. Wilderness.

[4] *Certain prospect*, i.e., Heaven.

[5] *Tenour*. Course or direction.

<50>

S. Wale del.   C. Grignion Sculp.

——————— Confess th' Almighty just:
And where you can't unriddle, learn to trust.

So, when a smooth expanse receives impress'd
Calm nature's image on its watery breast,
Down bend the banks, the trees depending grow,
And skies beneath with answering colours glow:
But if a stone the gentle sea divide,
Swift ruffling circles curl on every side,
And glimmering fragments of a broken sun,
Banks, trees, and skies, in thick disorder run.

To clear this doubt, to know the world by sight,
To find if books, or swains,[6] report it right,
(For yet by swains alone the world he knew,
Whose feet came wandering o'er the nightly dew,)
He quits his cell; the pilgrim-staff he bore,
And fix'd the scallop[7] in his hat before;
Then with the sun a rising journey went,
Sedate to think, and watching each event.

The morn was wasted in the pathless grass,
And long and lonesome was the wild to pass;
But when the southern sun had warm'd the day,
A Youth came posting o'er a crossing way;
His raiment decent,[8] his complexion fair,
And soft in graceful ringlets wav'd his hair.
Then near approaching, — "Father, hail!" he cried;
And — "Hail, my Son," — the reverend sire replied;
Words follow'd words, from question answer flow'd,
And talk of various kind deceiv'd the road;[9]
Till each with other pleas'd, and loth[10] to part,
While in their age they differ, join in heart:
Thus stands an aged elm in ivy bound,
Thus youthful ivy clasps an elm around.

---

[6] *Swains.* Rustic youths, probably shepherds in this instance.
[7] *Scallop.* A symbol worn by a pilgrim. Scallops from the seashore were a first proof that one had made a journey far from an inland home.
[8] *Decent.* Pleasing.
[9] *Deceiv'd the road.* Made the way seem shorter than it was.
[10] *Loth.* Reluctant.

<52>

Now sunk the sun; the closing hour of day
Came onward, mantled o'er with sober gray;
Nature in silence bid the world repose;
When near the road a stately palace rose:
There, by the moon, through ranks of trees they pass,
Whose verdure crown'd their sloping sides of grass,
It chanc'd, the noble master of the dome
Still made his house the wandering stranger's home:
Yet still the kindness, from a thirst of praise,
Prov'd the vain flourish of expensive ease.
The pair arrive: the liveried servants wait;
Their lord receives them at the pompous gate.
The table groans with costly piles of food,
And all is more than hospitably good.
Then led to rest, the day's long toil they drown,
Deep sunk in sleep, and silk, and heaps of down,

At length 'tis morn; and at the dawn of day,
Along the wide canals the Zephyrs play;
Fresh o'er the gay parterres the breezes creep,
And shake the neighbouring wood, to banish sleep,
Up rise the guests, obedient to the call:
An early banquet deck'd the splendid hall;
Rich luscious wine a golden goblet grac'd,
Which the kind master forced the guests to taste.
Then pleas'd, and thankful, from the porch they go;
And, but the landlord, none had cause of woe;
His cup was vanished; for, in secret guise,
The younger guest purloin'd the glitt'ring prize.

As one who spies a serpent in his way,
Glist'ning and basking in the summer ray,
Disorder'd stops, to shun the danger near,
Then walks with faintness on, and looks with fear;
So seem'd the sire; when, far upon the road,
The shining spoil his wily partner show'd.

<53>

He stopp'd with silence, walk'd with trembling heart,
And much he wish'd, but durst not ask, to part:
Murmuring, he lifts his eyes, and thinks it hard,
That generous actions meet a base reward.

    While thus they pass, the sun his glory shrouds,
The changing skies hang out their sable clouds;
A sound in air presaged approaching rain,
And beasts to covert, scud across the plain.
Warn'd by the signs, the wandering pair retreat,
To seek for shelter at a neighbouring seat:
'Twas built with turrets, on a rising ground,
And strong, and large, and unimprov'd around;
Its owner's temper, timorous and severe,
Unkind and griping,[11] caus'd a desert there.

As near the Miser's heavy doors they drew,
Fierce rising gusts with sudden fury blew;
The nimble light'ning, mix'd with show'rs, began,
And o'er their heads, loud-rolling thunder ran.
Here long they knock, but knock or call in vain,
Driven by the wind, and batter'd by the rain.
At length some pity warm'd the master's breast,
('Twas then his threshold first receiv'd a guest,)
Slow creaking turns the door, with jealous care,
And half he welcomes in the shivering pair;
One frugal faggot[12] lights the naked walls,
And nature's fervour, through their limbs recalls:
Bread of the coarsest sort, with meagre wine,
Each hardly granted,[13] serv'd them both to dine;
And when the tempest first appear'd to cease,
A ready warning bid them part in peace.

---

[11] *Griping*. Miserly.
[12] *Faggot*. Torch made from a bundle of sticks or dried branches.
[13] *Hardly granted*. Given grudgingly.

<54>

With still remark, the pond'ring Hermit view'd,
In one so rich, a life so poor and rude;
And why should such, within himself he cried,
Lock the lost wealth, a thousand want beside?
But what new marks of wonder soon took place,
In every settling feature of his face,
When from his vest, the young companion bore
That cup, the generous landlord own'd before,
And paid profusely with the precious bowl,
The stinted kindness of this churlish soul!

But now the clouds in airy tumult fly,
The sun emerging opes[14] an azure sky;
A fresher green the smelling leaves display,
And, glittering as they tremble, cheer the day;
The weather courts them from the poor retreat,
And the glad master bolts the wary gate.

While hence they walk, the Pilgrim's bosom wrought
With all the travail of uncertain thought;
His partner's acts, without their cause, appear,
'Twas there a vice, and seem'd a madness here:
Detesting that, and pitying this, he goes,
Lost and confounded with the various shows.

Now night's dim shades again involve the sky,
Again the wanderers want a place to lie,
Again they search, and find a lodging nigh.
The soil improved around, the mansion neat,
And neither poorly low, nor idly great:
It seem'd to speak its master's turn of mind,
Content, and not for praise, but virtue kind.

---

[14] *Opes*. Opens.

<55>

Hither the walkers turn, with weary feet,
Then bless the mansion, and the master greet:
Their greeting fair, bestow'd with modest guise,
The courteous master hears, and thus replies:

"Without a vain, without a grudging heart,
To Him who gives us all, I yield a part;
From Him you come, for Him accept it here,
A frank and sober, more than costly, cheer."

He spoke, and bid the welcome table spread,
Then talk'd of virtue till the time of bed,
When the grave household round his hall repair,
Warn'd by a bell, and close the hours with prayer.

At length the world, renew'd by calm repose,
Was strong for toil; the dappled morn arose;
Before the Pilgrims part, the younger crept
Near the clos'd cradle where an infant slept,
And writhed[15] his neck; the landlord's little pride —
O strange return! — grew black, and gasp'd, and died.
Horror of horrors! what, his only son!
How look'd our Hermit when the fact was done!?
Not hell, though hell's black jaws in sunder part,
And breathe blue fire, could more assault his heart.

Confus'd, and struck with silence at the deed,
He flies, but, trembling, fails to fly with speed.
His steps the Youth pursues: the country lay
Perplex'd with roads, a servant shew'd the way:
A river cross'd the path; the passage o'er
Was nice to find; the servant trode before;
Long arms of oaks an open bridge supplied,
And deep the waves, beneath the bending glide.

---

[15] *Writhed.* Twisted.

<56>

The Youth, who seem'd to watch a time to sin,
Approach'd the careless guide, and thrust him in;
Plunging he falls, and rising lifts his head,
Then flashing turns, and sinks among the dead.

Wild sparkling rage inflames the father's eyes,
He bursts the bands of fear, and madly cries:
— "Detested wretch!" — But scarce his speech began,
When the strange partner seem'd no longer man:
His youthful face grew more serenely sweet;
His robe turn'd white, and flow'd upon his feet;
Fair rounds of radiant points invest his hair;
Celestial odours breathe through purpled air;
And wings, whose colours glitter'd on the day,
Wide at his back their gradual plumes display.
The form ethereal bursts upon his sight,
And moves in all the majesty of light.

Though loud at first the pilgrim's passion grew,
Sudden he gazed, and wist not what to do;
Surprise in secret chains his words suspends,
And in a calm his settling temper ends.
But silence here the beauteous angel broke,
The voice of music ravish'd as he spoke:

— "Thy prayer, thy praise, thy life, to vice unknown,
In sweet memorial rise before the throne:
These charms, success in our bright region find,
And force an Angel down, to calm thy mind;
For this, commission'd, I forsook the sky,
Nay, cease to kneel — thy fellow-servant I.

<57>

"Then know the truth of government divine,
And let these scruples be no longer thine:

"The Maker justly claims that world he made,
In this the right of Providence is laid;
Its sacred majesty through all depends,
On using second means to work His ends:
'Tis thus, withdrawn in state from human eye,
The Power exerts his attributes on high;
Your actions uses, nor controls your will,
And bids the doubting sons of men 'be still.'

"What strange events can strike with more surprise,
Than those which lately struck thy wondering eyes?
Yet, taught by these, confess the Almighty just,
And where you can't unriddle, learn to trust.

"The great, vain man, who fared on costly food,
Whose life was too luxurious to be good;
Who made his ivory stands with goblets shine,
And forc'd his guests to morning draughts of wine,
Has, with the cup, the graceless custom lost,
And still he welcomes, but with less of cost.

"The mean, suspicious wretch, whose bolted door
Ne'er moved in duty to the wandering poor;
With him I left the cup, to teach his mind
That Heaven can bless, if mortals will be kind.
Conscious of wanting worth, he views the bowl,
And feels compassion touch his grateful soul.
Thus artists melt the sullen ore of lead,
With heaping coals of fire upon its head;
In the kind warmth the metal learns to glow,
And, loose from dross, the silver runs below.

<58>

"Long had our pious friend in virtue trod,
But now the child half wean'd his heart from God;
Child of his age, for him he liv'd in pain,
And measur'd back his steps to earth again.
To what excesses had his dotage run!
But God, to save the father, took the son.
To all but thee, in fits he seem'd to go,
And 'twas my ministry to deal the blow:
The poor fond parent, humbled in the dust,
Now owns, in tears, the punishment was just.

"But how had all his fortune felt a wrack,
Had that false servant sped in safety back;
This night his treasur'd heaps he meant to steal,
And what a fund of charity would fail!

"Thus Heaven instructs thy mind: this trial o'er,
Depart in peace, resign, and sin no more." —

On sounding pinions here the youth withdrew,
The Sage stood wondering as the seraph flew.
Thus look'd Elisha, when, to mount on high,
His master took the chariot of the sky;
The fiery pomp ascending left the view;
The Prophet gaz'd, and wish'd to follow too.

The bending Hermit here a prayer begun,
— "Lord! as in Heaven , on earth thy will be done" —
Then, gladly turning, sought his ancient place,
And pass'd a life of piety and peace.[16]

<hr>

[16] Note: I have edited this poem in accord with the 1855 collection of Parnell's poems by Gilfillan, to restore some necessary punctuation carelessly omitted by Lewis or his printer —BR.

<59>

Edwin of the Green [1]

THOMAS PARNELL

In Britain's isle, and Arthur's days,
When midnight faeries daunced the maze,
   Lived Edwin of the Green;
Edwin, I wis, a gentle youth,
Endow'd with courage, sense, and truth,
   Though badly shaped he'd been.

His mountain back mote[2] well be said
To measure heighth against his head,
   And lift itself above:[3]
Yet spite of all that nature did
To make his uncouth form forbid,
   This creature dared to love.

He felt the charms of Edith's eyes,
Nor wanted hope to gain the prize,
   Could ladies look within;
But one Sir Topaz dress'd with art,
And, if a shape could win a heart,
   He had a shape to win.

---

[1] Parnell titled this poem simply, "A Fairy Tale, in the Ancient English Style."
This 1714 poem is cast in octasyllabic couplets alternating with six-syllable lines,
"eights and sixes" with a rhyme scheme *aabccb*. The language is intentionally
archaic, probably more so than any other poem in this anthology. Despite its
antique style and vocabulary, the poem was much admired. Goldsmith wrote of
it: "never was the old manner of speaking more happily applied, or a tale better
told than this." (*"Beauties of English Poetry"* 563). Its early date makes it one of
the precursors of medievalist romanticism.
[2] *Mote*. Might.
[3] *His mountain back . . . itself above*. Edwin is a hunchback. Victims of this spinal
malformation were often kept in medieval court along with jesters, jugglers,
musicians and other entertainers. It was considered good luck to touch the
hump. The love-lorn, vengeful hunchback figures in later Romantic art,
especially via Hugo's play *Le Roi S'Amuse* (the basis of Verdi's opera, *Rigoletto*),
and *Notre Dame de Paris*, known in English-speaking countries as *The Hunchback
of Notre Dame*. Edgar Allan Poe's short story "Hop-Frog" is also in this tradition.

<60>

Edwin (if right I read my song,)
With slighted passion paced along
    All in the moony light:
'Twas near an old enchaunted court,
Where sportive faeries made resort,
    To revel out the night.

His heart was drear, his hope was cross'd,
'Twas late, 'twas far, the path was lost
    That reach'd the neighbour-town;
With weary steps he quits the shades,
Resolved, the darkling dome he treads,[4]
    And drops his limbs adown.

But scant he lays him on the floor,
When hollow winds remove the door,
    And trembling rocks the ground:
And (well I ween, to count aright,)
At once an hundred tapers light
    On all the walls around.

Now sounding tongues assail his ear,
Now sounding feet approachen near,
    And now the sounds increase;
And, from the corner where he lay,
He sees a train profusely gay
    Come pranckling[5] o'er the place.

---

[4] *Dome*. Probably a vaulted ceiling, perhaps in a ruined monastery.
[5] *Pranckling*. Parading and showing off their finery.

<61>

But (trust me, Gentles!)[6] never yet
Was dight a masking[7] half so neat,
   Or half so rich before;
The country lent the sweet perfumes,
The sea the pearl, the sky the plumes,
   The town its silken store.[8]

Now, whilst he gazed, a gallant dress'd
In flaunting robes above the rest,
   With awful accent cried:
— "What mortal of a wretched mind,
Whose sighs infect the balmy wind,
   Has here presumed to hide?" —

At this the swain, whope vent'rous soul
No fears of magic art control,
   Advanced in open sight:
— "Nor have I cause of dread," he said,
"Who view (by no presumption led,)
   Your revels of the night.

---

[6] *Gentles.* Polite contraction of "gentlefolk" or "ladies and gentlemen." The line is a nice interruption of the meter, setting the four-syllable "trust me, Gentles" one beat off on the line.

[7] *Dight a masking.* "Done" (performed) a masque. A masque is an entertainment where all the participants, in costume, take part in a choreographed musical-dramatic event. Masques reached their peak in seventeenth century France and England, with kings, queens and nobles portraying mythological or historical figures. Puritans and other Protestant sects regarded these events as indecent. A faerie masque is thus not only a supernatural event, but a blasphemous one, a parody of court excesses.

[8] *The town its silken store.* Fairies were blamed for the theft of valuables, a convenient scapegoat for sticky-fingered servants.

<62>

" 'Twas grief, for scorn of faithful love,
Which made my steps unweeting[9] rove
    Amid the nightly dew." —
" 'Tis well," the gallant cries again,
"We faeries never injure men
    Who dare to tell us true.

"Exalt thy love-dejected heart,
Be mine the task, or ere we part,
    To make thee grief resign;
Now take the pleasure of thy chaunce;
Whilst I with Mab,[10] my partner, daunce,
    Be Little Mable thine." —

He spoke, and all a sudden there
Light music floats in wanton air;[11]
    The Monarch leads the Queen:
The rest their faerie partners found,
And Mable trimly tript the ground
    With Edwin of the Green.

The dauncing past, the board was laid,
And siker[12] such a feast was made
    As heart and lip desire;
Withouten hands the dishes fly,
The glasses with a wish come nigh,
    And with a wish retire.

But now to please the Faerie King,
Full every deal they laugh and sing,
    And antick feats devise;
Some wind and tumble like an ape,
And other some transmute their shape
    In Edwin's wondering eyes.

---

9 *Unweeting.* Archaic form of "unwitting."
10 *Mab.* Queen of the Fairies, the Mab of Shakespeare's *Romeo and Juliet.*
11 *Wanton air.* A sung "air" or aria inducing wanton (lustful) feelings.
12 *Siker.* Archaic word. "Safe" or "secure," here probably meaning: safe from prying eyes.

<63>

Till one at last, that Robin hight,[13]
(Renown'd for pinching maids by night,)
    Has bent him up aloof;
And full against the beam he flung,
Where by the back the youth he hung,
    To spraul unneath the roof.

From thence, — "Reverse my charm," he cries,
"And let it fairly now suffice,
    The gambol has been shown." —
But Oberon answers with a smile,
— "Content thee, Edwin, for a while,
    The vantage is thine own." —

Here ended all the phantome play:
They smelt the fresh approach of day,
    And heard a cock to crow;[14]
The whirling wind that bore the crowd
Has clapp'd the door, and whistled loud,
    To warn them all to go.

Then screaming all at once, they fly,
And all at once the tapers die;
    Poor Edwin falls to floor;
Forlorn his state, and dark the place,
Was never wight in sike a case,[15]
    Through all the land before.

But soon as Dan Apollo[16] rose,
Full jolly creature, home he goes,
    He feels his back the less;
His honest tongue and steady mind,
Had rid him of the lump behind,
    Which made him want[17] success.

---

13 *Robin hight.* The fairy "hight" (named) Robin is Puck.
14 The rooster's crow always interrupts fairy or witch revels.
15 *Was never wight...* There was never a person in such a state.
16 *Dan Apollo.* Master or Sir Apollo, the Sun.
17 *Want.* Lack.

<64>

With lusty livelyhed he talks,
He seems a daucing as he walks;
   His story soon took wind;
And beauteous Edith sees the youth,
Endow'd with courage, sense, and truth,
   Without a hunch behind,[18]

The story told, Sir Topaz moved,
The youth of Edith erst approved,
   To see the revel scene.
At close of eve he leaves his home,
And wends to find the ruin'd dome
   All on the gloomy plain.

As there he bides, it so befell,
The wind came rustling down a dell,
   A shaking seized the wall:
Up spring the tapers as before,
The faeries bragly[19] foot the floor,
   And music fills the hall.

But certes[20] sorely sunk with woe
Sir Topaz sees the Elfin show, —
   His spirits in him die:
When Oberon[21] cries, — "A man is near,
A mortal passion, cleeped[22] fear,
   Hangs flagging in the sky." —

---

[18] *Hunch*. The 1801 edition says, erroneously, "bunch."
[19] *Bragly*. Boldly.
[20] *Certes*. Latin. "Truly."
[21] *Oberon*. King of the Fairies, as in Shakespeare's *A Midsummer Night's Dream*.
[22] *Cleeped*. Named.

<65>

With that Sir Topaz, (hapless youth!)
In accent faultering, ay for ruth,
   Intreats them pity graunt;
For als he been a mister wight,[23]
Betray'd by wandering in the night,
   To tread the circled haunt;

— "Ah, Losell[24] vile!" at once they roar,
"And little skill'd of faerie lore,
   Thy cause to come, we know:
Now has thy kestrell courage fell;[25]
And Faeries, since a lie you tell,
Are free to work thee woe." —

Then Will, who bears the wispy fire[26]
To trail the swains among the mire,
   The caitive upward flung;[27]
There, like a tortoise in a shop,
He dangled from the chamber-top,
   Where whilome[28] Edwin hung.

---

[23] *For als he been a mister wight.* For as he was just an ordinary person, i.e., a simple tradesman.

[24] *Losell.* Worthless person or scoundrel.

[25] *Now has thy kestrell courage fell,* i.e., "Now your hawk-like courage has fallen from the sky."

[26] *Will ... wispy fire.* The Will o'the Wisp, or fairy light, a natural phenomenon. They became a more prominent part of the supernatural when Goethe personified and introduced them in *Faust*; Hector Berlioz crafted an exquisite musical number, "Minuet of the Will o' the Wisps" in his *Damnation of Faust.*

[27] *Caitive.* Captive.

[28] *Whilome.* "Previously." The suspension of characters from the ceiling in this poem may have directly inspired the events in Edgar Allan Poe's "Hop Frog," although Poe combines suspension with burning alive, based on an account of royals catching fire at a masque in the 14th century.

<66>

The revel now proceeds apace,
Deftly they frisk it o'er the place,
   They sit, and drink, and eat:
The time with frolic mirth beguile,
And poor Sir Topaz hangs the while,
   Till all the rout retreat.

By this the stars began to wink,
They shriek, they fly, the tapers sink,
   And down ydrops the Knight:[29]
For never a spell by faerie laid
With strong enchantment bound a glade,
   Beyond the length of night.

Chill, dark, alone, adreed,[30] he lay,
Till up the welkin rose the day,
   Then deem'd the dole was o'er;[31]
But wot[32] ye well his harder lot?
His seely[33] back the hunch had got
   Which Edwin lost afore.

This tale a Sybil-nurse[34] ared;[35]
She softly stroked my youngling head,
   And when the tale was done,
— "Thus some are born, my son," she cries,
"With base impediments to rise,
   And some are born with none.

---

[29] *Ydrops the Knight*. The archaic "ydrops," especially followed by "Knight," evokes the earlier poems of Spenser or even Chaucer. Parnell peppers this poem with archaisms going all the way back to the 1400s.

[30] *Adreed*. Full of dread.

[31] *Then deem'd the dole was o'er*. Then he thought the danger had passed.

[32] *Wot*. Know.

[33] *Seely*. Poor, defenseless.

[34] *Sybil-nurse*. The Sybils were prophetesses in the ancient Greek world, hideous truth-tellers.

[35] *Ared*. Aired, or told.

<67>

"But virtue can itself advance
To what the favourite fools of chance
   By fortune seem'd design'd;
Virtue can gain the odds of fate,
And from itself shake off the weight
   Upon th' unworthy mind." —

<68>

Theodore and Honoria[1]

[JOHN] DRYDEN

Of all the cities in Romanian lands,[2]
The chief and most renowned Ravenna[3] stands;
Adorned in ancient times with arms and arts,
And rich inhabitants with generous hearts.
But Theodore the brave,[4] above the rest,
With gifts of fortune and of nature blessed,
The foremost place for wealth and honour held,
And all in feats of chivalry excell'd.

This noble youth to madness loved a dame
Of high degree, Honoria was her name;
Fair as the fairest, but of haughty mind,
And fiercer than became so soft a kind;
Proud of her birth (for equal she had none),
The rest she scorned, but hated him alone;
His gifts, his constant courtship, nothing gain'd;
For she, the more he loved, the more disdain'd,
He lived with all the pomp he could devise,
At tilts and tournaments obtained the prize;
But found no favour in his lady's eyes:

---

[1] Originally published in 1700 as part of Dryden's *Fables Ancient and Modern*. John Dryden's epigraph reads "From Boccace," i.e., Boccaccio's *Decameron*, where this tale is called "Nastagio degli Onesti" (Day 5, Novel 8). Sir Walter Scott notes that Dryden was not the first to render this misogynistic tale into verse: Dryden was preceded by "A Notable History of Nastagio and Traversary, no less pitiful than pleasant; translated out of Italian into English Verse," by a mysterious Mr. "C.T." and printed in London in 1569.
[2] *Romanian lands*. The Romagna region of Italy.
[3] *Ravenna*. Italian city near the Adriatic coast, capital of the Western Roman Empire from 402 to 476 CE, and later ruled by the Ostrogoths. It was the city of Dante's exile, and the place of his burial. Ravenna was also Boccaccio's home.
[4] Theodore the brave, suggestive of Ravenna's Theodoric the Great (454-526 CE).

<69>

Relentless as a rock, the lofty maid
Turn'd all to poison that he did or said:
Nor prayers, nor tears, nor offer'd vows could move;
The work went backward; and the more he strove
T' advance his suit, the farther from her love.

Wearied at length, and wanting remedy,
He doubted oft, and oft resolved to die.
But pride stood ready to prevent the blow,
For who would die to gratify a foe?
His generous mind disdain'd so mean a fate;
That pass'd, his next endeavour was to hate.
But vainer that relief than all the rest;
The less he hoped, with more desire possess'd;
Love stood the siege, and would not yield his breast.
Change was the next, but change deceived his care;
He sought a fairer, but found none so fair.
He would have worn her out by slow degrees,
As men by fasting starve th' untamed disease;
But present love required a present ease.
Looking, he feeds alone his famish'd eyes,
Feeds lingering death, but, looking not, he dies.
Yet still he chose the longest way to fate,
Wasting at once his life and his estate.

His friends beheld, and pitied him in vain.
For what advice can ease a lover's pain?
Absence, the best expedient they could find,
Might save the fortune, if not cure the mind:
This means they long proposed, but little gain'd,
Yet after much pursuit at length obtain'd.

Hard you may think it was to give consent,
But struggling with his own desires he went;
With large expense, and with a pompous train,
Provided as to visit France or Spain,
Or for some distant voyage o'er the main.
But Love had clipp'd his wings, and cut him short,
Confin'd within the purlieus of his court.

<70>

Three miles he went, nor farther could retreat;
His travels ended at his country seat:
To Chassi's[5] pleasing plains he took his way,
There pitched his tents, and there resolved to stay.

The spring was in the prime, the neighbouring grove
Supplied with birds, the choristers of love:
Music unbought, that minister'd delight
To morning walks, and lull'd his cares by night:
There he discharged his friends, but not the expense
Of frequent treats and proud magnificence.
He lived as kings retire, though more at large
From public business, yet with equal charge;
With house and heart still open to receive;
As well content as love would give him leave:
He would have lived more free; but many a guest,
Who could forsake the friend, pursued the feast.

It happed one morning, as his fancy led,
Before his usual hour he left his bed,
To walk within a lonely lawn, that stood
On every side surrounded by the wood;
Alone he walked, to please his pensive mind,
And sought the deepest solitude to find;
'Twas in a grove of spreading pines[6] he strayed;
The winds within the quivering branches played,
And dancing trees a mournful music made;
The place itself was suiting to his care,
Uncouth and savage as the cruel fair.
He wandered on, unknowing where he went,
Lost in the wood, and all on love intent:
The day already half his race had run,
And summoned him to due repast at noon,
But Love could feel no hunger but his own.

---

5 *Chassi.* This is the town of Classis, one of the quarters of old Ravenna, site of a basilica. The town, other than the basilica, had been razed by the Lombards in the eighth century.

6 *A grove of speading pines.* The *Pineta*, or Pini Forest, extends for 25 miles along the Adriatic. These woods have been celebrated by Dante, Boccaccio and Byron.

<71>

A portion of Botticelli's 1483 painting depicting the story of Nastagio degli Onesti from Boccaccio's *Decameron*.

While listening to the murmuring leaves he stood,
More than a mile immersed within the wood,
At once the wind was laid; the whispering sound
Was dumb; a rising earthquake rocked the ground;
With deeper brown the grove was overspread;
A sudden horror seized his giddy head,
And his ears tinkled, and his colour fled.
Nature was in alarm; some danger nigh
Seemed threaten'd, though unseen to mortal eye.
Unused to fear, he summon'd all his soul,
And stood collected in himself, and whole;
Not long: for soon a whirlwind rose around,
And from afar he heard a screaming sound,
As of a dame distress'd, who cried for aid,
And fill'd with loud laments the secret shade.

<72>

A thicket close beside the grove there stood,
With briers and brambles choked, and dwarfish wood;
From thence the noise, which now approaching near
With more distinguished notes invades his ear;
He raised his head, and saw a beauteous maid,
With hair dishevel'd issuing through the shade;
Stripped of her clothes, and e'en those parts revealed
Which modest nature keeps from sight conceal'd.
Her face, her hands, her naked limbs were torn,
With passing through the brakes and prickly thorn;
Two mastiffs gaunt and grim her flight pursued,
And oft their fastened fangs in blood imbrued:
Oft they came up, and pinched her tender side,
—"Mercy, O mercy, Heaven!" — she ran, and cried;
When Heaven was named, they loosed their hold again.
Then sprung she forth, they followed her amain.

Not far behind, a knight of swarthy face,
High on a coal-black steed pursued the chase;
With flashing flames his ardent eyes were fill'd,
And in his hands a naked sword he held.
He cheer'd the dogs to follow her who fled,
And vowed revenge on her devoted head.

As Theodore was born of noble kind,
The brutal action roused his manly mind;
Moved with unworthy usage of the maid,
He, though unarmed, resolved to give her aid.
A sapling pine he wrenched from out the ground,
The readiest weapon that his fury found.
Thus, furnish'd for offence, he crossed the way
Betwixt the graceless villain and his prey.

<73>

The knight came thundering on, but, from afar,
Thus in imperious tone forbad the war:
—"Cease, Theodore, to proffer vain relief,
Nor stop the vengeance of so just a grief;
But give me leave to seize my destined prey,
And let eternal justice take the way:
I but revenge my fate, disdained, betrayed,
And suffering death for this ungrateful maid."—

He said, at once dismounting from the steed;
For now the hell-hounds with superior speed
Had reach'd the dame, and, fastening on her side,
The ground with issuing streams of purple dyed.
Stood Theodore surprised in deadly fright,
With chattering teeth, and bristling hair upright;
Yet armed with inborn worth, — "Whate'er," said he,
"Thou art, who knows't me better than I thee;
Or prove thy rightful cause, or be defied."
The spectre fiercely staring, thus replied:

"Know, Theodore, thy ancestry I claim,
And Guido Cavalcanti[7] was my name.
One common sire our fathers did beget,
My name and story some remember yet;
Thee, then a boy, within my arms I laid,
When, for my sins, I loved this haughty maid;
Not less adored in life, nor served by me,
Than proud Honoria now is loved by thee.
What did I not her stubborn heart to gain?
But all my vows were answered with disdain:
She scorned my sorrows, and despised my pain.
Long time I dragged my days in fruitless care;
Then loathing life, and plunged in deep despair,
To finish my unhappy life I fell
On this sharp sword, and now am damned in hell.

---

[7] *Guido Cavalcanti.* Florentine poet, Dante's best friend. The poet's father, an
atheist, is depicted in Dante's *Inferno*. The ghost huntsman is named Guido degli
Anastagi in Boccaccio's *Decameron*.

<74>

"Short was her joy; for soon the insulting maid
By Heaven's decree in the cold grave was laid;
And as in unrepenting sin she died,
Doomed to the same bad place, is punished for her pride:
Because she deemed I well deserved to die,
And made a merit of her cruelty.
There, then, we met; both tried, and both were cast,
And this irrevocable sentence pass'd —
That she, whom I so long pursued in vain,
Should suffer from my hands a lingering pain:
Renewed to life, that she might daily die,
I daily doomed to follow, she to fly;
No more a lover, but a mortal foe,
I seek her life (for love is none below);
As often as my dogs with better speed
Arrest her flight, is she to death decreed:
Then with this fatal sword, on which I died,
I pierce her opened back or tender side,
And tear that hardened heart from out her breast,
Which with her entrails makes my hungry hounds a feast.
Nor lies she long, but as her fates ordain,
Springs up to life, and fresh to second pain,
Is saved to-day, to-morrow to be slain."—

This, versed in death, th' infernal Knight relates,
And then for proof fulfilled their common fates;
Her heart and bowels through her back he drew,
And fed the hounds that helped him to pursue.
Stern looked the fiend, as frustrate of his will,
Not half sufficed, and greedy yet to kill.
And now the soul, expiring through the wound,
Had left the body breathless on the ground,
When thus the grisly Spectre spoke again:
—"Behold the fruit of ill-rewarded pain!:
As many months as I sustained her hate,
So many years is she condemned by fate
To daily death; and every several place
Conscious of her disdain and my disgrace,
Must witness her just punishment, and be

<75>

A scene of triumph and revenge to me.
As in this grove I took my last farewell,
As on this very spot of earth I fell,
As Friday saw me die, so she my prey
Becomes even here, on this revolving day."[8]—

Thus while he spoke, the Virgin from the ground
Upstarted fresh, already closed the wound,
And unconcerned for all she felt before,
Precipitates her flight along the shore:
The hell-hounds, as ungorged with flesh and blood,
Pursue their prey, and seek their wonted food:
The fiend remounts his courser, mends his pace,
And all the vision vanished from the place.

Long stood the noble youth oppressed with awe
And stupid[9] at the wondrous things he saw,
Surpassing common faith, transgressing nature's law:
He would have been asleep, and wish'd to wake,
But dreams, he knew, no long impression make,
Though strong at first; if vision, to what end,
But such as must his future state portend?
His love the damsel, and himself the fiend.
But yet reflecting that it could not be
From heaven, which cannot impious acts decree,
Resolved within himself to shun the snare,
Which hell for his destruction did prepare;
And as his better genius should direct,
From an ill cause to draw a good effect.

Inspired from heaven he homeward took his way,
Nor pall'd his new design with long delay;
But of his train a trusty servant sent
To call his friends together at his tent.
They came, and, usual salutations paid,
With words premeditated thus he said:
"What you have often counsel'd, to remove

---

[8] *Revolving day*, i.e., every Friday.
[9] *Stupid*, i.e., stupefied.

<76>

My vain pursuit of unregarded love,
By thrift my sinking fortune to repair,
Though late, yet is at last become my care:
My heart shall be my own; my vast expense
Reduced to bounds by timely providence:
This only I require; invite for me
Honoria, with her father's family,
Her friends and mine; the cause I shall display,
On Friday next, for that's the appointed day."—

Well pleased were all his friends, the task was light,
The father, mother, daughter they invite;
Hardly the dame was drawn to this repast;
But yet resolved, because it was the last.
The day was come, the guests invited came,
And with the rest th' inexorable Dame:
A feast prepared with riotous expense,
Much cost, more care, and most magnificence.
The place ordain'd was in that haunted grove
Where the revenging ghost pursued his love:
The tables in a proud pavilion spread,
With flowers below, and tissue[10] overhead;
The rest in rank, Honoria, chief in place,
Was artfully contrived to set her face
To front the thicket and behold the chase.
The feast was served, the time so well forecast,
That just when the dessert and fruits were placed,
The fiend's alarm began; the hollow sound
Sung in the leaves, the forest shook around,
Air blacken'd, roll'd the thunder, groan'd the ground.

Nor long before the load laments arise,
Of one distress'd, and mastiffs' mingled cries;
And first the Dame came rushing through the wood,
And next the famished hounds that sought their food,
And grip'd her flanks, and oft essay'd their jaws in blood.
Last came the Felon on the sable steed,
Armed with his naked sword, and urged his dogs to speed.

---

10 *Tissue.* A fine cloth, interwoven with silver or gold.

<77>

She ran, and cried, her flight directly bent
(A guest unbidden) to the fatal tent,[11]
The scene of death, and place ordain'd for punishment.
Loud was the noise, aghast was every guest,
The woman shriek'd, the men forsook the feast;
The hounds at nearer distance hoarsely bay'd;
The hunter close pursued the visionary maid,
She rent the heaven with loud laments, imploring aid.

The gallants, to protect the Lady's right,
Their faulchions[12] brandished at the grisly spright;
High on his stirrups he provoked the fight;
Then on the crowd he cast a furious look,
And wither'd all their strength before he spoke:[13]
—"Back on your lives! let be," said he, "my prey,
And let my vengeance take the destined way:
Vain are your arms, and vainer your defence,
Against the eternal doom of Providence:
Mine is th' ungrateful maid by Heaven design'd:
Mercy she would not give, nor mercy shall she find." —
At this the former tale again he told
With thundering tone, and dreadful to behold:
Sunk were their hearts with horror of the crime,
Nor needed to be warned a second time,
But bore each other back; some knew the face,
And all had heard the much lamented case
Of him who fell for love, and this the fatal place.

And now th' infernal minister advanced,
Seized the due victim, and with fury lanced[14]
Her back, and piercing through her inmost heart,
Drew backward as before th' offending part.
The reeking entrails next he tore away,
And to his meagre mastiffs made a prey.

[11] This moment is illustrated in a masterful Botticelli painting of 1487,
The Banquet in the Pine Forest.
[12] *Faulchion*. A broadsword with one curved edge.
[13] *Spoke*. Dryden wrote "strook," a better rhyme but a vaguer meaning. Lewis
changed this to "spoke," only a near-rhyme to "look," an unusual change since
Lewis was a stickler for rhyme.
[14] Lanced. Lewis's weary typesetter set this as "launch'd," certainly an error.

<78>

The pale assistants on each other stared,
With gaping mouths for issuing words prepared;
The stillborn sounds upon the palate hung,
And died imperfect on the faltering tongue.
The fright was general; but the female band,
(A helpless train) in more confusion stand;
With horror shuddering, on a heap they run,
Sick at the sight of hateful justice done;
For conscience rung th' alarm, and made the case their own.

So spread upon a lake, with upward eye,
A plump of fowl behold their foe on high;
They close their trembling troop; and all attend
On whom the sousing eagle will descend.

But most the proud Honoria feared the event,
And thought to her alone the vision sent.
Her guilt presents to her distracted mind
Heaven's justice, Theodore's revengeful kind,
And the same fate to the same sin assign'd;
Already sees herself the monster's prey,
And feels her heart and entrails torn away.
'Twas a mute scene of sorrow, mix'd with fear;
Still on the table lay th' unfinish'd cheer:
The Knight and hungry mastiffs stood around,
The mangled Dame lay breathless on the ground;
When on a sudden, re-inspired with breath,
Again she rose, again to suffer death;
Nor stay'd the hell-hounds, nor the hunter stay'd,
But followed, as before, the flying maid:
The avenger took from earth the avenging sword,
And mounting light as air his sable steed he spurr'd:
The clouds dispelled, the sky resumed her light,
And Nature stood recovered of her fright.

But fear, the last of ills, remained behind,
And horror heavy sat on every mind.
Nor Theodore encouraged more his feast,
But sternly look'd, as hatching in his breast

<79>

Some deep design, which when Honoria view'd
The fresh impulse her former fright renew'd:
She thought herself the trembling dame who fled,
And him the grisly ghost that spurr'd th' infernal steed:
The more dismayed, for when the guests withdrew,
Their courteous host saluting all the crew,
Regardless passed her o'er, nor graced with kind adieu.
That sting infixed within her haughty mind,
The downfall of her empire she divined;
And her proud heart with secret sorrow pined.
Home as they went, the sad discourse renew'd,
Of the relentless dame to death pursued,
And of the sight obscene so lately view'd.
None durst arraign the righteous doom she bore,
Even they who pitied most yet blamed her more:
The parallel they needed not to name,
But in the dead they damn'd the living dame.

At every little noise she look'd behind,
For still the knight was present to her mind;
And anxious oft she started on the way,
And thought the horseman-ghost came thundering for his prey.
Returned, she took her bed with little rest,
But in short slumbers dreamt the funeral feast;
Awak'd, she turned her side, and slept again;
The same black vapours mounted in her brain,
And the same dreams returned with double pain.

Now forc'd to wake, because afraid to sleep,
Her blood all fevered, with a furious leap
She sprung from bed, distracted in her mind,
And feared, at every step, a twitching sprite behind.
Darkling and desperate, with a staggering pace,
Of death afraid, and conscious of disgrace,
Fear, pride, remorse, at once her heart assail'd;
Pride put remorse to flight, but fear prevail'd.

<80>

Friday, the fatal day, when next it came,
Her soul forethought the fiend would change his game,
And her pursue, or Theodore be slain,
And two ghosts join their packs to hunt her o'er the plain.

This dreadful image so possess'd her mind,
That, desperate any succour else to find,
She ceas'd all farther hope; and now began
To make reflection on the unhappy man.
Rich, brave, and young, who past expression lov'd,
Proof to disdain, and not to be remov'd:
Of all the men respected and admir'd,
Of all the dames, except herself, desir'd:
Why not of her? preferr'd above the rest
By him with knightly deeds, and open love profess'd?
So had another been, where he his vows address'd.
This quell'd her pride, yet other doubts remain'd,
That once disdaining, she might be disdain'd.
The fear was just, but greater fear prevail'd,
Fear of her life by hellish hounds assail'd:
He took a lowering leave; but who can tell
What outward hate might inward love conceal?
Her sex's arts she knew, and why not, then,
Might deep dissembling have a place in men?
Here hope began to dawn; resolv'd to try,
She fixed on this her utmost remedy;
Death was behind, but hard it was to die:
'Twas time enough at last on death to call,
The precipice in sight, a shrub was all
That kindly stood betwixt to break the fatal fall.

One maid she had, beloved above the rest:
Secure of her, the secret she confessed;
And now the cheerful light her fears dispell'd,
She with no winding turns the truth conceal'd,
But put the woman off, and stood reveal'd:
With faults confess'd, commission'd her to go,
If pity yet had place, and reconcile her foe.
The welcome message made was soon received;

<81>

'Twas what he wished and hoped, but scarce believed:
Fate seem'd a fair occasion to present,
He knew the sex, and feared she might repent,
Should he delay the moment of consent.
There yet remain'd to gain her friends (a care
The modesty of maidens well might spare);
But she with such a zeal the cause embraced,
(As women, where they will, are all in haste);
The father, mother, and the kin beside,
Were overborne by fury of the tide;
With full consent of all she changed her state;
Resistless in her love, as in her hate.

By her example warn'd, the rest beware;
More easy, less imperious, were the fair;
And that one hunting, which the Devil designed
For one fair female, lost him half the kind.

<82>

NASTAGIO DEGLI ONESTI
(THE DECAMERON, DAY V, NOVEL VIII)

In Ravenna, that most ancient city of Romagna, there dwelt of yore noblemen and gentlemen not a few, among whom was a young man, Nastagio degli Onesti by name, who by the death of his father and one of his uncles inherited immense wealth. Being without a wife, Nastagio, as 'tis the way with young men, became enamoured of a daughter of Messer Paolo Traversaro, a damsel of much higher birth than his, whose love he hoped to win by gifts and the like modes of courting, which, albeit they were excellent and fair and commendable, not only availed him not, but seemed rather to have the contrary effect, so harsh and ruthless and unrelenting did the beloved damsel shew herself towards him; for whether it was her uncommon beauty or her noble lineage that puffed her up, so haughty and disdainful was she grown that pleasure she had none either in him or in aught that pleased him. The burden of which disdain Nastagio found so hard to bear, that many a time, when he had made his moan, he longed to make away with himself. However he refrained therefrom, and many a time resolved to give her up altogether, or, if so he might, to hold her in despite, as she did him: but 'twas all in vain, for it seemed as if, the more his hope dwindled, the greater grew his love.

And, as thus he continued, loving and spending inordinately, certain of his kinsfolk and friends, being apprehensive lest he should waste both himself and his substance, did many a time counsel and beseech him to depart Ravenna, and go tarry for a time elsewhere, that so he might at once cool his flame and reduce his charges. For a long while Nastagio answered their admonitions with banter; but as they continued to ply him with them, he grew weary of saying no so often, and promised obedience. Whereupon he equipped himself as if for a journey to France or Spain, or other distant parts, got on horseback and sallied forth of Ravenna, accompanied by not a few of his friends, and being come to a place called Chiassi, about three miles from Ravenna, he halted, and having sent for tents and pavilions, told his companions that there he meant to stay, and they might go back to Ravenna.

So Nastagio pitched his camp, and there commenced to live after as fine and lordly a fashion as did ever any man, bidding divers of his friends from time to time to breakfast or sup with him, as he had been wont to do. Now it so befell that about the beginning of May, the season being very fine, he fell a brooding on the cruelty of his mistress, and, that his meditations might be the less disturbed, he bade all his servants leave him, and sauntered slowly, wrapt in thought, as far as the pinewood. Which he had threaded for a good half-mile, when, the fifth hour of the day being

<83>

well-nigh past, yet he recking neither of food nor of aught else, 'twas as if he heard a woman wailing exceedingly and uttering most piercing shrieks: whereat, the train of his sweet melancholy being broken, he raised his head to see what was toward, and wondered to find himself in the pinewood; and saw, moreover, before him running through a grove, close set with underwood and brambles, towards the place where he was, a damsel most comely, stark naked, her hair dishevelled, and her flesh all torn by the briers and brambles, who wept and cried piteously for mercy; and at her flanks he saw two mastiffs, exceeding great and fierce, that ran hard upon her track, and not seldom came up with her and bit her cruelly; and in the rear he saw, riding a black horse, a knight sadly accoutred, and very wrathful of mien, carrying a rapier in his hand, and with despiteful, blood-curdling words threatening her with death.

Whereat he was at once amazed and appalled, and then filled with compassion for the hapless lady, whereof was bred a desire to deliver her, if so he might, from such anguish and peril of death. Wherefore, as he was unarmed, he ran and took in lieu of a cudgel a branch of a tree, with which he prepared to encounter the dogs and the knight.

Which the knight observing, called to him before he was come to close quarters, saying:—"Hold off, Nastagio, leave the dogs and me alone to deal with this vile woman as she has deserved." And, even as he spoke, the dogs gripped the damsel so hard on either flank that they arrested her flight, and the knight, being come up, dismounted.

Whom Nastagio approached, saying:—"I know not who thou art, that knowest me so well, but thus much I tell thee: 'tis a gross outrage for an armed knight to go about to kill a naked woman, and set his dogs upon her as if she were a wild beast: rest assured that I shall do all I can to protect her." Whereupon: —"Nastagio," replied the knight, "of the same city as thou was I, and thou wast yet a little lad when I, Messer Guido degli Anastagi by name, being far more enamoured of this damsel than thou art now of her of the Traversari, was by her haughtiness and cruelty brought to so woeful a pass that one day in a fit of despair I slew myself with this rapier which thou seest in my hand; for which cause I am condemned to the eternal pains.

"Nor was it long after my death that she, who exulted therein over measure, also died, and for that she repented her not of her cruelty and the joy she had of my sufferings, for which she took not blame to herself, but merit, was likewise condemned to the pains of hell. Nor had she sooner made her descent, than for her pain and mine 'twas ordained, that she should flee before me, and that I, who so loved her, should pursue her, not as my beloved lady, but as my mortal enemy, and so, as often as I come up with her, I slay her with this same rapier with which I slew myself, and having ripped her up by the back, I take out that hard and cold heart, to

<84>

which neither love nor pity had ever access, and therewith her other inward parts, as thou shalt forthwith see, and cast them to these dogs to eat. And in no long time, as the just and mighty God decrees, she rises even as if she had not died, and recommences her dolorous flight, I and the dogs pursuing her. And it so falls out that every Friday about this hour I here come up with her, and slaughter her as thou shalt see; but ween not that we rest on other days; for there are other places in which I overtake her, places in which she used, or devised how she might use, me cruelly; on which wise, changed as thou seest from her lover into her foe, I am to pursue her for years as many as the months during which she shewed herself harsh to me. Wherefore leave me to execute the decree of the Divine justice, and presume not to oppose that which thou mayst not avail to withstand."

Affrighted by the knight's words, insomuch that there was scarce a hair on his head but stood on end, Nastagio shrank back, still gazing on the hapless damsel, and waited all a tremble to see what the knight would do. Nor had he long to wait; for the knight, as soon as he had done speaking, sprang, rapier in hand, like a mad dog upon the damsel, who, kneeling, while the two mastiffs gripped her tightly, cried him mercy; but the knight, thrusting with all his force, struck her between the breasts, and ran her clean through the body.

Thus stricken, the damsel fell forthwith prone on the ground sobbing and shrieking: whereupon the knight drew forth a knife, and having therewith opened her in the back, took out the heart and all the circumjacent parts, and threw them to the two mastiffs, who, being famished, forthwith devoured them. And in no long time the damsel, as if nought thereof had happened, started to her feet, and took to flight towards the sea, pursued, and ever and anon bitten, by the dogs, while the knight, having gotten him to horse again, followed them as before, rapier in hand; and so fast sped they that they were quickly lost to Nastagio's sight.

Long time he stood musing on what he had seen, divided between pity and terror, and then it occurred to him that, as this passed every Friday, it might avail him not a little. So, having marked the place, he rejoined his servants, and in due time thereafter sent for some of his kinsfolk and friends, and said to them: — "'Tis now a long while that you urge me to give up loving this lady that is no friend to me, and therewith make an end of my extravagant way of living; and I am now ready so to do, provided you procure me one favour, to wit, that next Friday Messer Paolo Traversaro, and his wife and daughter, and all the ladies, their kinswomen, and as many other ladies as you may be pleased to bid, come hither to breakfast with me: when you will see for yourselves the reason why I so desire." A small matter this seemed to them; and so, on their return to Ravenna, they lost no time in conveying Nastagio's message to his intended guests: and,

<85>

albeit she was hardly persuaded, yet in the end the damsel that Nastagio loved came with the rest.

Nastagio caused a lordly breakfast to be prepared, and had the tables set under the pines about the place where he had witnessed the slaughter of the cruel lady; and in ranging the ladies and gentlemen at table he so ordered it, that the damsel whom he loved was placed opposite the spot where it should be enacted. The last course was just served, when the despairing cries of the hunted damsel became audible to all, to their no small amazement; and each asking, and none knowing, what it might import, up they all started intent to see what was toward; and perceived the suffering damsel, and the knight and the dogs, who in a trice were in their midst. They hollaed amain to dogs and knight, and not a few advanced to succour the damsel: but the words of the knight, which were such as he had used to Nastagio, caused them to fall back, terror-stricken and lost in amazement. And when the knight proceeded to do as he had done before, all the ladies that were there, many of whom were of kin to the suffering damsel and to the knight, and called to mind his love and death, wept as bitterly as if 'twere their own case.

When 'twas all over, and the lady and the knight had disappeared, the strange scene set those that witnessed it pondering many and divers matters: but among them all none was so appalled as the cruel damsel that Nastagio loved, who, having clearly seen and heard all that had passed, and being ware that it touched her more nearly than any other by reason of the harshness that she had ever shewn to Nastagio, seemed already to be fleeing from her angered lover, and to have the mastiffs on her flanks. And so great was her terror that, lest a like fate should befall her, she converted her aversion into affection, and as soon as occasion served, which was that very night, sent a trusty chambermaid privily to Nastagio with a request that he would be pleased to come to her, for that she was ready in all respects to pleasure him to the full. Nastagio made answer that he was greatly flattered, but that he was minded with her consent to have his pleasure of her in an honourable way, to wit, by marrying her. The damsel, who knew that none but herself was to blame that she was not already Nastagio's wife, made answer that she consented. Wherefore by her own mouth she acquainted her father and mother that she agreed to marry Nastagio; and, they heartily approving her choice, Nastagio wedded her on the ensuing Sunday, and lived happily with her many a year. Nor was it in her instance alone that this terror was productive of good: on the contrary, it so wrought among the ladies of Ravenna that they all became, and have ever since been, much more compliant with men's desires than they had been wont to be. [15]

---

[15] Boccaccio. *The Decameron*. Translated by J. M. Riggs, London 1930.

<86>

Dreams

[JOHN] DRYDEN

[Two Episodes] From the Tale of "The Cock and the Fox."[1]

[Madam, quoth he, gramercy for your care,
  But Cato, whom you quoted, you may spare:
'Tis true, a wise and worthy man he seems,
And (as you say) gave no belief to dreams:
But other men of more authority,
And, by the immortal powers! as wise as he,
Maintain, with sounder sense, that dreams forebode;
For Homer plainly says they come from God.
Nor Cato said it: but some modern fool
Imposed in Cato's name on boys at school.
Believe me, madam, morning dreams foreshow
The events of things, and future weal or woe:
Some truths are not by reason to be tried,
But we have sure experience for our guide.
An ancient author, equal with the best,
Relates this tale of dreams among the rest.][2]

---

[1] Dryden's poem is an adaptation and expansion of "The Nun Priest's Tale" from
Chaucer's *Canterbury Tales*. This poem was widely read and admired, and Sir
Walter Scott wrote in praise of Dryden's clever additions to the original. Critic
Tom Mason describes Dryden's adaptation of Chaucer thus: "The degree of
approximation of Dryden's English to the original varies passage by passage, line
by line, almost phrase by phrase. Some passages are modeled closely on
Chaucer's, and some lines taken over almost verbatim, to an extent that is
impossible when translating dead languages; but there are also long passages
appearing to have little Chaucerian basis, and alterations are made to character
and plot. It is as if Dryden were impelled to push his techniques, particularly of
addition, to the extreme" (Mason 2).
[2] Lewis has selected a free-standing episode from The Nun's Priest's Tale, lines
210-355. I have inserted, in square brackets, the prefatory and concluding
passages from Dryden. Lewis's excerpting from Dryden's and Chaucer's
narrative conceals the fact that the poem is a beast fable, and that the speaker is a
rooster.

<87>

Two friends or brothers, with devout intent,
On some far pilgrimage together went.
It happen'd so that, when the sun was down,
They just arrived by twilight at a town:
That day had been the baiting of a bull,
'Twas at a feast, and every inn so full,
That no void room in chamber, or on ground,
And but one sorry bed was to be found:
And that so little it would hold but one,
Though till this hour they never lay alone.

So were they forced to part; one staid behind,
His fellow sought what lodging he could find:
At last he found a stall where oxen stood,
And that he rather chose than lie abroad.
'Twas in a farther yard without a door;
But, for his ease, well litter'd[3] was the floor.

His fellow, who the narrow bed had kept,
Was weary, and without a rocker[4] slept:
Supine he snored; but in the dead of night
He dream'd his friend appear'd before his sight,
Who, with his ghastly look and doleful cry,

Said, "Help me, brother, or this night I die:
Arise, and help, before all help be vain,
Or in an ox's stall I shall be slain." —
Roused from his rest, he waken'd in a start,
Shivering with horror, and with aching[5] heart;
At length to cure himself by reason tries;
— "'Tis but a dream, and what are dreams but lies?" —
So thinking, changed his side, and closed his eyes.
His dream returns; his friend appears again:
— "The murderers come, now help, or I am slain!" —
'Twas but a vision still, and visions are but vain.

---

[3] *Well-litter'd*, i.e., covered with straw.
[4] *Rocker.* Not in Chaucer. Usually refers to a servant or attendant who rocks an infant's cradle.
[5] *Aching.* Lewis's version reads "aking."

<88>

He dreamt the third: but now his friend appear'd
Pale, naked, pierced with wounds, with blood besmear'd:
Thrice warn'd, — "Awake," said he; "relief is late,
The deed is done; but thou revenge my fate:
Tardy of aid, unseal thy heavy eyes;
Awake, and with the dawning day arise:
Take to the western gate thy ready way,
For by that passage they my corpse convey:
My corpse is in a tumbril[6] laid, among
The filth and ordure, and enclosed with dung;
That cart arrest, and raise a common cry;
For sacred hunger of my gold, I die:" —
Then shew'd his grisly wound; and last he drew
A piteous sigh, and took a long adieu.
The frighted friend arose by break of day,
And found the stall where late his fellow lay.
Then of his impious host inquiring more,
Was answer'd that his guest was gone before:
"Muttering he went," said he, "by morning light,
And much complain'd of his ill rest by night."
This raised suspicion in the pilgrim's mind;
Because all hosts are of an evil kind,
And oft, to share the spoils, with robbers join'd.

His dream confirm'd his thought: with troubled look
Straight to the western gate his way he took:
There, as his dream foretold, a cart he found,
That carried compost forth to dung the ground.
This when the pilgrim saw, he stretch'd his throat,
And cried out "Murder!" with a yelling note.
"My murder'd fellow in this cart lies dead,
Vengeance and justice on the villain's head;
You, magistrates, who sacred laws dispense,
On you I call to punish this offence."

---

6 *Tumbril.* A dung-cart.

<89>

The word thus given, within a little space,
The mob came roaring out, and throng'd the place.
All in a trice they cast the cart to ground,
And in the dung the murder'd body found;
Though breathless, warm, and reeking from the wound.
Good Heaven, whose darling attribute we find
Is boundless grace and mercy to mankind,
Abhors the cruel; and the deeds of night
By wondrous ways reveals in open light:
Murder may pass unpunish'd for a time,
But tardy justice will o'ertake the crime.
And oft a speedier pain the guilty feels;
The hue and cry of Heaven pursues him at the heels,
Fresh from the fact; as in the present case,
The criminals are seized upon the place:
Carter and host confronted face to face.
Stiff in denial, as the law appoints,
On engines they distend their tortured joints:[7]
So was confession forced, th' offence was known,
And public justice on th' offenders[8] done.

—"Here may you see that visions are to dread;
And in the page that follows this, I read," —

— Of two young merchants, whom the hope of gain
Induced in partnership to cross the main:
Waiting till willing winds their sails supplied,
Within a trading town they long abide,
Full fairly situate on a haven's side.
One evening it befell, that, looking out,
The wind they long had wish'd was come about:
Well pleased, they went to rest; and if the gale
Till morn continued, both resolved to sail.
But as together in a bed they lay,
The younger had a dream at break of day.

---

[7] *On engines...* The accused are subjected to the rack or other instruments of torture.
[8] *Th' offense ... th' offenders.* Lewis elides "the offense" and "the offenders" to keep Dryden's meter intact. Lewis also includes judicious punctuation not found in later editions of Dryden.

<90>

A man, he thought, stood frowning at his side;
Who warn'd him for his safety to provide,
Nor put to sea, but safe on shore abide.

—"I come, thy genius,[9] to command thy stay;
Trust not the winds, for fatal is the day,
And death, unhoped, attends the watery way" —

The vision said: and vanish'd from his sight:
The dreamer waken'd in a mortal fright:
Then pull'd his drowsy neighbour, and declared
What in his slumber he had seen and heard.
His friend smiled scornful, and with proud contempt
Rejects, as idle, what his fellow dreamt.
— "Stay, who will stay; for me no fears restrain,
Who follow Mercury,[10] the god of gain;
Let each man do as to his fancy seems,
I wait not, I, till you have better dreams.
Dreams are but interludes which fancy makes;
When monarch Reason sleeps, this mimic wakes:
Compounds a medley of disjointed things,
A mob of cobblers, and a court of kings:
Light fumes are merry, grosser fumes[11] are sad;
Both are the reasonable soul run mad:
And many monstrous forms in sleep we see,
That neither were, nor are, nor e'er can be.
Sometimes forgotten things, long cast behind,
Rush forward in the brain, and come to mind.
The nurse's legends are for truths received,
And the man dreams but what the boy believed.

---

9 *Genius*. Guardian spirit or angel.
10 Some irony here, as the god Mercury (the Greek Hermes) is also the messenger
delivering information from the gods in the form of dreams. Dryden
underscores the cost of failing to study one's classics.
11 *Fumes*. "Something which 'goes to the head' and clouds the faculties or the
reason" (OED).

<91>

"Sometimes we but rehearse a former play,
The night restores our actions done by day;
As hounds in sleep will open for their prey.
In short, the farce of dreams is of a piece:
Chimeras all; and more absurd, or less:
You, who believe in tales, abide alone;
Whate'er I get this voyage is my own." —

Thus while he spoke, he heard the shouting crew
That call'd aboard, and took his last adieu.
The vessel went before a merry gale,
And for quick passage put on every sail:
But when least fear'd, and even in open day,
The mischief overtook her in the way:
Whether she sprung a leak, I cannot find,
Or whether she was overset with wind,
Or that some rock below her bottom rent;
But down at once with all her crew she went:
Her fellow ships from far her loss descried;
But only she was sunk, and all were safe beside.

[By this example you are taught again,
That dreams and visions are not always vain:][12]

---

[12] I have appended Dryden's lines which elide this dream narrative to the one
which follows in the Chaucer original. Again, bear in mind that the speaker is
Chanticleer, a rooster.

<92>

History of Porsenna, King of Russia

[THOMAS] LISLE[1]

> *Arva, beata,*
> *Petamus arva, divites et insulas*
> — Hor. Epod. 16[2]

BOOK I.

In Russia's frozen clime, some ages since,
There dwelt, historians say, a worthy prince,
Who to his people's good confin'd his care,
And fix'd the basis of his empire there;
Enlarg'd their trade, the liberal arts improved,
Made nations happy, and himself belov'd;

---

[1] *Lisle.* The Rev. Thomas Lisle (b. ?? - d. 1767) is now but a footnote in literature. He was the son of Edward Lisle, of Crux Easton, Hampshire, one of twenty siblings. This long poem is steeped in same-sex affection, and a between-the-lines reading of Lisle's career indicates his likely inclinations. At Magdalen College he was one of three men in a scandal involving "blasphemy and other vile practices." He was the only one to escape expulsion or prosecution, but half a decade or so of discreet exile followed, with the poet serving as a chaplain in Smyrna. He was in Cairo in 1734 and in Marseilles in 1735, and then found a position as a rector on the Isle of Wight. The scandal was well behind him when his mother secured him the vicarage at Burghclere, Hampshire, where he spent the rest of his days (Courtney 404). Lewis's penchant for texts by social "outsiders" comes to the fore in the selection of this poem, which is a mythological/pastoral fantasy with some Gothic trappings.

Lewis's source for this text was most likely Volume 6 of J. Dodsley's series, *A Collection of Poems in Six Volumes by Several Hands*. Lisle's poem is there in full on pp. 178-210. Lewis could also have found the poem as pp. 109-143 in J.G.A. Stoupe's 1779 Paris anthology, *A Collection of Poems by Several Hands*, which also includes Parnell's "The Hermit." Scott mentions "Porsenna" as a familiar poem in his "Essay on Imitations of Ancient Ballads," so Lisle's work must have been known to him before Lewis chose it. The narrative appears to be pure invention, although Lisle alludes to other poetic texts. Sabine Baring-Gould, in his 1868 *Curious Myths of the Middle Ages*, mentions this poem and compares the story told therein with other medieval legends of The Blessed Isles (282-283).

[2] *Arva, beata.* From Epode 16 of Horace. This Latin poem, whose opening refers to Lars Porsena, an Etruscan enemy of Rome, may have suggested to Lisle the name "Porsenna," which is not Russian at all. The phrase "Arva beata" is a powerful demarcation of the concept of Utopian "blessed isles," a haven for refugees, and the phrase was used gratefully to describe Great Britain as it aligned itself with Protestant groups, who had occasion to seek haven there from Continental oppression. The lines from Horace are *"Nos manet Oceanus circumvagus: arva, beata/ Petamus arva, divites et insulas,"* which translates as "The Ocean remains around us: we seek fields, blessed fields and fortunate isles." Of course, this also plays on the origin of Lisle's own family name, *de L'Isle*.

<93>

To all the neighbouring states a terror grown,
The dear delight and glory of his own.
Not like those kings, who vainly seek renown
From countries ruin'd, and from battles won;
Those mighty Nimrods,[3] who mean laws despise,
Call murder but a princely exercise,
And, if one bloodless sun should steal away,
Cry out, with Titus,[4] they have lost a day;
Who, to be more than men, themselves debase
Beneath the brute, their Maker's form deface,
Raising their titles by their God's disgrace.
Like fame to bold Erostratus[5] we give,
Who scorn'd by less than sacrilege to live;
On holy ruins rais'd a lasting name,
And in the temple's fire diffus'd his shame.
Far different praises, and a brighter fame,
The virtues of the young Porsenna[6] claim;
For by that name the Russian king was known,
And sure a nobler ne'er adorn'd the throne.
In war he knew the deathful sword to wield,
And sought the thickest dangers of the field,
A bold commander; but, the storm o'erblown,
He seem'd as he were made for peace alone;
Then was the golden age again restor'd,
Nor less his justice honour'd, than his sword.
All needless pomp, and outward grandeur spar'd,
The deeds that grac'd him were his only guard;
No private views beneath a borrow'd name;
His and the public interest were the same.
In wealth and pleasure let the subject live;
But virtue is the king's prerogative:

---

[3] *Nimrod*. Mythical Old Testament figure, possibly of Assyrian origin, associated with rebellion against God and with the construction of the Tower of Babel.

[4] *Titus*. Titus Flavius Vespasianus (CE 39-81). Roman legate who conquered Jerusalem in 70 CE, become Roman Emperor in 79 CE, known for his cruelty before becoming Emperor. His reign, more temperate, belied his reputation.

[5] *Erostratus*. Arsonist who set fire to the Temple of Diana at Ephesus, on the same day in 356 BCE on which the future Alexander the Great was born. Erostratus wanted immortal fame for the deed, and he gains it, as a footnote.

[6] *Porsenna*. Porsenna is not a Slavic name: it is Etruscan, nor was there a kingdom called "Russia" in antiquity.

<94>

Porsenna there without a rival stood,
And would maintain his right of doing good.
Nor did his person less attraction wear,
Such majesty and sweetness mingled there:
Heaven, with uncommon art, the clay refin'd,
A proper mansion for so fair a mind;
Each look, each action, bore peculiar grace,
And love itself was painted on his face.
In peaceful time he suffered not his mind
To rust in sloth, though much to peace inclin'd;
Nor wanton in the lap of pleasure lay,
And, lost to glory, loiter'd life away:
But active rising ere the prime of day.
Through woods and lonely deserts lov'd to stray;
With hounds and horns to wake the furious bear,
Or rouse the tawny lion from his lair,
To rid the forest of the savage brood,
And whet his courage for his country's good.
One day, as he pursued the dangerous sport,
Attended by the nobles of his court,
It chanc'd, a beast of more than common speed
Sprang from the brake, and through the desert fled.
The ardent Prince, impetuous as the wind,
Rush'd on, and left his lagging train behind.
Fir'd with the chase, and full of youthful blood,
O'er plains, and vales, and woodland wilds, he rode,
Urging his courser's speed, nor thought the day,
How wasted, nor how intricate the way:
Nor, till the night in dusky clouds came on,
Restrain'd his pace, or found himself alone.
Missing his train, he strove to measure back
The road he came, but could not find the track;
Still turning to the place he left before,
And only lab'ring to be lost the more.
The bugle horn, which o'er his shoulders hung,
So loud he winded, that the forest rung;
In vain, no voice but Echo[7] from the ground,
And vocal woods make mockery of the sound.

---

[7] *Echo*. Personification of the acoustic effect of the echo, usually as a mountain nymph.

<95>

And now the gathering clouds began to spread
O'er the dun face of night a deeper shade;
And the hoarse thunder, growling from afar,
With herald voice proclaim'd th' approaching war;
Silence awhile ensued, then by degrees
A hollow wind came muttering through the trees.
Sudden the full-fraught sky discharg'd its store,
Of rain and rattling hail a mingled shower;
The active lightning ran along the ground;
The fiery bolts by fits were hurl'd around,
And the wide forests trembled at the sound.
Amazement seiz'd the Prince; where could he fly?
No guide to lead, no friendly cottage nigh.
Pensive and unresolv'd awhile he stood
Beneath the scanty covert of the wood;
But, drove from thence, soon sallied forth again,
As chance directed, on the dreary plain;
Constrain'd his melancholy way to take
Through many a loathsome bog, and thorny brake,
Caught in the thicket, flound'ring in the lake.
Wet with the storm, and wearied with the way,
By hunger pinch'd, himself to beasts a prey;
Nor wine to cheer his heart, nor fire to burn,
Nor place to rest, nor prospect to return.
Drooping and spiritless, at life's despair,
He bade it pass, not worth his farther care;
When suddenly he 'spied a distant light,
That faintly twinkled through the gloom of night,
And his heart leap'd for joy, and bless'd the welcome sight.
Oft times he doubted, it appear'd so far,
And hung so high, 'twas nothing but a star,
Or kindled vapour wand'ring through the sky,[8]
But still press'd on his steed, still kept it in his eye;
Till much fatigue, and many dangers past,
At a huge mountain he arriv'd at last.
There, lighting from his horse, on hands and knees
Grop'd out the darksome road by slow degrees,
Crawling or clamb'ring o'er the rugged way;

---

[8] *Kindled vapour, i.e*, the Northern Lights.

<96>

Lapland witch summons winds to destroy a sailing ship.
From Olaus Magnus, *Historia de Gentibus Septentrionalibus*, 1555

The thunder rolls above, the flames around him play.
Joyful at length he gain'd the sleepy height.
And found the rift whence sprang the friendly light —
And here he stopp'd to rest his wearied feet,
And weigh the perils he had still to meet;
Unsheath'd his trusty sword, and dealt his eyes
With caution round him to prevent surprise;
Then summon'd all the forces of his mind,
And, entering boldly, cast his fears behind,
Resolv'd to push his way, whate'er withstood,
Or perish bravely, as a monarch should.
While he the wonders of the place survey'd,
And through the various cells at random stray'd;
In a dark corner of the cave he view'd
Somewhat, that in the shape of woman stood;
But more deform'd than dreams can represent
The midnight hag, or poet's fancy paint
The Lapland witch, ⁹ when she her broom bestrides,

---

⁹ *Lapland Witch.* Lapland was long associated with witches (both male and female), whose
specialty was the creation, and even sale, of the power of the winds. Milton mentions these
Arctic-circle witches with some dread: "Follow the night-hag, when called/ In secret,
riding through the air she comes,/ Lured with the smell of infant blood, to dance/ With
Lapland witches, while the labouring moon/ Eclipses at their charms" (*Paradise Lost*, ii,
622-66) Frank Edgar Farley traced the entry of translations, real or imaginative, from
Laplandish during the Seventeenth Century, adding an even more primitive and rustic
tone to the literature around Odin and the gloomy north. Specifics of the witch lore came
from Johan Scheffer's *Lapponia* (1673 in Latin), and *The History of Lapland* (1674 in
English, Oxford).

<97>

And scatters storms and tempests as she rides.
She look'd as nature made her to disgrace
Her kind, and cast a blot on all the race;
Her shrivel'd skin, with yellow spots besmear'd,
Like mouldy records seem'd; her eyes were blear'd;
Her feeble limbs with age and palsy shook;
Bent was her body, haggard was her look.
From the dark nook out crept the filthy crone,
And, propp'd upon her crutch, came tottering on.
The Prince in civil guise approach'd the Dame,
Told her his piteous case, and whence he came,
And till Aurora[10] should the shades expel,
Implor'd a lodging in her friendly cell.
"Mortal, whoe'er thou art," the Fiend began,
And, as she spake, a deadly horror ran
Through all his frame; his cheeks the blood forsook,
Chatter'd his teeth, his knees together struck.
"Whoe'er thou art, that with presumption rude
Dar'st on our sacred privacy intrude,
And without licence in our court appear,
Know, thou'rt the first that ever enter'd here.
But since thou plead'st excuse, thou'rt hither brought
More by thy fortune than thy own default,
Thy crime, though great, an easy pardon finds,
For mercy ever dwells in royal minds;
And would you learn from whose indulgent hand
You live, and in whose awful presence stand,
Know farther, through yon wide extended plains
Great Eolus[11] the King of Tempests reigns,
And in this lofty palace makes abode
Well suited to his state, and worthy of the God.
The various elements his empire own,
And pay their humble homage at his throne;
And hither all the storms and clouds resort,
Proud to increase the splendour of his court.

---

[10] *Aurora*. Spirit or nymph of the dawn.
[11] *Eolus*. Aeolus, one of the Greek wind spirits.

<98>

His Queen am I,[12] from whom the beauteous race
Of winds arose, sweet fruit of our embrace!"
She scarce had ended, when, with wild uproar
And horrid din, her sons impetuous pour
Around the cave; came rushing in amain
Lybs,[13] Eurus,[14] Boreas,[15] all the boist'rous train;
And, close behind them, on a whirlwind rode,
In clouded majesty, the Blust'ring God.
Their locks a thousand ways were blown about;
Their cheeks like full-blown bladders strutted out;
Their boasting talk was of the feats they'd done,
Of trees uprooted, and of towns o'erthrown;
And, when they kindly turn'd them to accost
The Prince, they almost pierc'd him with their frost.
The gaping hag in fix'd attention stood,
And at the close of every tale, cried "Good!"
Blessing with outstretched arms each darling son,
In due proportion to the mischief done.
"And where," said she, "does little Zephyr[16] stray?
Know ye, my sons, your brother's route to-day?
In what bold deeds does he his hours employ?
Grant heaven no evil has befall'n my boy!
Ne'er was he known to linger thus before."
Scarce had she spoke, when at the cavern door
Came lightly tripping in a form more fair
Than the young poet's fond ideas are,
When, fir'd with love, he tries his utmost art
To paint the beauteous tyrant of his heart,
A satin vest his slender shape confin'd,
Embroider'd o'er with flowers of every kind,
Flora's own work, when first the goddess strove
To win the little wanderer to her love.

---

12 *His queen am I.* Lisle interpolates his witch in place of Aeolus's traditional wife, an Athenian princess named Oreithya. Lisle's marriage of the Lapland witch queen to the King of the Winds, although eminently logical, is a bizarre synthesis of Greek and Nordic myth.

13 *Lybs.* Lips, or Libonotus, the Southwest wind, often depicted holding the stern of a sailing ship.

14 *Eurus.* The East Wind, an unlucky spirit.

15 *Boreas.* The North Wind.

16 *Zephyr.* The West Wind.

<99>

Of burnish'd silver were his sandals made,
Silver his buskins, and with gems o'erlaid;
A saffron-colour'd robe behind him flow'd,
And added grace and grandeur as he trod.
His wings, than lilies whiter to behold,
Sprinkled with azure spots, and streak'd with gold;
So thin their form, and of so light a kind,
That they forever danc'd, and flutter'd in the wind.
Around his temples, with becoming air,
In wanton ringlets curl'd his auburn hair,
And o'er his shoulders negligently spread;
A wreath of fragrant roses crown'd his head.
Such his attire; but O! no pen can trace,
No words can shew the beauties of his face;
So kind! so winning! so divinely fair!
Eternal youth and pleasure flourish'd there;
There all the little Loves and Graces meet,
And ev'ry thing that's soft, and ev'ry thing that's sweet.
"Thou vagrant," cried the Dame in angry tone,
"Where could'st thou loiter thus so long alone?
Little thou car'st what anxious thoughts molest,
What pangs are labouring in a mother's breast.
Well do you sue, our duty by your haste,
For thou, of all my sons, art always last;
A child less fondled would have fled more fast.
Sure, 'tis a curse on mothers, doom'd to mourn,
Where best they love, the least and worst return."
"My dear mama!" the gentle youth replied,
And made a low obeisance, "cease to chide,
Nor wound me with your words, for well you know
Your Zephyr bears a part in all your woe;
How great must be his sorrow then to learn,
That he himself's the cause of your concern!
Nor had I loiter'd thus, had I been free,
But the fair Princess of Felicity
Intreated me to make some short delay;
And ask'd by her, who could refuse to stay?
Surrounded by the damsels of her court,
She sought the shady grove, her lov'd resort;

<100>

Fresh rose the grass, the flowers were mix'd between,
Like rich embroidery on a ground of green,
And in the midst, protected by the shade,
A crystal stream in wild meanders play'd;
While in its banks, the trembling leaves among,
A thousand little birds in concert sung.
Close by a mount, with fragrant shrubs o'ergrown,
On a cool mossy couch she laid her down;
Her air, her posture, all conspir'd to please;
Her head, upon her snowy arm at ease
Reclin'd, a studied carelessness express'd;
Loose lay her robe, and naked heav'd her breast.
Eager I flew to that delightful place,
And pour'd a shower of kisses on her face;
Now hover'd o'er her neck, her breast, her arms,
Like bees o'er flowers, and tasted all her charms;
And then her lips, and then her cheeks I tried,
And fann'd, and wanton'd round on every side.
'O Zephyr,' cried the fair, 'thou charming boy,
Thy presence only can create me joy;
To me thou art beyond expression dear,
Nor can I quit the place while thou art here.'
Excuse my weakness, madam, when I swear
Such gentle words, join'd with so soft an air,
Pronounc'd so sweetly from a mouth so fair,
Quite ravish'd all my sense; nor did I know
How long I staid, or when or where to go.
Meanwhile the damsels, debonair and gay,
Prattled around, and laugh'd the time away:
These in soft notes address'd the ravish'd ear,
And warbled out so sweet, 'twas heaven to hear;
And those in rings, beneath the greenwood shade,
Danc'd to the melody their fellows made.
Some, studious of themselves, employ'd their care
In weaving flowery wreaths to deck their hair;
While others to some favourite plant convey'd
Refreshing showers, and cheer'd its drooping, head.

<101>

The winged Zephyr in a seductive embrace with Apollo's lover Hyacinthus.

Joy so general spread through all the place,
such satisfaction dwelt on every face,
The nymphs so kind, so lovely look'd the queen,
That never eye beheld a sweeter scene."
Porsenna like a statue fix'd appeared,
And, wrapp'd in silent wonder, gaz'd and heard;
Much he admir'd the speech, the speaker more,
And dwelt on every word, and griev'd to find it o'er.
— "Oh gentle youth," he cried, "proceed to tell,
In what fair country does this princess dwell;
What regions unexplor'd, what hidden coast

<102>

Can so much goodness, so much beauty boast?" —
To whom the winged god, with gracious look,
Numberless sweets diffusing while he spoke,
Thus answer'd kind, "These happy gardens lie
Far hence remov'd, beneath a milder sky;
Their name the Kingdom of Felicity.
Sweet scenes of endless bliss, enchanted ground,
A soil for ever sought, but seldom found;
Though in the search all human kind in vain
Weary their wits, and waste their lives in pain.
In different parties different paths they tread,
As reason guides them, or as follies lead;
These wrangling for the place they ne'er shall see,
Debating those, if such a place there be;
But not the wisest, nor the best, can say
Where lies the point, or mark the certain way.
Some few, by Fortune favour'd for her sport,
Have sail'd in sight of this delightful port:
In thought already seiz'd the bless'd abodes,
And in their fond delirium rank'd with gods.
Fruitless attempt! all avenues are kept
By dreadful foes, sentry that never slept.
Here fell Detraction darts her pois'nous breath
Fraught with a thousand stings, and scatters death;
Sharp-sighted Envy there maintains her post,
And shakes her flaming brand, and stalks around the coast.
These on the helpless bark their fury pour,
Plunge in the waves, or dash against the shore;
Teach wretched mortals they were doom'd to mourn,
And ne'er must rest but in the silent urn.
But say, young Monarch, for what name you bear
Your mein, your dress, your person, all declare;
And though I seldom fan the frozen north,
Yet have I heard of brave Porsenna's worth.
My brother Boreas through the world has flown,
Swelling his breath to spread forth your renown;

<103>

Say, would you choose to visit this retreat,
And view the world where all these wonders meet?
Wish you some friend o'er that tempestuous sea
To bear you safe, behold that friend in me.
My active wings, shall all their force employ,
And nimbly waft you to the realms of joy;
As once, to gratify the God of Love,
I bore fair Psyche to the Cyprian grove;[17]
Or as Jove's bird, descending from on high,
Snatch'd the young Trojan trembling to the sky.[18]
There perfect bliss thou may'st for ever share,
Scap'd from the busy world, and all its care;
There in the lovely princess thou shall find
A mistress ever blooming, ever kind."—

All ecstasy on air Porsenna trod,
And to his bosom strain'd the little God:
With grateful sentiments his heart o'erflow'd,
And in the warmest words millions of thanks bestow'd.
When Eolus in surly humour broke
Their strict embrace, and thus abruptly spoke:
— "Enough of compliment; I hate the sport
Of meanless words: this is no human court,
Where plain and honest are discarded quite,
For the more modish title of polite;
Where in soft speeches hypocrites impart
The venom'd ills that lurk beneath the heart;
In friendship's holy guise their guilt improve,
And kindly kill with specious shew of love.
For us, my subjects are not used to wait,
And waste their hours to hear a mortal prate.
They must abroad before the rising sun,
And hie 'em to the seas: there's mischief to be done.
Excuse my plainness, Sir, but business stands,

---

[17] *Psyche*. A maiden kidnapped on behalf of the love-god Cupid.
[18] The abduction of Ganymede, the Trojan boy carried off by Zeus, in the form of an eagle. The wind god here is boasting of a deed he was not involved in. A homoerotic element is added here, therefore, since the beauteous Zephyr has just offered to carry off Porsenna, a man he has just met for the first time. (Zephyr was also involved in a love triangle with Apollo and Hyacinthus, another god-young man love tale.)

<104>

And we have storms and shipwrecks on our hands." —
He ended frowning, and the noisy rout
Each to his several cell went puffing out.
But Zephyr, far more courteous than the rest,
To his own bower convey'd the royal guest;
There on a bed of roses neatly laid,
Beneath the fragrance of a myrtle shade,
His limbs to needful rest the Prince applied;
His sweet companion slumbering by his side.

BOOK II

No sooner in her silver chariot rose
The ruddy Morn, than, sated with repose,
The Prince address'd his host; the God awoke,
And leaping from his couch, thus kindly spoke:
"This early call, my lord, that chides my stay,
Requires my thanks, and I with joy obey.
Like you, I long to reach the blissful coast,
Hate the slow night, and mourn the moments lost.
The bright Rosinda, loveliest of the fair
That crowd the Princess' court, demands my care;
E'en now with fears and jealousies o'erborne
Upbraids, and calls me cruel and forsworn.
What sweet rewards on all my toils attend,
Serving at once my mistress and my friend!
Just to my love and to my duty too,
Well paid in her, well pleas'd in pleasing you."
This said, he led him to the cavern gate,
And clasp'd him in his arms, and pois'd his weight;
Then, balancing his body here and there,
Stretch'd forth his agile wings, and launch'd in air;
Swift as the fiery meteor from on high
Shoots to its goal, and gleams athwart the sky.
Here with quick fan his lab'ring pinions play;
There glide at ease along the liquid way:
Now lightly skim the plain with even flight;
Now proudly soar above the mountain's height.
Spiteful Detraction, whose envenom'd hate
Sports with the sufferings of the good and great,

<105>

Spares not our Prince, but with opprobious sneer
Arraigns him of the heinous sin of fear;
That he, so tried in arms, whose very name
Infus'd a secret panic where it came,
E'en he, as high above the clouds he flew,
And 'spied the mountains less'ning to the view,
Nought round him but the wide expanded air,
Helpless, abandoned to a stripling's care,
Struck with the rapid whirl, and dreadful height,
Confess'd some faint alarm, some little fright.
The friendly God, who instantly divin'd
The terrors that possess'd his fellow's mind,
To calm his troubled thoughts, and chear the way,
Describ'd the nations that beneath them lay,
The name, the climate, and the soil's increase,
Their arms in war, their government in peace;
Shew'd their domestic arts, their foreign trade,
What interest they pursued, what leagues they made.
The sweet discourse so charm'd Porsenna's ear,
That, lost in joy, he had no time for fear.
From Scandinavia's cold inclement waste
O'er wide Germania's various realms they pass'd,
And now on Albion's fields[19] suspend their toil,
And hover for a while, and bless the soil.
O'er the gay scene the Prince delighted hung,
And gaz'd in rapture, and forgot his tongue;
Till bursting forth at length: "Behold," cried he,
The promis'd isle, the land I long'd to see;
Those plains, those vales, and fruitful hills, declare
My queen, my charmer must inhabit there." —
Thus rav'd the Monarch, and the gentle Guide,
Pleas'd with his error, thus in smiles replied:
— "I must applaud, my lord, the lucky thought;
E'en I, who know th' original, am caught,
And doubt my senses, when I view the draught.
The slow-ascending hill, the lofty wood
That mantles o'er its brow, the silver flood

---

[19] *Albion's fields*. They have come to the British Isles. It may well be that Lisle has Zephyr
linger over the Arcadian grottos of his own family's estate. The poet's long separation from
home and country may add to the pathos of this description.

<106>

Wand'ring in mazes through the flow'ry mead,
The herd that in the plenteous pastures feed,
And every object, every scene, excites
Fresh wonder in my soul, and fills with new delights:
Dwells cheerful Plenty there, and learned Ease,
And Art with Nature seems at strife to please.
There Liberty, delightful goddess, reigns,
Gladdens each heart, and gilds the fertile plains;
There, firmly seated, may she ever smile,
And shower her blessings o'er her favourite isle!
But see, the rising sun reproves our stay." —
He said, and to the ocean wing'd his way,
Stretching his course to climates then unknown,
Nations that swelter in the burning zone.
There, in Peruvian vales, a moment staid,
And smooth'd his wings beneath the citron shade;
Then swift his oary pinions plied again,
Cross'd the new world, and sought the Southern main;
Where, many a wet and weary league o'erpast,
The wish'd-for Paradise appeared at last.
With force abated, now they gently sweep
O'er the smooth surface of the shining deep;
The Dryads[20] hail'd them from the distant shore,
The Nereids play'd around, the Tritons swam before, [21]
While soft Favonius[22] their arrival greets,
And breathes his welcome in a thousand sweets.
Nor pale disease, nor health-consuming care,
Nor wrath, nor foul revenge, can enter there:
No vapour'd foggy gloom imbrowns the sky;
No tempests rage, no angry lightnings fly;
But dews, and soft refreshing airs are found,
And pure ethereal azure shines around.

---

[20] *Dryads.* Tree nymphs.
[21] *Nereids . . . Tritons.* Sea nymphs, and mermaids and mermen.
[22] *Favonius.* Roman name for Zephyr.

<107>

Whate'er the sweet Sabaean soil[23] can boast,
Or Mecca's plains, or India's spicy coast;
What Hybla's hills,[24] or rich Cabalia's fields,[25]
Or flow'ry vale of famed Hymettus[26] yields;
Or what of old th' Hesperian orchard[27] grac'd,

All that was e'er delicious to the taste,
Sweet to the smell, or lovely to the view,
Collected there with added beauty grew.
High tow'ring to the Heavens the trees are seen,
Their bulk immense, their leaf forever green!
So closely interwove, the tell-tale sun
Can ne'er descry the deeds beneath them done,
But where by fits the sportive gales divide
Their tender tops, and fan the leaves aside.
Like a smooth carpet, at their feet lies spread
The matted grass, by bubbling fountains fed;
And on each bough the feather'd choir employ
Their melting notes, and nought is heard but joy.
The painted flowers exhale a rich perfume,
The fruits are mingled with eternal bloom,
And Spring and Autumn hand in hand appear,
Lead on the merry months, and join to clothe the year.
Here, o'er the mountain's shaggy summit pour'd,
From rock to rock the tumbling torrent roar'd,
While beauteous Iris[28] in the vale below
Paints on the rising fumes her radiant bow.
Now through the meads the mazy current stray'd,
Now hid its wand'rings in the myrtle shade;
Or in a thousand veins divides its store,
Visits each plant, refreshes ev'ry flow'r;
O'er gems and golden sands in murmurs flows,
And sweetly soothes the soul, and lulls to soft repose.
If hunger call, no sooner can the mind

---

[23] *Sebaean.* Yemen, the legendary home of the Queen of Sheba.
[24] *Hybla.* The Hyblaean mountains in Sicily.
[25] *Cabalia.* Region of Persia.
[26] *Hymettus.* Mountain near Athens, famed for its thyme-flavored honey.
[27] *Hesperian.* The goddess Hera's garden, where grew the apples of immortality; in this context, the ultimate garden.
[28] *Iris.* Goddess of the Rainbow.

<108>

Express her will to needful food inclin'd,
But in some cool recess, or op'ning glade,
The seats are plac'd, the tables neatly laid,
And instantly convey'd by magic hand
In comely rows the costly dishes stand;
Meats of all kinds that nature can impart,
Prepared in all the nicest forms of art.
A troop of sprightly nymphs array'd in green,
With flow'ry chaplets crown'd, come scudding in:
With fragrant blossoms these adorn the feast,
Those with officious zeal attend the guest;
Beneath his feet the silken carpet spread,
Or sprinkle liquid odours o'er his head.
Others in ruby cups with roses bound,
Delightful! deal the sparkling nectar round;
Or weave the dance, or tune the vocal lay;
The lyres resound, the merry minstrels play;
Gay health, and youthful joys overspread the place,
And swell each heart, and triumph in each face.
So, when embolden'd by the vernal air,
The busy bees to blooming fields repair;
For various use employ their chymic[29] power;
One culls the snowy pounce, one sucks the flower;
Again to different works returning home,
Some steeve[30] the honey, some erect the comb;
All for the general good in concert strive,
And every soul's in motion, every limb's alive.
And now descending from his flight, the God
On the green turf releas'd his precious load;
There, after mutual salutations past,
And endless friendship vow'd, they part in haste;
Zephyr impatient to behold his love,
The Prince in raptures wand'ring through the grove;
Now skipping on, and singing as he went,
Now stopping short to give his transports vent;
With sudden gusts of happiness oppress'd,
Or stands entranc'd, or raves like one possess'd;
His mind afloat, his wand'ring senses quite

---

[29] *Chymic.* From chime: the juice or sap of plants.
[30] *Steeve.* To secure.

<109>

Overcome with charms, and frantic with delight;
From scene to scene by random steps convey'd,
Admires the distant views, explores the secret shade,
Dwells on each spot, with eager eye devours
The woods, the lawns, the buildings, and the bowers;
New sweets, new joys at every glance arise,
And every turn creates a fresh surprise.
Close by the borders of a rising wood,
In a green vale a crystal grotto stood;
And o'er its side, beneath a beechen shade,
In broken falls a silver fountain play'd.
Hither, attracted by the murmuring stream,
And cool recess, the pleas'd Porsenna came,
And on the tender grass reclining chose
To wave his joys awhile, and take a short repose.
The scene invites him, and the wanton breeze
That whispers through the vale, the dancing trees,
The warbling birds, and rills that gently creep,
All join their music to prolong his sleep.
The Princess for her morning walk prepar'd,
The female troops attend, a beauteous guard.
Array'd in all her charms appear'd the fair;
Tall was her stature, unconfin'd her air;
Proportion deck'd her limbs, and in her face
Lay love inshrin'd, lay sweet attractive grace
Temp'ring the awful beams her eyes convey'd,
And like a lambent flame around her play'd.
No foreign aids, by mortal ladies worn,
From shells and rocks her artless charms adorn;
For grant that beauty were by gems increas'd,
'Tis rendered more suspected at the least;
And foul defects, that would escape the sight,
Start from the piece, and take a stronger light.
Her chestnut hair in careless rings around
Her temples wav'd, with pinks and jasmine crown'd,
And, gather'd in a silken cord behind,
Curl'd to the waist, and floated in the wind;
O'er these a veil of yellow gauze she wore,
With amaranths and gold embroider'd o'er.

<110>

Her snowy neck half naked to the view
Gracefully fell; a robe of purple hue
Hung loosely o'er her tender shape, and tried
To shade those beauties, that it could not hide.
The damsels of her train with mirth and song
Frolic behind, and laugh and sport along.
The birds proclaim their Queen from every tree;
The beasts run frisking through the groves to see;
The Loves, the Pleasures, and the Graces meet
In antic rounds, and, dance before her feet.
But whatever fancy led, it chanc'd that day
They through the secret valley took their way,
And to the crystal grott[31] advancing 'spied
The Prince, extended by the fountain's side.
He look'd as, by some skilful hand express'd,
Apollo's youthful form retired to rest;

---

[31] *Grott.* Grotto. A grotto is a secluded, landscaped area, incorporating a natural or artificial cave. Some grottos were constructed to enclose family tombs, while others were purely ornamental. The construction of grottos such as those found in Renaissance Italian villas, and the raising of faux Druid standing stones and other pagan relics became a great pastime of the country gentleman, the best one could do if one did not inherit a crumbling abbey or a Roman hill-fort.

Alexander Pope spent over 20 years on his grotto on leased land in Twickenham, and the fame of his construction inspired many others to create beautifully-situated artificial caves (see Willson's detailed history of the poet's grotto). Lisle's father constructed a handsome rural grotto which was the subject of poems by Dryden and other poets, some featured in Dodsley's volume. The Lisle grotto at Crux Easton was faced with flint stone, the interior decorated with shells, stones of iron ore and other materials. The poet's nine sisters each had a seat in the grotto, permitting them to form a circle corresponding to the Nine Muses of antiquity. A niche was used for poetry reading or oracular pronouncements, with Pope serving at least once as Apollo. (Courtney 404). The Lisle grotto at Crux Easton was described thus by Pope:

Here, shunning, idleness at once and praise,
    This radiant pile nine sisters raise;
The glittering emblem of each spotless dame,
Clear as her soul and shining as her frame;
    Beauty which nature only can impart,
    And such a polish as disgraces art;
But fate disposed them in his humble sort,
And hid in deserts what would charm a court.
                — (Dodsley, vi., 161-62)

<111>

An English grotto at Ascot, 1831

When with the chase fatigued he quits the wood
For Pindus' vale,[32] and Aganippe's flood;[33]
There sleeps secure, his careless limbs display'd
At ease, encircled by the laurel shade;
Beneath his head his sheaf of arrows lie,
His bow unbent hangs negligently by.
The slumb'ring Prince might boast an equal grace,
So turn'd his limbs, so beautiful his face.
Waking, he started from the ground in haste,
And saw the beauteous choir around him plac'd;

[32] *Pindus*. Mountain range in northern Greece. See also the following note.

[33] *Aganippe*. A fountain at the base of Mt. Helicon, a very poetic choice since this locale was sacred to the Muses. Pausanias has given us a detailed description of the Muses' grove and spring (*Description of Greece*, ix, 29). An echo of the family circle at Crux Easton is contained in Pausanius' speculation about how the Muses grew in number from the original three to nine: "Pierus, a Macedonian ... came to Thespiae and established nine Muses, changing their names to the present ones ... There are some who say that Pierus himself had nine daughters, that their names were the same as those of the goddesses, and that those whom the Greeks called the children of the Muses were sons of the daughters of Pierus" (295). Lisle, father and son and sisters, were thus re-enacting Pausanius at their English grotto.

The Aganippe fountain is mentioned in passing along with Pindus, in Virgil's *Eclogues*: "nam neque Parnasi vobis iuga, nam neque Pindi/ ulla moram fecere, neque Aonie Aganippe" (x, 11-12): "For no heights of Parnassus or of Pindus, no Aonian Aganippe made you tarry."

<112>

Then, summoning his senses, ran to meet
The Queen, and laid him humbly at her feet.
"Deign, lovely Princess, to behold," said he,
"One, who has travers'd all the world to see
Those charms, and worship thy divinity:
Accept thy slave, and with a gracious smile
Excuse his rashness, and reward his toil."
Stood motionless the fair, with mute surprise,
And read him over with admiring eyes;
And while she steadfast gaz'd, a pleasing smart
Ran thrilling through her veins, and reach'd her heart.
Each limb she scann'd, considered every grace,
And sagely judg'd him of the Phoenix'[34] race:
An animal like this she ne'er had known,
And thence concluded there could be but one;
The creature too had all the Phoenix' air;
None but the Phoenix could appear so fair.
The more she look'd, the more she thought it true,
And call'd him by that name, to shew she knew.
— "O handsome Phoenix, for that such you are
We know; your beauty does your breed declare;
And I with sorrow own through all my coast
No other bird can such perfection boast;
For Nature form'd you single and alone,
Alas! what pity 'tis there is but one!
Was there a queen so fortunate to shew
An aviary of charming birds like you,
What envy would her happiness create
In all who saw the glories of her state!" —
The Prince laugh'd inwardly, surprised to find
So strange a speech, so innocent a mind.
The compliment indeed did some offence
To reason, and a little wrong'd her sense;
He could not let it pass, but told his name,
And what he was, and whence, and why he came;
And hinted other things of high concern
For him to mention and for her to learn;

---

[34] *Phoenix.* Some gender ambiguity enters here again, as the Phoenix (which lays an egg) is a female, or at best a creature of indeterminate gender that self-regenerates asexually after being consumed by a fire.

<113>

And she had a piercing wit, of wond'rous reach
To comprehend whatever he could teach.
Thus hand in hand they to the palace walk,
Pleas'd and instructed with each other's talk.
Here should I tell the furniture's expence,
And all the structure's vast magnificence,
Describe the walls of shining sapphire made,
With emerald and pearl the floors inlaid,
And how the vaulted canopies unfold
A mimic heaven, and flame with gems and gold;
Or how Felicity regales her guest,
The wit, the mirth, the music, and the feast;
And on each part bestow the praises due,
'Twould tire the writer, and the reader too.

My amorous tale a softer path pursues:
Love and the happy pair demand my Muse.[35]
O could her art in equal terms express
The lives they lead, the pleasures they possess!
Fortune had ne'er so plenteously before
Bestow'd her gifts, nor can she lavish more.
'Tis heaven itself, 'tis ecstasy of bliss,
Uninterrupted joy, untir'd excess;
Mirth following mirth the moments dance away;
Love claims the night, and friendship rules the day.
Their tender care no cold indifference knows;
No jealousies disturb their sweet repose;
No sickness, no decay; but youthful grace,
And constant beauty shines in either face.
Benumbing age may mortal charms invade,
Flowers of a day, that do but bloom and fade;
Far different here on them it only blows
The lily's white, and speeds the blushing rose;
No conquest o'er those radiant eyes can boast;

[35] *My amorous tale.* This is the only intrusion into the poem of the poet's personal voice,
and the only Muse invocation in the work. Since the work lacks an opening invocation of a
Muse, the intrusion seems awkward. The preceding stanza, ending with "'Twould tire the
writer, and the reader too," also removes the reader from engagement with the narrative to
a consideration of author-and-reader. Lisle, perhaps, realizes that he has reached the limit
of his reader's attention span, and he is not quite sure how to end one canto and start
another.

<114>

They, like the stars, shine brighter in its frosty
Nor fear its rigour, nor its rule obey;
All seasons are the same, and every month is May,
Alas! how vain is happiness below!
Man, soon or late, must have his share of woe;
Slight are his joys, and fleeting as the wind;
His griefs wound home, and leave a sting behind.
His lot distinguish'd from the brute appears
Less certain by his laughter than his tears;
For ignorance too oft our pleasure breeds,
But sorrow from the reasoning soul proceeds.
If man on earth in endless bliss could be,
The boon, young Prince, had been bestow'd on thee.
Bright shone thy stars, thy fortune flourish'd fair,
And seem'd secure beyond the reach of care,
And so might still have been, but anxious thought
Has dash'd thy cup, and thou must taste the draught.
It so befel: as on a certain day
This happy couple toy'd their time away,
He ask'd how many charming hours were flown,
Since on her slave her heaven of beauty shone.
— "Should I consult my heart," cried he, "the rate
Were small, a week would be the utmost date:
But when my mind reflects on actions past,
And counts its joys, time must have fled more fast;
Perhaps I might have said, three months are gone." —
— "Three months!" replied the fair, "three months alone!
Know that three hundred years have roll'd away,
Since at my feet the lovely Phoenix lay." —
— "Three hundred years!" re-echo'd back the Prince,
"A whole three hundred years completed since
I landed here! O! whither then are flown
My dearest friends, my subjects, and my throne?
How strange, alas! how alter'd shall I find
Each earthly thing, each scene I left behind!
Who knows me now? on whom shall I depend
To wain[36] my rights? where shall I find a friend?
My crown, perhaps, may grace a foreign line,

---

[36] *Wain.* To convey or carry a report; in this case to convey his royal title and rights after an absence of three centuries.

<115>

A race of kings, that knows not me nor mine;
Who reigns may wish my death, his subjects treat
My claim with scorn, and call their Prince a cheat.
Oh had my life been ended as begun!
My destin'd stage, my race of glory run,
I should have died well pleas'd; my honour'd name
Had liv'd, had flourished in the list of fame;
Reflecting now, my mind with horror sees
The sad survey, a scene of shameful ease,
The odious blot, the scandal of my race,
Scarce known, and only mention'd with disgrace." —
The Fair beheld him with impatient eye,
And red with anger made this warm reply.
— "Ungrateful man! Is this the kind return
My love deserves? and can you thus with scorn
Reject what once you priz'd, what once you swore
Surpass'd all charms, and made e'en glory poor ?
What gifts have I bestow'd, what favours shewn!
Made you partaker of my bed and throne;
Three centuries preserv'd in youthful prime,
Safe from the rage of death and injuries of time.
Weak arguments! for glory reigns above
The feeble ties of gratitude and love.
I urge them not, nor would request your stay;
The phantom glory calls, and I obey;
All other virtues are regardless quite,
Sunk and absorb'd in that superior light.
Go then, barbarian, to thy realms return,
And shew thyself unworthy my concern;
Go tell the world, your tender heart could give
Death to the Princess, by whose care you live." —
At this a deadly pale her cheeks o'erspread,
Cold trembling seiz'd her limbs, her spirits fled;
She sunk into his arms: the Prince was mov'd,
Felt all her griefs, for still he greatly lov'd.
He sigh'd, he wish'd he could forget his throne,
Confine his thoughts, and live for her alone;
But glory shot him deep, the venom'd dart
Was fix'd within, and rankled at his heart;

<116>

He could not hide its wounds, but pin'd away
Like a sick flower, and languished in decay.
An age no longer like a month appears,
But every month becomes a hundred years.
Felicity was griev'd, and could not bear
A scene so chang'd, a sight of so much care.
She told him with a look of cold disdain,
And seeming ease, as women well can feign,
He might depart at will; a milder air
Would mend his health; he was no prisoner there;
She kept him not, and wish'd he ne'er might find
Cause to regret the place he left behind;
Which once he lov'd, and where he still must own
He had at least some little pleasure known.
If these prophetic words awhile destroy
His peace, the former balance it in joy.
He thank'd her for her kind concern, but chose
To quit the place, the rest let heaven dispose.
For Fate, on mischiefs bent, perverts the will,
And first infatuates whom it means to kill.
Aurora now, not, as she wont to rise,
In gay attire ting'd with a thousand dyes,
But sober-sad in solemn state appears,
Clad in a dusky veil bedew'd with tears.
Thick mantling clouds beneath her chariot spread,
A faded wreath hangs drooping from her head.
The sick'ning sun emits a feeble ray,
Half drown'd in fogs, and struggling into day.
Some black event the threat'ning skies foretell;
Porsenna rose to take his last farewell.
A curious vest the mournful Princess brought,
And armour by the Lemnian artist[37] wrought;
A shining lance with secret virtue stor'd,
And of resistless force a magic sword;
Caparisons and gems of wond'rous price,
And loaded him with gifts and good advice;
But chief she gave, and what he most would need,
The fleetest of her stud, a flying steed.

[37] *Lemnian artist.* The god Hephaestus, blacksmith and weapons-maker to the
Gods, is associated with the island of Lemnos.

<117>

— "The swift Grisippo," said th' afflicted fair,
(Such was the courser's name) "with speed shall bear,
And place you safely in your native air;
Assist against the foe, with matchless might
Ravage the field, and turn the doubtful fight;
With care protect you till the danger cease,
Your trust in war, your ornament in peace.
But this, I warn, beware; whate'er shall lay
To intercept your course, or tempt your stay,
Quit not your saddle, nor your speed abate,
Till safely landed at your palace gate.
On this alone depends your weal or woe;
Such is the will of Fate, and so the Gods foreshew." —
He in the softest terms repaid her love,
And vow'd, nor age, nor absence, should remove
His constant faith, and sure she could not blame
A short divorce due to his injur'd fame.
The debt discharg'd, then should her soldier come
Gay from the field, and flush'd with conquest home;
With equal ardour her affection meet,
And lay his laurels at his mistress' feet.
He ceas'd, and sighing took a kind adieu;
Then urg'd his steed; the fierce Grisippo flew;
With rapid force outstripp'd the lagging wind,
And left the blissful shores, and weeping fair behind;
Now o'er the seas pursued his airy flight,
Now scower'd the plains, and climb'd the mountain's height.
Thus driving on at speed the Prince had run
Near half his course, when, with the setting sun,
As through a lonely lane he chanc'd to ride,
With rocks and bushes fenc'd on either side,
He 'spied a waggon full of wings, that lay
Broke and o'erturn'd across the narrow way.
The helpless driver on the dirty road
Lay struggling, crush'd beneath the incumbent load.
Never in human shape was seen before
A wight[38] so pale, so feeble, and so poor;
Comparisons of age would do him wrong,

---

[38] *Wight.* Person.

<118>

For Nestor's[39] self, if plac'd by him, were young.
His limbs were naked all, and worn so thin,
The bones seem'd starting through the parchment skin,
His eyes half drown'd in rheum, his accents weak,
Bald was his head, and furrow'd was his cheek.
The conscious steed stopp'd short in deadly fright,
And back recoiling stretch'd his wings for flight.
When thus the wretch with supplicating tone
And rueful face, began his piteous moan,
And, as he spake, the tears ran trickling down.
— "O gentle youth, if pity e'er inclin'd
Thy soul to generous deeds, if e'er thy mind
Was touch'd with soft distress, extend thy care
To save an old man's life, and ease the load I bear.
So may propitious heaven your journey speed,
Prolong your days, and all your vows succeed." —
Mov'd with the prayer the kind Porsenna staid,
Too nobly-minded to refuse his aid,
And, prudence yielding to superior grief,
Leap'd from his steed, and ran to his relief;
Removed the weight, and gave the prisoner breath,
Just choak'd, and gasping on the verge of death.
Then reach'd his hand, when lightly with a bound
The grizly Spectre, vaulting from the ground,
Seized him with sudden gripe, th' astonish'd Prince
Stood horror-struck, and thoughtless of defence.
"O King of Russia," with a thundering sound
Bellow'd the ghastly Fiend, "at length thou'rt found.
Receive the ruler of mankind, and know,
My name is Time, thy ever dreaded foe.
These feet are founder'd, and the wings you see
Worn to the pinions in pursuit of thee;
Through all the world in vain for ages sought,
But Fate has doom'd thee now, and thou art caught."

---

[39] *Nestor.* The oldest man among the Greeks in *The Iliad,* possibly over 100 years old.

<119>

Then round his neck his arms he nimbly cast,
And seiz'd him by the throat, and grasp'd him fast;
Till forc'd at length the soul forsook its seat,
And the pale breathless corse[40] fell bleeding at his feet.
Scarce had the cursed spoiler left his prey,
When so it chanc'd, young Zephyr pass'd that way[41]
Too late his presence to assist his friend,
A sad, but helpless witness of his end.
He chafes, and fans, and strives in vain to cure
His streaming wounds; the work was done too sure.
Now lightly with a soft embrace uprears
The lifeless load, and bathes it in his tears;
Then to the blissful seat with speed conveys,
And graceful on the mossy carpets lays
With decent care, close by the fountain's side,
Where first the Princess had her Phoenix spied.
There with sweet flowers his lovely limbs he strew'd,
And gave a parting kiss, and sighs and tears bestow'd.
To that sad solitude the weeping Dame,
Wild with her loss, and swol'n with sorrow, came.
There was she wont to vent her griefs, and mourn
Those dear delights that must no more return.
Thither that morn with more than usual care
She sped, but oh what joy to find him there!
As just arriv'd, and weary with the way,
Retir'd to soft repose her Hero lay.
Now near approaching she began to creep
With careful steps, loth to disturb his sleep;
Till quite o'ercome with tenderness she flew,
And round his neck her arms in transport threw.

----

[40] *Corse.* Corpse.

[41] *Young Zephyr passed that way*. Lisle reintroduces male friendship at the end of the poem, an untarnished affection apparently not susceptible to jealousy or alienation. By returning the dead Porsenna to the "blessed isle," Porsenna's narrative is broken, and the reader is left with no idea how this story came to be told, since Porsenna vanished three hundred years earlier. This is a pure Arcadian classical fantasy, and in it Lisle escapes responsibility for reconnecting his hero to any historical timeline. In the tradition of the court masque, it is quite possible that this elaborate poem alludes to actual persons and was written more for their entertainment than for the general reader. It is the longest poem Lewis chose for his anthology, and its mix of Arcadian and Gothic (and its coded same-sex affections) must have appealed to him.

<120>

But, when she found him dead, no tongue can tell
The pangs she felt; she shriek'd, and swooning fell.
Waking, with loud laments she pierc'd the skies,
And fill'd th' affrighted forest with her cries.
That fatal hour the palace gates she barr'd,
And had around the coast a stronger guard:
Now rare appearing, and at distance seen,
With crowds of black misfortunes plac'd between;
Mischiefs of every kind, corroding care,
And fears and jealousies, and dark despair.
And since that day (the wretched world must own
These mournful truths by sad experience known)
No mortal e'er enjoy'd that happy clime,
And every thing on earth submits to Time.

<121>

The fatal Sisters

From the Norse Tongue. [THOMAS] GRAY [1]

To be found in the *Orcades* of Thermodus Torfaeus, Hafniae, 1691, folio; and also in Bartholinus.[2]

Vitt er orpit fyrir valfalli, &c.

In the eleventh century Sigurd, Earl of the Orkney Islands, went with a fleet of ships and a considerable body of troops into Ireland, to the assistance of Sigtrygg with the silken beard, who was then making war on his father-in-law, Brian, King of Dublin. The Earl and all his forces were cut to pieces, and Sigtrygg was in danger of a total defeat; but the enemy had a greater loss in the death of Brian their king, who fell in the action. On Christmas-day (the day of the battle),[3] a native of Scotland saw, at a distance, a number of persons on horseback riding full speed towards a hill, and seeming to enter into it. Curiosity led him to follow them, till looking through an opening in the rocks, he saw twelve gigantic figures resembling women: they were all employed about a loom; and as they wove, they sung the following dreadful song; which, when they had finished, they tore the web into twelve pieces, and (each taking her portion) galloped six to the north, and as many to the south. These were the Valkyriur,[4] female divinities, servants of Odin (or Woden) in the Gothic mythology. Their name signifies Choosers of the Slain. They were mounted

---

[1] Thomas Gray (1716-1771), a shy, reclusive poet, was bullied by his fellow students at college. He was given to passionate male friendships and spent a great deal of time playing the harpsichord. He produced only 13 poems, many of them gestating for years, including his masterpiece graveyard poem, "Elegy in a Country Churchyard." He wrote his two Norse Odes in 1761, but they were not published until 1768. His life's work in poetry consists of less than 1,000 lines.

[2] *Darraðarljoð,* as this poem-song is titled, remained in Orkney oral tradition until the 18th century. *The Saga of Burnt Njal* contains the song and its framing narrative. Gray found the material in Latin and Icelandic in Bartholin and in Torfaeus's *Orcades*. The curious reader can find the Icelandic, Latin, and a comparison between Gray's and Percy's versions in Wawn, *Vikings*, pp. 28-29.

[3] The Battle of Clontarf, April 23, 1014 CE, not Christmas Day as Gray indicates. The battle effectively ended the Viking kingdom in Ireland. *The Saga of Burnt Njal* places the Valkyrie sighting on Good-Friday. Good-Friday, among the superstitious, has often been regarded as a time of spiritual darkness during which the powers of pagan magic might be more prone to break through.

[4] Actually, these women are a combination of Valkyries, who carry off the chosen slain, and the Norns, who spin the web of destiny and determine, in advance, who will die.

<122>

on swift horses, with drawn swords in their hands; and in the throng of battle selected such as were destined to slaughter, and conducted them to Valhalla, the hall of Odin, or Paradise of the Brave, where they attended the banquet, and served the departed heroes with horns of mead and ale.

Now the storm begins to lower,
(Haste, the loom of hell prepare,)
Iron-sleet of arrowy shower[5]
Hurtles in the darken'd air.

Glittering lances are the loom,
Where the dusky warp we strain,
Weaving many a soldier's doom,
Orkney's woe, and Randver's bane.

See the grisly texture grow!
('Tis of human entrails made)
And the weights, that play below,
Each a gasping warrior's head.

Shafts for shuttles, dipp'd in gore,
Shoot the trembling cords along.
Sword, that once a monarch bore,
Keep the tissue close and strong.

Mista, black terrific Maid,
Sangrida, and Hilda, see!
Join the wayward work to aid:
'Tis the woof of victory.

---

[5] An allusion to Milton: "How quick they wheel'd, and flying, behind them shot/ Sharp sleep of arrow'y show'r—" *Paradise Regained* III, 323-24.

<123>

Thomas Gray

Ere the ruddy sun be set,
Pikes must shiver, javelins sing,
Blade with clattering buckler meet,
Hauberk crash, and helmet ring.

(Weave the crimson web of war)
Let us go, and let us fly,
Where our friends the conflict share,
Where they triumph, where they die.

<124>

As the paths of Fate we tread,
Wading through th' ensanguin'd field,
Gondula, and Geira, spread
O'er the youthful King your shield.

We the reins to slaughter give,
Ours to kill, and ours to spare:
Spite of danger he shall live.
(Weave the crimson web of war.)

They, whom once the desert beach
Pent within its bleak domain,
Soon their ample sway shall stretch
O'er the plenty of the plain.

Low the dauntless Earl is laid,
Gor'd with many a gaping wound:
Fate demands a nobler head;
Soon a King shall bite the ground.

Long his loss shall Eirin[6] weep,
Ne'er again his likeness see;
Long her strains in sorrow steep;
Strains of immortality!

Horror covers all the heath,
Clouds of carnage blot the sun.
Sisters, weave the web of death:
Sisters, cease: the work is done.

Hail the task, and hail the hands!
Songs of joy and triumph sing!
Joy to the victorious bands;
Triumph to the younger King!

---

[6] *Eirin.* Ireland.

<125>

Mortal, thou that hear'st the tale,
Learn the tenor of our song.
Scotland, through each winding vale
Far and wide the notes prolong.

Sisters, hence with spurs of speed:
Each her thundering faulchion wield
Each bestride her sable steed.
Hurry, hurry to the field.

WALTER SCOTT ON THE ORIGINAL
IN ORAL TRADITION

"[T]he old Norwegian sagas were preserved and often repeated by the fishermen of Orkney and Zetland, while that language was not yet quite forgotten. . . . A clergyman, who was not long deceased, remembered well when some remnants of the Norse were still spoken in the island called North Ronaldshaw. When Gray's Ode, entitled the "Fatal Sisters," was first published, or at least first reached that remote island, the reverend gentleman had the well-judged curiosity to read it to some of the old persons of the isle, as a poem which regarded the history of their own country. They listened with great attention to the preliminary stanzas:

> *Now the storm begins to lour,*
> *Haste the doom of hell prepare,*
> *Iron sleet of arrowy shower*
> *Hurtles in the darkened air.*

But when they had heard a verse or two more, they interrupted the reader, telling him that they knew the song well in the Norse language, and had often sung it to him when he asked them for an old song. They called it the Magicians or the Enchantresses. It would have been singular news to the elegant translator, when executing his version from the text of Bartholine, to have learned that the Norse original was still preserved by tradition in a remote corner of the British dominions.[7]

---

[7] Sir Walter Scott, *The Pirate*. Waverly Novels Volume 23. 1821. Note 6.

<126>

SUPERNATURAL TIDINGS FROM THE BATTLE OF CLONTARF, FROM *THE SAGA OF BURNT NJAL*[8]

On Good Friday that event happened in Caithness that a man whose name was Daurrud went out. He saw folk riding twelve together to a bower, and there they were all lost to his sight. He went to that bower and looked in through a window slit that was in it, and saw that there were women inside, and they had set up a loom. Men's heads were the weights, but men's entrails were the warp and weft, a sword was the shuttle, and the reels were arrows.

They sang these songs, and he learnt them by heart —

THE WOOF OF WAR.

"See! warp is stretched
For warriors' fall,
Lo! weft in loom
'Tis wet with blood;
Now fight foreboding,
'Neath friends' swift fingers,
Our gray woof waxeth
With war's alarms,
Our warp bloodred,
Our weft corseblue.[9]
This woof is y-woven
With entrails of men,

This warp is hardweighted
With heads of the slain,
Spears blood-besprinkled
For spindles we use,
Our loom ironbound,
And arrows our reels;

---

[8] This Victorian translation of the poem and its framing text gives a good example of the enthusiastic reception of Norse myth among the British. From George Webbe Dasent's 1861 translation, pp. 338-343.
[9] *Corseblue*. Corpse-blue.

<127>

With swords for our shuttles
This war-woof we work;
So weave we, weird sisters.
Our warwinning woof.

Now War-winner walketh
To weave in her turn,
Now Swordswinger steppeth,
Now Swiftstroke, now Storm;
When they speed the shuttle
How spear-heads shall flash!
Shields crash, and helmgnawer[10]
On harness bite hard!

Wind we, wind swiftly
Our warwinning woof,
Woof erst for king youthful
Foredoomed as his own,
Forth now we will ride.
Then through the ranks rushing
Be busy where friends
Blows blithe give and take.

Wind we, wind swiftly
Our warwinning woof,
After that let us steadfastly
Stand by the brave king;
Then men shall mark mournful
Their shields red with gore,
How Swordstroke and Spearthrust
Stood stout by the prince.

---

[10] *Helmgnawer.* A sword that bites helmets.

<128>

Wind we, wind swiftly
Our warwinning woof;
When sword-bearing rovers
To banners rush on.
Mind, maidens, we spare not
One life in the fray!
We corse-choosing sisters
Have charge of the slain.

Now new-coming nations
That island shall rule.
Who on outlying headlands
Abode ere the fight;
I say that King mighty
To death now is done.
Now low before spearpoint
That Earl bows his head.

Soon over all Ersemen
Sharp sorrow shall fall,
That woe to those warriors
Shall wane nevermore;
Our woof now is woven,
Now battle-field waste,
O'er land and o'er water
War tidings shall leap.
Now surely 'tis gruesome
To gaze all around,
When bloodred through heaven
Drives cloudrack o'er head;
Air soon shall be deep hued
With dying men's blood
When this our spaedom[11]
Comes speedy to pass.

---

[11] *Spaedom.* Iceland word for "prophecy."

<129>

So cheerily chant we
Charms for the young king,
Come maidens lift loudly
His warwinning lay;
Let him who now listens
Learn well with his ears,
And gladden brave swordsmen
With bursts of war's song.

Now mount we our horses.
Now bare we our brands.
Now haste we hard, maidens.
Hence far, far, away.

Then they plucked down the woof and tore it asunder, and each kept what she had hold of.

Now Daurrud goes away from the slit, and home; but they got on their steeds and rode six to the south, and the other six to the north.

A like event befell Brand Gneisti's son in the Faroe Isles. At Swinefell, in Iceland, blood came on the priest's stole on Good Friday, so that he had to put it off.

At Thvattwater the priest thought he saw on Good Friday a long deep of the sea hard by the altar, and there he saw many awful sights, and it was long ere he could sing the prayers.

This event happened in the Orkneys, that Hareck thought he saw Earl Sigurd, and some men with him. Then Hareck took his horse and rode to meet the Earl. Men saw that they met and rode under a brae, but they were never seen again, and not a scrap was ever found of Hareck.

Earl Gilli in the Southern Isles dreamed that a man came to him and said his name was Hostfinn, and told him he was come from Ireland.

The Earl thought he asked him for tidings thence, and then he sang this song:

I have been where warriors wrestled,
High in Erin sang the sword,
Boss to boss met many bucklers,
Steel rung sharp on rattling helm;

<130>

I can tell of all their struggle;
Sigurd fell in flight of spears;
Brian fell, but kept his kingdom
Ere he lost one drop of blood.

Those two, Flosi and the Earl, talked much of this dream. A week after, Hrafn the red came thither, and told them all the tidings of Brian's battle, the fall of the king, and of Earl Sigurd, and Brodir, and all the Vikings.

"What," said Flosi, "hast thou to tell me of my men?"

"They all fell there," says Hrafn, "but thy brother-in-law Thorstein took peace from Kerthialfad, and is now with him."

Flosi told the Earl that he would now go away, "for we have our pilgrimage south to fulfil."

The Earl bade him go as he wished, and gave him a ship and all else that he needed, and much silver.

Then they sailed to Wales, and stayed there a while.

<131>

The Descent of Odin

FROM THE NORSE TONGUE .... [THOMAS] GRAY

[The original is] To be found in Bartholinus, *De causis contemnendae mortis;* Hafniae, 1689, quarto.[1]

Upreis Odinn Allda gautr, &c.

Uprose the King of Men with speed,
And saddled straight his coal-black steed;
Down the yawning steep he rode,
That leads to Hela's drear abode.[2]
Him the Dog of Darkness[3] spied,
His shaggy throat he open'd wide,
While from his jaws, with carnage fill'd,
Foam and human gore distill'd:
Hoarse he bays with hideous din,
Eyes that glow, and fangs that grin;
And long pursues, with fruitless yell,
The Father of the powerful spell.

---

[1] Gray's interest in these poems was antiquarian and literary, as he explains in the "Advertisement" to his Norse translations: "The author once had thoughts (in concert with a friend) of giving a history of English poetry: in the introduction of it he meant to have produced some specimens of the style that reigned in ancient times among the neighboring nations, or those who had subdued the greater part of this island, and were our progenitors ... He afterwards dropped his design; specially after he had heard that it was already in the hands of a person well qualified to do it justice both by his taste and his researches into antiquity" (Gray, 1782, p. 61). Gray makes clear his indebtedness to Bartholin, Mallat, and Bishop Percy in the course of his notes —BR.
The original of this poem is *Baldr's Dreams (Baldrs Draumar),* a poem of 14 stanzas in the *Poetic Edda,* a work dating to the 10th Century CE. Fine modern renderings of this poem can be found in Bellows (195-200) and in Terry (241-43). There is also a translation by W.H. Auden and P.B. Taylor — BR.
[2] Niflheimr, the hell of the Gothick nations, consisted of nine worlds, to which were devoted all such as died of sickness, old age, or by any other means than in battle; over it presided Hela, the Goddess of Death— TG.
[3] The *Edda* gives this dog the name of Managarmr; he fed upon the lives of those that were to die —TG or his editor.

<132>

13th Century Icelandic manuscript shows Odin riding Sleipnir, his eight-legged horse.

Onward still his way he takes,
(The groaning earth beneath him shakes,)
Till full before his fearless eyes
The portals nine of Hell arise.
   Right against the eastern gate,
By the moss-grown pile, he sate;
Where long of yore to sleep was laid
The dust of the prophetic Maid.
Facing to the northern clime,
Thrice he trac'd the Runic rhyme;
Thrice pronounc'd, in accents dread,

<133>

The thrilling verse that wakes the dead;
Till from out the hollow ground
Slowly breath'd a sullen sound.

PROPHETESS.
What call unknown, what charms, presume
To break the quiet of the tomb?
Who thus afflicts my troubled sprite,
And drags me from the realms of night?
Long on these mouldering bones have beat
The winter's snow, the summer's heat,
The drenching dews, and driving rain!
Let me, let me sleep again.
Who is he, with voice unbless'd,
Calls me from the bed of rest?

ODIN.
A traveler, to thee unknown,[4]
Is he that calls, a warrior's son.
Thou the deeds of light shalt know;
Tell me what is done below,[5]
For whom yon glitt'ring board is spread,
Dress'd for whom yon golden bed?

PROPHETESS.
Mantling in the goblet see
The pure bev'rage of the bee;
O'er it hangs the shield of gold;
'Tis the drink of Balder bold:
Balder's head to death is giv'n.
Pain can reach the Sons of Heav'n!
Unwilling I my lips unclose:
Leave me, leave me to repose.

---

[4] It is unthinkable to summon a spirit without giving one's name. In the poem, Odin tells the witch he is Vegtam ("The Wanderer"), son of Valtam ("The Fighter") —BR.

[5] *What is done below.* Odin, we find both from this Ode and the *Edda*, was solicitous about the fate of his son Balder, who had dreamed that he was soon to die. The *Edda* mentions the manner of his death when killed by Odin's other son Hoder; and also that Hoder was himself slain afterwards by Vali, the son of Odin and Rinda, consonant with this prophecy —TG (or his editor).

<134>

A suggestion of the imagined size of Wolf Fenrir, one of the dreaded monsters to be unleashed at Ragnarok.

ODIN.
Once again my call obey:
Prophetess, arise, and say,
What dangers Odin's child await,
Who the author of his fate?

PROPHETESS.
In Hoder's hand the Hero's doom;
His brother sends him to the tomb,
Now my weary lips I close;
Leave me, leave me to repose.

ODIN.
Prophetess, my spell obey,
Once again arise, and say,
Who th' Avenger of his guilt,
By whom shall Hoder's blood be spilt?

<135>

PROPHETESS.
In the caverns of the west,
By Odin's fierce embrace compress'd,
A wond'rous boy shall Rinda bear,
Who ne'er shall comb his raven-hair,
Nor wash his visage in the stream,
Nor see the sun's departing beam,
Till he on Hoder's corse[6] shall smile,
Flaming on the funeral pile.
Now my weary lips I close;
Leave me, leave me to repose.

ODIN.
Yet awhile my call obey;
Prophetess, awake, and say,
What virgins these, in speechless woe,
That bend to earth their solemn brow,
That their flaxen tresses tear,
And snowy veils that float in air?
Tell me whence their sorrows rose:
Then I leave thee to repose.

PROPHETESS.
Ha! no Traveler art thou,
King of Men,[7] I know thee now;
Mightiest of a mighty line —

---

[6] *Corse.* Corpse.
[7] *King of Men.* Gray's epithet associating Odin with man rather than the Asgardian gods also makes the reader think of King Saul's quest for prophecy from the Witch of Endor in *I Samuel.* The Biblical witch also enjoys a moment of sudden recognition of her royal guest. Odin's discomfort at begging prophecy parallels that of King Saul, who likewise was denied the ability to see the future events closest to his heart. Gray omits the first five stanzas of the original, which more clearly set a pagan tone, and set apart a vow among the gods not to permit harm to come to Balder, versus the gods' ignorance of Destiny, the realm of the Norns —BR.

<136>

ODIN.
No boding maid of skill divine
Art thou, nor Prophetess of good;
But mother of the giant-brood![8]

PROPHETESS.
Hie thee hence, and boast at home,
That never shall enquirer come,
To break my iron sleep again:
Till Lok[9] has burst his tenfold chain;
Never, till substantial Night
Has reassum'd her ancient right;
Till wrapp'd in flames, in ruin hurl'd,
Sinks the fabric of the world.

---

[8] The exchange of insults is a standard device in Norse poetry. Here, Odin
besmears the Prophetess as a daughter of the unsavory Giant race, i.e., one of the
malevolent Norns, and the Prophetess mocks Odin as a foredoomed king. If she
is indeed one of the primal Norns, Odin got more than he bargained for: if she is
the Norn who gave birth to the terrible monster Wolf Fenrir who will one day
devour Odin, he has ventured to the worst possible source of prophecy —BR.
[9] Lok[i] is the Evil Being, who continues in chains till the *Twilight of the Gods*
approaches; when he shall break his bonds; the human-race, the stars and sun,
shall disappear, the earth sink in the seas, and fire consume the skies; even Odin
himself, and his kindred deities, shall perish. For a farther explanation of this
mythology see *Introduction a l'Histoire de Dannemarc par Mons. Mallat, 1755, 4to;*
or rather a translation of it published in 1770, and entitled *Northern Antiquities,*
in which some mistakes in the original are judiciously corrected —TG or his
editor.

<137>

The Witch of Wokey

DR. [HENRY] HARRINGTON

Wokey-hoh is a noted cavern in Somersetshire, which has given birth to as many wild fanciful stories as the Sybil's Cave, in Italy. Through a very narrow entrance, it opens into a very large vault, the roof whereof, either on account of its height, or the thickness of the gloom, cannot be discovered by the light of torches. It goes winding a great way under ground, is crost by a stream of very cold water, and is all horrid with broken pieces of rock; many of these are evident petrifactions; which, on account of their singular forms, have given rise to the fables alluded to in this poem. [1]

In aunciente days tradition showes
A base and wicked elfe arose,
The Witch of Wokey hight:[2]
Oft have I heard the fearful tale
From Sue and Roger of the vale.

On some long winter's night.
Deep in the dreary dismal cell,
Which seem'd and was ycleped[3] hell,

---

[1] This epigraph is actually by Bishop Thomas Percy, who printed the poem in his *Reliques of Ancient English Poetry*, Vol I, Book III, xiv, pp. 344-347. Lewis omitted Percy's further background about the work:

> — was published in a small collection of poems, intitled *Euthemia, or the Power of Harmony, &c.* 1756, written, in 1748, by the ingenious Dr. Harrington, of Bath, who never allowed them to be published, and withheld his name till it could no longer be concealed. The following copy was furnished by the late Mr. Shenshione, with some variations and corrections of his own, which he had taken the liberty to propose, and for which the Author's indulgence was intreated. In this Edition it was intended to reprint the Author's own original copy; but as that may be seen correctly given in Pearch's Collection, Vol. I. 1783, p. 161, it was thought that the Reader of Taste would wish to have the variations preserved; they are therefore still retained here, which it is hoped the worthy Author will excuse with his wonted liberality.

[2] *Hight.* Called.
[3] *Yclepted* or *yclept.* Named, described as.

<138>

This blear-eyed Hag did hide:
Nine wicked elves, as legends sayne,
She chose to form her guardian trayne,

And kennel near her side.
Here screeching owls oft made their nest,
While wolves its craggy sides possest,

Night-howling thro' the rock:
No wholesome herb could here be found:
She blasted every plant around,
And blister'd every flock.

Her haggard face was foul to see;
Her mouth unmeet a mouth to bee;
Her eyne⁴ of deadly leer:
She nought clevis'd,⁵ but neighbour's ill;
She wreak'd on all her wayward will,
And marr'd all goodly chear.

All in her prime, have poets sung,
No gaudy youth, gallant and young,
E'er blest her longing armes;
And hence arose her spight to vex,
And blast the youth of either sex,
By dint of hellish charms.

From Glaston came a lerned wight,⁶
Full bent to marr her fell despight,⁷
And well he did, I ween:
Sich mischief never had been known,
And, since his mickle⁸ lerninge shown,
Sich mischief ne'er has been.
He chauntede out his godlie book,
He crost the water, blest the brooke,⁹

---

⁴ *Eyen.* Eyes.
⁵ *She nought clevis'd.* She devoted herself to nothing.
⁶ *Wight.* Person.
⁷ *Fell despight.* Cruel and contemptuous behavior.
⁸ *Mickle.* Much.

<139>

Then pater noster[10] done,
The ghastly hag he sprinkled o'er;
When lo! where stood a hag before,
Now stood a ghastly stone.[11]

Full well 'tis known adown the dale;
Tho' passing strange indeed the tale,
And doubtfull may appear,
I'm bold to say, there's never a one,
That has not seen the witch in stone,
With all her household gear.

But tho' this lernede Clerke[12] did well,
With grieved heart, alas! I tell,
She left this curse behind:
That Wokey-nymphs forsaken quite,
Tho' sense and beauty both unite,
Should find no leman[13] kind.

For lo! even, as the Fiend did say,
The sex have found it to this day,
That men are wond'rous scant:
Here's beauty, wit, and sense combin'd,
With all that's good and virtuous join'd,
Yet hardly one gallant.

---

[9] *Crost the water*... Made Holy Water by blessing the brook.
[10] *Pater Noster*. The Lord's Prayer in Latin.
[11] *Ghastly stone*. The witch's figure is a stalagmite in the first chamber of the caves. The Wokey caves have been used for millennia and are cool enough for storing cheese. The cave, which is frequented by cave divers, and has an adjacent (now defunct) paper mill, is a tourist attraction. Television shows on the Wokey Witch legend brought renewed attention to the locale in recent years. The ghost of a drowned cave diver is now said to keep the witch company. A 1975 Doctor Who adventure, *Revenge of the Cybermen*, was filmed in the caves.
[12] *Clerke*. At this period, a deacon, priest or bishop.
[13] *Leman*. Lover.

<140>

Shall then sich maids unpitied moane?
They might as well, like her, be stone,
As thus forsaken dwell.
Since Glaston now can boast no clerks;[14]
Come down from Oxenford, ye sparks,
And, oh! revoke the spell.

Yet stay nor thus despond, ye fair;
Virtue's the gods' peculiar care;
I hear the gracious voice:
Your sex shall soon be blest agen,
We only wait to find sich men,
As best deserve your choice.

---

[14] The Abbey at Glastonbury was dissolved in 1539.

<141>

The Marriage of Sir Gawaine

From Percy's *Reliques of Ancient English Poetry.*[1]

PART I.

King Arthur lives in merry Carleile,
And seemly is to see;
And there with him Queene Guenever,
That bride soe bright of blee.[2]

And there with him Queene Guenever,
That bride so bright in bowre:
And all his barons about him stoode,
That were both stiffe and stowre.[3]

The King a royale Christmasse kept,
With mirth and princelye cheare;
To him repaired many a knighte,
That came both farre and neare.

And when they were to dinner sette,
And cups went freely round;
Before them came a fair damselle,
And knelt upon the ground.

---

[1] This ballad is found in Volume III of Bishop Percy's *Reliques of Ancient English Poetry*, pp. 11-24, with the note, "[It] is chiefly taken from the fragment of an old ballad in the Editor's MS. which he has reason to believe more ancient than the time of Chaucer, and what furnished that bard with his Wife of Bath's Tale. The original was so extremely mutilated, half of every leaf being torn away, that without large supplements, &c. it would have been improper for this collection: these it has therefore received, such as they are." Chaucer's variant telling, "The Wife of Bath's Tale" in *The Canterbury Tales*, was written sometime between 1392 to 1395 CE. A variant of it also appears in Gower's *Confessio Amantis*, written 1386-1390. The poem is Child Ballad No. 31.
[2] *Blee.* Color or hue.
[3] *Stiffe and stowre.* Strong in a fight.

<142>

— "A boone, a boone, O king Arthure,
I beg a boone of thee;
Avenge me of a carlish[4] knighte,
Who hath shent[5] my love and mee.

"At Tearne-Wadling[6] his castle stands,
Near to that lake so fair,
And proudlye rise the battlements,
And streamers deck the air.

"Noe gentle knighte, nor lady gay,
May pass that castle-walle:
But from that foul discourteous knighte,
Mishappe will them befalle.

"Hee's twice the size of common men,
Wi' thewes, and sinewes stronge,
And on his backe he bears a clubb,
That is both thicke and longe.

"This grimme Barone 'twas our harde happe,
But yester morne to see;
When to his bowre he bare my love,
And sore misused mee.

"And when I told him, King Arthure
As lyttle shold him spare;
'Goe tell,' say'd hee, that cuckold kinge,
To meete mee if he dare.'" —

---

4 *Carlish.* Coarse, vulgar or rude; ill-mannered.
5 *Shent.* Disgraced.
6 Tearne-Wadling is the name of a small lake near Hasketh in Cumberland, on
the road from Penrith to Carlisle. There is a tradition, that an old castle once
stood near the lake, the remains of which were not long since visible. Tearn, in
the dialect of that country, signifies a small lake, and is still in use —Percy (12).

<143>

Upp then sterted King Arthure,
And sware by hille and dale,
He ne'er wolde quitt that grimme Barone,
Till he had made him quail.

— "Goe fetch my sword Excalibar:
Goe saddle mee my steede;
Nowe, by my faye,[7] that grimme Barone
Shall rue this ruthfulle deede." —

And when he came to Tearne-Wadling,
Benethe the castle walle:
— "Come forth; come forth; thou proude Barone,
Or yielde thyself my thralle."[8] —

On magicke ground that castle stoode,
And fenc'd with many a spelle:
Noe valiant knight could tread thereon,
But straite his courage felle.

Forth then rush'd that carlish Knight,
King Arthure felte the charm:
His sturdy sinewes lost their strengthe,
Down sunke his feeble arme.

— "Nowe yield thee, yield thee, King Arthure,
Now yield thee unto mee;
Or fighte with mee, or lose thy lande,
Noe better terms maye bee.

"Unless thou sweare upon the rood,[9]
And promise on thy faye,
Here to returne to Tearne-Wadling,
Upon the new-yeare's daye;

---

[7] *Faye.* Probably "faith." Not in OED, so this is perhaps another Percy invention.
[8] *Thralle.* Thrall: servant or subject.
[9] *Rood.* Cross.

<144>

"And bringe me worde what thing it is
All women most desyre;
This is thy ransome, Arthur," he sayes,
"I'll have no other hire." —

King Arthur then helde up his hande,
And sware upon his faye,
Then took his leave of the grimme Barone,
And faste hee rode awaye.

And he rode east, and he rode west,
And did of all inquyre,
What thing it is all women crave,
And what they most desyre.

Some told him riches, pompe, or state;
Some rayment fine and brighte;
Some told him mirthe; some flatterye;
And some a jollye knighte.

In letters all King Arthur wrote,
And seal'd them with his ringe:
But still his minde was helde in doubte,
Each tolde a different thinge.

As ruthfulle he rode over a more,[10]
He saw a Ladye sette
Between an oke, and a greene holleye,
All clad in red scarlette.

Her nose was crookt and turnd outwarde,
Her chin stood all awrye;
And where as shoulde have been her mouthe,
Lo! there was set her eye:

---

[10] *More.* Moor.

<145>

Her haires, like serpents, clung aboute
Her cheeks of deadlye hewe:
A worse-form'd ladye than she was,
No man mote ever viewe.

To hail the King in seemelye sorte
This ladye was fulle faine,
But King Arthure all sore amaz'd,
No aunswere made againe.

— "What wight art thou," the Ladye say'd,
"That wilt not speake to mee;
Sir, I may chance to ease thy paine,
Though I bee foule to see." —

— "If thou wilt ease my paine," he sayd,
And helpe me in my neede;
Ask what thou wilt, thou grimme Ladye,
And it shall bee thy meede." —

— "O sweare mee this upon the roode,[11]
And promise on thy faye;
And here the secrette I will telle,
That shall thy ransome paye." —

King Arthur promis'd on his faye,
And sware upon the roode:
The secrette then the Ladye told,
As lightlye well she cou'de.

— "Now this shall be my paye, sir King,
And this my guerdon bee,
That some young, fair and courtly knight,
Thou bringe to marry mee." —

---

[11] *Roode.* Cross.

<146>

Fast then pricked King Arthure
Ore hille, and dale, and downe:
And soone he founde the Barone's bowre,
And soone the grimme Baroune.

He bare his clubbe upon his backe,
Hee stoode bothe stiffe and stronge;
And, when he had the letters reade,
Awaye the letters flunge.

— "Nowe yielde thee, Arthur, and thy lands,
All forfeit unto mee;
For this is not thy paye, sir King,
Nor may thy ransome bee." —

— "Yet hold thy hand, thou proud Barone,
I praye thee hold thy hand;
And give mee leave to speake once more
In reskewe of my land.

"This morne, as I came over a more,
I saw a Ladye sette,
Betwene an oke, and a greene holleye,
All clad in red scarlette;

"She sayes, all women will have their wille,
This is their chief desyre;
Now yield, as thou art a Barone true,
That I have payd mine hyre." —

— "An earlye vengeance light on her!"
The carlish Baron swore:
(Shee was my sister tolde thee this,
And she's a misshapen whore.)

<147>

"But here I will make mine avowe,
To do her as ill a turne:
For an ever I may that foule theefe gette,
In a fyre I will her burne." —

PART II.

Homewarde pricked[12] King Arthure,
And a wearye man was hee;
And soone he mette Queene Guenever,
That bride so bright of blee.

— "What newes! what newes! thou noble King,
Howe, Arthur, hast thou sped?
Where hast thou hung the carlish Knighte?
And where bestow'd his head?" —

— "The carlish Knight is safe for mee,
And free fro mortal harme:
On magicke grounde his castle stands,
And fenc'd with many a charme.

"To bowe to him I was fulle faine,
And yielde mee to his hand;
And but for a lothly Ladye, there
I should have lost my land.

"And nowe this fills my hearte with woe,
And sorrowe of my life;
I swore a yonge and courtlye knight,
Sholde marry her to his wife."

---

[12] *Pricked.* Hurrying, spurring his horse on.

<148>

Then bespake him Sir Gawaine,
That was ever a gentle knighte:
"That lothly Ladye I will wed;
Therefore be merrye and lighte." —

— "Nowe naye, nowe naye, good Sir Gawaine;
My sister's sonne yee bee;
This lothlye Ladye's all too grimme,
And all too foule for yee.

"Her nose is crookt, and turn'd outwarde;
Her chin stands all awrye;
A worse form'd ladye than shee is
Was never seen with eye." —

— "What though her chin stand all awrye,
And shee be foule to see:
I'll marry her, unkle, for thy sake,
And I'll thy ransome bee." —

— "Nowe thankes, nowe thankes, good Sir Gawaine;
And a blessing thee betyde!
To-morrow wee'll have knights and squires,
And wee'll goe fetch thy bride.

"And wee'll have hawkes, and wee'll have houndes,
To cover our intent;
And wee'll away to the greene forest,
As wee hunting went." 13 —

Sir Lancelot, Sir Stephen bolde,
They rode with them that daye;
And foremost of the companye
There rode the stewarde Kaye:

---

13 *As wee hunting went.* As though we were hunting.

<149>

Soe did Sir Banier and Sir Bore,
And eke Sir Garratte keene;
Sir Tristram too, that gentle knight,
To the forest freshe and greene.

And when they came to the greene forrest,
Beneathe a faire holley tree,
There sate that Ladye in red scarlette
That unseemelye was to see.

Sir Kay beheld that Lady's face,
And looked upon her sweere;[14]
"Whoever kisses that Ladye," he sayes,
"Of his kisse he stands in feare."

Sir Kay beheld that Ladye againe,
And looked upon her snout;
"Whoever kisses that Ladye," he sayes,
"Of his kisse he stands in doubt." —

— "Peace, brother Kay," sayde Sir Gawaine,
"And amend thee of thy life;
For there is a Knight amongst us all,
Must marry her to his wife." —

— "What, marry this foule queane," quoth Kay,
"In the devil's name anone;
Gett mee a wife wherever I maye,
In sooth shee shall be none." —

Then some tooke up their hawkes in haste,
And some tooke up their houndes;
And said they wolde not marry her,
For cities, nor for townes.

---

[14] *Sweere.* Neck.

<150>

Then bespake him King Arthure,
And sware there by this daye;
— "For a little foule sighte and mislikinge,
Yee shall not say her naye." —

— "Peace, Lordlings, Peace!" Sir Gawaine sayd,
"Nor make debate and strife;
This lothlye Ladye I will take,
And marry her to my wife." —

— "Nowe thankes, nowe thankes, good Sir Gawaine,
And a blessinge be thy meede!
For as I am thine owne ladye,
Thou never shalt rue this deede." —

Then up they took that lothlye Dame,
And home anone they bringe:
And there Sir Gawaine he her wed,
And married her with a ringe.

And when they were in wed-bed laid,
And all were done awaye:
"Come turne to mee, mine owne wed-lord,
Come turne to mee I praye."

Sir Gawaine scant could lift his head,
For sorrowe and for care;
When, lo! instead of that lothlye Dame,
Hee sawe a young Ladye faire.

Sweet blushes stayn'd her rud-red cheeke,
Her eyen were blacke as sloe:
The ripening cherrye swellde her lippe,
And all her neck was snowe.

<151>

Sir Gawaine kiss'd that Lady faire,
Lying upon the sheete:
And swore, as he was a true Knighte,
The spice was never soe sweete.

Sir Gawaine kiss'd that Lady brighte,
Living there by his side:
"The fairest flower is not soe faire:
Thou never can'st bee my bride." —

— "I am thy bride, mine owne deare Lorde,
The same whiche thou didst knowe,
That was soe lothtye, and was wont
Upon the wild more to goe.

"Nowe, gentle Gawaine, chuse," quoth shee,
"And make thy choice with care;
Whether by night, or else by daye,
Shall I be foule or faire?" —

— "To have thee foule still in the night,
When I with thee should playe!
I had rather farre, my lady deare,
To have thee foul by daye." —

— "What, when gaye ladyes goe with their lordes
To drink the ale and wine;
Alas! tho I must hide myself,
I must not goe with mine?" —

— "My faire ladye," Sir Gawaine sayd,
"I yield me to thy skille;
Because thou art mine owne ladye,
Thou shalt have all thy wille." —

<152>

— "Nowe blessed be thou, sweete Gawaine,
And the daye that I thee see;
For as thou seest mee at this time,
Soe shall I ever bee.

"My father was an aged knighte,
And yet it chanced soe,
He tooke to wife a false ladye,
Whiche broughte me to this woe.

"Shee witch'd mee, being a fair yonge maide,
In the greene forest to dwelle;
And there to abyde in lothlye shape,
Most like a fiend of helle.

"Midst mores[15], and mosses; woods, and wilds;
To lead a lonesome life:
Till some yonge faire and courtlye knighte
Wolde marry me to his wife:

"Nor fully to gaine mine owne trewe shape,
Such was her devilish skille;
Until he wolde yielde to be rul'd by mee,
And let mee have all my wille.

"She witch'd my brother to a carlish boore,
And made him stiffe and stronge
And built him a bowre on magicke grounde,
To live by rapine and wrong.

"But now the spelle is broken throughe,
And wronge is turnde to righte;
Henceforth I shall be a fair ladye,
And hee be a gentle knighte."

---

[15] *Mores*. Moors.

<153>

King Arthur's Death

A FRAGMENT

From Percy's *Reliques of Ancient English Poetry*

[The subject of this ballad is evidently taken from the old romance
Morte [d']Arthur, but with some variations, especially in the
concluding stanzas; in which the author seems rather to follow the
traditions of the old Welsh Bards, who 'believed that King Arthur
was not dead, but conveied awaie by the Fairies into some pleasant
place, where he should remain for a time, and then returne againe
and reign in as great authority as ever.' —Holingshed. B.5.c. 14 or as
it is expressed in an old Chronicle printed at Antwerp 1493 by Ger.
de Leew, "The Bretons supposen, that he [K. Arthur] — shall come
yet and conquere all Bretaigne, for certes this is the prophicye of
Merlyn: He sayd, that his death shall be doubteous; and sayd soth,
for men thereof yet have doubte, and shullen for ever more — for
men wyt not whether that he lyveth or is deade.' See more ancient
testimonies in Selden's *Notes on Polyolbion,* Song III.
This fragment being very incorrect and imperfect in the original
MS. hath received some conjectural emendations, and even a
supplement of three or four stanzas composed from the Romance of
Morte [d']Arthur.][1]

On Trinitye Mondaye in the morne,
　This sore battayle was doom'd to bee,
Where manye a knighte cry'd, Well-away!
　Alacke, it was the more pittìe.

Ere the first crowinge of the cocke,
　When as the kinge in his bed laye,
He thoughte Sir Gawaine to him came,
　And there to him these wordes did saye:

---

[1] Epigraph inserted from Percy, *Reliques of Ancient English Poetry.* Vol. III, p.
28—BR.

<154>

"Nowe, as you are mine unkle deare,
  And as you prize your life, this daye
O meet not with your foe in fight;
  Putt off the battayle, if yee maye,

"For Sir Launcelot is nowe in Fraunce,
  And with him many an hardye knighte:
Who will within this moneth be backe,
  And will assiste yee in the fighte."

The kinge then call'd his nobles all,
  Before the breakinge of the daye;
And told them howe Sir Gawaine came,
  And there to him these wordes did saye.

His nobles all this counsayle gave,
  That earlye in the morning, hee
Should send awaye an herauld-at-armes,
  To aske a parley faire and free.

Then twelve good knightes King Arthur chose,
  The best of all that with him were,
To parley with the foe in field,
  And make with him agreement faire.

The king he charged all his hoste,
  In readinesse there for to bee;
But noe man shold noe weapon sturre,
  Unlesse a sword drawne they shold see.

And Mordred, on the other parte,
  Twelve of his knights did likewise bringe,
The best of all his companye,
  To hold the parley with the kinge.

<155>

Sir Mordred alsoe charged his hoste,
    In readinesse there for to bee;
But noe man sholde noe weapon sturre,
    But if a sworde drawne they shold see.

For he durste not his unkle truste,
    Nor he his nephewe, sothe to tell;
Alacke! it was a woefulle case,
    As ere in Christentye befelle.

But when they were together mette,
    And both to faire accordance broughte,
And a month's league betweene them sette,
    Before the battayle shoulde be foughte,

An addere crept forth of a bushe,
    Stunge one o' th' king's knightes on the knee;
Alacke! It was a woefulle chance,
    As ever was in Christentìe.

When the knighte found him wounded sore,
    And sawe the wild-worm hanginge there,
His sworde he from his scabberde drewe;
    A piteous case, as ye shall heare.

For when the two hostes sawe the sworde,
    They joyned battayle instantlye;
Till of soe manye noble knightes,
    On one side there were left but three.

For all were slain that durst abide,
    And but some fewe that fled awaye:
Ay mee! it was a bloodye fielde,
    As ere was foughte on a summer's daye.

<156>

Upon King Arthur's own partyè,
  Onlye himselfe escaped there,
And Lukyn Duke of Gloster free,
  And the king's butler Bedevere.

And when the king beheld his knightes
  All dead and scattered on the molde,
The teares fast trickled downe his face;
  That manlye face in fight so bolde.

— "Nowe reste yee all, brave knights," he said,
  "Soe true and faithful to your trust:
And must ye then, ye valiant hearts,
  Be lefte to moulder into dust!

"Most loyal have yee been to mee,
  Most true and faithful unto deathe:
And, oh! to rayse yee up againe,
  How freelye could I yield my breathe!

"But see, the traitor's yet alive!
  Lo where hee stalkes among the deade!
Nowe bitterlye he shall abye:
  And vengeance fall upon his head."

"O staye, my liege," then sayd the duke;
  "O staye for love and charitìe;
Remember what the vision spake,
  Nor meete your foe, if it may bee."

"O staye mee not, thou worthye wight,
  This debt my loyal knights I owe:
Betide my life, betide me death,
  I will avenge them of their foe." —

<157>

Then straite he grasp'd his trustye speare,
  And on his horse then mounted hee:
As his butler holpe him to his horse,
  His bowels gushed to his knee.

— "Alas!" then sayd the noble king,
  "That I should live this sight to see!
To see this good knight here be slaine,
  All for his love in helping mee!" —

He put his speare into his reste.
  And to Sir Mordred loud gan crye:
— "Nowe sette thyself upon thy guarde,
  For, traitor, nowe thy death is nye." —

Sir Mordred lifted up his sworde,
  And fierce to meet the king ran hee:
The king his speare he through him thrust,
  A fathom thorow his bodìe.

When Mordered felt the stroke of death,
  And found that he was wounded soe,
He thrust himselfe upon the speare,
  And strucke the king a deadlye blowe.

Then grimmlye dyed Sir Mordered,
  Presentlye upon that tree:
And bloody streames ranne from the kinge,
  Ere to the duke returned hee.

Sir Lukyn then he thus bespake:
— "Sir Knighte, thou hast been faithfulle tryde;
Nowe take my sworde Excalibar,
  That hangs so freelye by my syde;

<158>

King Arthur's fatal combat with Mordred, by Arthur Rackham.

"O take my sword Excalibar,
    And there into the river throwe:
For here, henceforth, benethe this tree,
    All use of weapons I forgoe.

"And fare thee well, thou trustye sword,
    A better neer had valiant knighte;
With thee full ofte, and many a daye,
    Have I withstood my foe in fighte.

"With this good faulchion[2] in my hande,
    Oft have I reapd the bloody feelde:
But nowe the fatalle houre is come,
    That never more I may thee weelde."

The duke to the river side he went,
    And there his owne sword in threwe he;
But he kept back Excalibar,
    He kept it back in privitie.

For all of coleyne[3] was the blade,
    And all the hilte of precious stone:
"And ever alacke!" then sayd the knighte,
    "Must such a sword awaye be throwne?"

Then backe he came unto the kinge,
    Who sayd, "Sir Lukyn, what did yee see?" —
— "Nothing, my liege, save that the winde
    Blewe oer the waters faire and free." —

— "O goe againe," then said the kinge,
    "O good Sir Lukyn, goe againe:
Into the rivere throwe my sword,
    Nor keepe me lingering here in paine."—

---

[2] *Faulchion.* A broadsword with one curved edge.
[3] *Coleyne.* Uncertain, possibly "cold iron," an archaic name for either iron or steel, referring to its supposed ability to repel fairies and melavolent spirits.

<160>

The duke then to the river went,
   And the king's scabberd in threwe hee;
But he kept backe Excalibar,
   And hid it undernethe a tree.

Then backe he came to tell the kinge,
   Who sayde, "Sir Lukyn, sawe ye oughte?" —
— "Nothinge, my liege, save that the winde
   Nowe with the angrye waters fought." —

— "O Lukyn, Lukyn," said the kinge,
   "Twice haste thou dealt deceytfullye:
Alacke, whom may wee ever truste,
   When suche a knighte soe false can bee!

"Saye, wouldst thou have thy master dead,
   All for a sword that wins thine eye?
Now goe againe, and throwe it in,
   Or here the one of us shall dye." —

The duke, all shent[4] with this rebuke,
   No aunswere made unto the kinge;
But to the rivere tooke the sworde,
   And threwe it far as he coulde flinge.

A hande and an arme did meete the sworde,
   And flourishd three times in the air;
Then sunke benethe the renninge streme,
   And of the duke was seene noe mair.

All sore astonied stood the duke,
   He stood as still, as still mote bee;
Then hastened backe to telle the kinge,
   But he was gone from under the tree.

---

[4] *Shent.* Disgraced.

<161>

But to what place he cold not tell,[5]
  For never after hee did him spye;
But hee sawe a barge goe from the land,
  And hee heard ladyes howle and crye.[6]

And whether the kinge were there or not,
  Hee never knewe, nor ever colde,
For from that sad and direfulle daye,
  Hee never more was seene on molde.[7]

---

[5] Malory's *Morte D'Arthur* ends with a similar air of mystery. The wounded Arthur tells Sir Bedwere, "I [will] into the vale of Avylon to hele me of my grevous wounds." Arthur is then carried off on a barge by three women: his sorceress sister Morgan le Fay, the Queen of North Galis, and the Queen of the Waste Lands. Bedwere later comes upon a chapel and hermitage where he is told that three ladies had brought a corpse for interment. Malory, saying cryptically that "here in thys worlde he chaugned his lyff," ends his epic romance by saying "Thus of Arthur I fynde no more wrytten in bokis that bene auctorysed, nothir more of the verrye sertaynte of hys deathe harde I never rede" (fol 482r). The hint of Arthur's survival, real or supernatural, is enforced by the legend of what is inscribed on Arthur's tomb: *Hic iacet Arthurus, rex quondam rexque futurus* (Here lies Arthur, the once and future King).
[6] *Ladyes howle and crye*. A supernatural possibility here, as "ladyes" in this era and genre frequently meant fairies or nymphs.
[7] *On molde*. Obsc., probably meaning "on land."

<162>

fair Margaret and Sweet William

From Percy's *Reliques of Ancient English Poetry*.[1]

As it fell out on a long summer's day
    Two lovers they sat on a hill;
They sat together that long summer's day,
    And could not talk their fill.

— "I see no harm by you, Margarèt,
    And you see none by mee;
Before to-morrow at eight o' the clock
    A rich wedding you shall see." —

Fair Margaret sat in her bower-window,
    Combing her yellow hair;
There she spied Sweet William and his bride,
    As they were a-riding near.

Then down she layd her ivory combe,
    And braided her hair in twain:
She went alive out of her bower,
    But ne'er came alive in't again.

When day was gone, and night was come,
    And all men fast asleep,
Then came the spirit of fair Marg'ret,
    And stood at William's feet.

— "Are you awake, sweet William?" she said;
    "Or, sweet William, are you asleep?
God give you joy of your gay bride-bed,
    And me of my winding sheet." —

---

[1] Percy, *Reliques*, Vol III, pp. 120-24. For a discussion of variants of the comings
and goings of ballad ghosts named Margaret and William, see Lowry Wimberly's
Folklore in English and Scottish Ballads, pp. 250-253.

<163>

When day was come, and night was gone,
    And all men wak'd from sleep,
Sweet William to his lady said,
    — "My dear, I have cause to weep:

"I dreamt a dream, my dear ladyè,
    Such dreames are never good:
I dreamt my bower was full of red wine,
    And my bride-bed full of blood." —

He called up his merry men all,
    By one, by two, and by three;
Saying, — "I'll away to fair Marg'ret's bower,
    By the leave of my ladyè." —

And when he came to fair Marg'ret's bower,
    He knocked at the ring;
And who so ready as her seven brethrèn
    To let Sweet William in.

Then he turned up the covering-sheet,
    — "Pray let me see the dead;
Methinks she looks all pale and wan,
    She hath lost her cherry red.

"I'll do more for thee, Margarèt,
    Than any of thy kin;
For I will kiss thy pale wan lips,
    Though a smile I cannot win." —

With that bespake the seven brethren,
    Making most piteous mone:
— "You may go kiss your jolly brown bride,
    And let our sister alone." —

<164>

— "If I do kiss my jolly brown bride,
    I do but what is right;
I ne'er made a vow to yonder poor corpse
    By day, nor yet by night.

"Deal on, deal on, my merry men all,
    Deal on your cake and your wine:[2]
For wha'ever is dealt at her funeral to-day
    Shall be dealt to-morrow at mine." —

Fair Margaret died to-day, to-day,
    Sweet William died the morrow:
Fair Margaret died for pure true love,
    Sweet William died for sorrow.

Margaret was buryed in the lower chancèl,
    And William in the higher:
Out of her breast there sprang a rose,
    And out of his a briar.

They grew till they grew unto the church-top,
    And then they could grow no higher;
And there they tyed in a true lovers' knot,
    Which made all the people admire.

Then came the clerk of the parish,
    As you the truth shall hear,
And by misfortune cut them down,
    Or they had now been there.

---

[2] *Cake and wine*. Alluding to the dole anciently given at funerals —MGL.

<165>

Sweet William's Ghost

From Allan Ramsay's *Tea-Table Miscellany*. [1]

There came a Ghost to Margaret's door,
    With many a grievous grone,[2]
And ay he tided at the pin;[3]
    But answer made she none.

— "Is this my father Philip?
    Or is't my brother John?
Or is't my true love Willie,
    From Scotland new come home?" —

— "'Tis not thy father Philip;
    Nor yet thy brother John:
But 'tis thy true love Willie
    From Scotland new come home.

"O sweet Margret! O dear Margret!
    I pray thee speak to mee:
Give me my faith and troth, Margret,
    As I gave it to thee." —

— "Thy faith and troth thou'se nevir get,
    Of me shall nevir win,
Till that thou come within my bower,
    And kiss my cheek and chin." —

---

[1] Ramsay's collections of ballads for singing commenced in 1724 and went through many editions. This ballad is found in the 1740 edition, Vol II, p. 118. Lewis almost certainly obtained this material from Percy's *Reliques of Ancient English Poetry*, Vol III, Book II, p. 127, from which he copies Percy's alterations to spelling. This item is Child Ballad No. 77a. This ballad, transported to Germany with changed locales, is believed to be the inspiration for Bürger's "Lenore."

[2] This is spelled *groan* in Ramsay, and changed to *grone* by Percy.

[3] *Tided at the pin.* Attempted to open the door-latch. The ghost, therefore, is a voice calling through a closed door.

<166>

— "If I should come within thy bower,
    I am no earthly man:
And should I kiss thy rosy lipp,
    Thy days will not be lang.

"O sweet Margret, O dear Margret,
    I pray thee speak to me:
Give me my faith and troth, Margret,
    As I gave it to thee." —

— "Thy faith and troth thou'se nevir get,
    Of me shall nevir win,
Till thou take me to yon kirk yard,
    And wed me with a ring." —

— "My bones are buried in a kirk yard
    Afar beyond the sea,
And it is but my sprite, Margret,
    That's speaking now to thee."—

She stretched out her lily-white hand,
    As for to do her best:
— "Hae there your faith and troth, Willie,
    God send your soul good rest." —

Now she has kilted her robes of green,
    A piece below her knee:
And a' the live-lang winter night
    The dead corpse followed shee.

— "Is there any room at your head, Willie?
    Or any room at your feet?
Or any room at your side, Willie,
    Wherein that I may creep?"

<167>

—"There's nae room at my head, Margret,
   There's nae room at my feet,
There's nae room at my side, Margret,
   My coffin is made so meet."[4] —

Then up and crew the red red cock,
   And up then crew the gray:
— "'Tis time, 'tis time, my dear Margret,
   That I were gane away." —

No more the Ghost to Margret said,
   But, with a grievous grone,
Evanish'd in a cloud of mist,
   And left her all alone.

— "O stay, my only true love, stay,"—
   The constant Margret cried:
Wan grew her cheeks, she clos'd her een,
   Stretch'd her saft limbs, and died.[5]

[4] *Meet.* Narrow, tightly-fitting.
[5] Percy believed this final stanza to be a modern addition.

<168>

The Boy and the Mantle

[ANON., Adapted by M.G. LEWIS]

From Percy's *Reliques of Ancient English Poetry*[1].

In Carleile dwelt King Arthur,
  A prince of passing might;
And there maintain'd his table round,
  Beset with many a knight.

And there he kept his Christmas
  With mirth and princely cheare,
When, lo! a straunge and cunning boy
  Before him did appeare.

A kirtle, and a mantle,
  This boy had him upon,
With brooches, rings, and owches,
  Full daintily bedone.

---

[1] Percy took the original ballad as found and merely modernized the language and spelling a little. Despite the epigraph, however, Lewis has made major changes, and this really should be considered as an original adaptation by Lewis. Where the original is a sly satire on infidelity with Guenevere as only the highest among many offenders, Lewis moves the boy's accusation of Guenevere to the very end of the poem, thus making her guilt (and hypocrisy) the apparent point of the whole piece. Lewis can be credited with giving the poem a better framing opening stanza, and with solving a dilemma: in the original ballad, the boy sees a live boar, kills it, and brings in its head, yet the knights commence the effort to carve and eat "morsels" of it without its ever having been roasted. Some lines that might have been offensive in 1801 were also removed by Lewis, or his printer. The differences between the Percy transcription and Lewis's version are so substantial that I feel it necessary to present Percy's version as well. Within its classic structure of three trials of fidelity (one directed at the women, the other two mocking the offended husbands), the original is a broader satire, and it frames, without spotlighting it, the dilemma of Arthur, the last to know or believe in his Queen's infidelity. By ending the poem with the boy's taunt at Arthur, Lewis seems to hurl down a gauntlet against the aristocrats of his own time, obsessed with morals yet sinning in the manner of their ancestors. The original version of this ballad is preserved as Child Ballad No. 29. Herder translated in into German in his *Volkslied*, Vol. I, 249-61.

<169>

He had a sarke[2] of silk
    About his middle meet;[3]
And thus, with seemely curtesy,
    He did King Arthur greet.

— "God speed thee, brave King Arthur,
    Thus feasting in thy bowre;
And Guenever thy goodly Queen,
    That fair and peerlesse flowre.

"Ye gallant Lords, and Lordings,
    I wish you all take heed,
Lest, what ye deem a blooming rose
    Should prove a cankred weed." —

Then straitway from his bosome
    A little wand he drew;
And with it eke a mantle[4]
    Of wondrous shape, and hew.

— "Now have thou here, King Arthur,
    Have this here of mee,
And give unto thy comely Queen,
    All-shapen[5] as you see.

"No wife it shall become,
    That once hath been to blame." —
Then every Knight in Arthur's court
    Slye glaunced at his dame.

And first came lady Guenever,
    The mantle she must trye.
This dame, she was new-fangled,[6]
    And of a roving eye.

---

[2] *Sarke.* Shirt.
[3] *Meet.* Tightly-fitting.
[4] *Mantle.* A loose, sleeveless cloak.
[5] *All-shapen.* In this instance, shapeless.
[6] *New-fangled.* Fond of novelty.

<170>

When she had tane[7] the mantle,
  And all was with it cladde,
From top to toe it shiver'd down,
As tho' with sheers beshradde.[8]

One while it was too long,
  Another while too short,
And wrinkled on her shoulders
  In most unseemly sort.

Now green, now red it seemed,
  Then all of sable hue.
— "Beshrew me," quoth King Arthur,
  "I think thou beest not true." —

Down she threw the mantle,
  Ne longer would not stay;
But storming like a fury,
  To her chamber flung away.

She curst the whoreson weaver,
  That had the mantle wrought:
And doubly curst the froward[9] impe,
  Who thither it had brought.

— "I had rather live in desarts
  Beneath the green-wood tree,
Than here, base King, among thy groomes,
  The sport of them and thee." —

Sir Kay call'd forth his Lady,
  And bade her to come near:
— "Yet dame, if thou be guilty,
I pray thee now forbear." —

---

[7] *Tane.* Taken.
[8] *As tho' with sheers beshradde.* As though shredded with scissors.
[9] *Froward.* Perverse or ill-disposed.

<171>

This lady pertly giggling,
    With forward step came on,
And boldly to the little boy
    With fearless face is gone.

When she had tane the mantle,
    With purpose for to wear:
It shrunk up to her shoulder,
    And left her b— side[10] bare.

Then every merry knight,
    That was in Arthur's court,
Gibed, and laught, and flouted,
    To see that pleasant sport.

Downe she threw the mantle,
    No longer bold or gay,
But with a face all pale and wan,
    To her chamber slunk away.

Then forth came an old knight,
    A pattering o'er his creed;[11]
And proffer'd to the little boy
    Five nobles[12] to his meed;[13]

— "And all the time of Christmass
    Plumb-porridge shall be thine,
If thou wilt let my lady fair
    Within the mantle shine." —

A saint his lady seemed,
    With step demure, and slow,
And gravely to the mantle
    With mincing pace doth goe.

---

[10] *B—side.* Backside, apparently censored by Lewis's printer. Child and Percy
have "buttockes."
[11] *Creed.* Missal or prayer book.
[12] *Nobles.* Gold coin.
[13] *Meed.* Reward, or, in this case, a bribe.

<172>

When she the same had taken,
    That was so fine and thin,
It shrivell'd all about her,
    And show'd her dainty skin.

Ah! little did HER mincing,
    Or HIS long prayers bestead;
She had no more hung on her,
    Than a tassel and a thread.

Down she threwe the mantle,
    With terror and dismay,
And, with a face of scarlet,
    To her chamber hyed away.

Sir Cradock call'd his lady,
    And bade her to come neare:
— "Come win this mantle, lady,
    And do me credit here.

"Come win this mantle, lady,
    For now it shall be thine,
If thou hast never done amiss,
    Sith first I made thee mine." —

The lady gently blushing,
    With modest grace came on,
And now to trye the wond'rous charm
    Courageously is gone.

When she had tane the mantle,
    And put it on her backe,
About the hem it seemed
    To wrinkle and to cracke.

<173>

— "Lye still, she cried, O mantle!
    And shame me not for nought,
I'll freely own whate'er amiss,
    Or blameful I have wrought.

"Once I kist Sir Cradocke
    Beneathe the green wood tree:
Once I kist Sir Cradocke's mouth
    Before he married mee." —

When thus she had her shriven,
    And her worst fault had told,
The mantle soon became her
    Right comely as it shold.

Most rich and fair of colour,
    Like gold it glittering shone:
And much the knights in Arthur's court
    Admir'd her every one.

Then towards King Arthur's table
    The boy he turn'd his eye:
Where stood a boar's-head garnished
    With bayes and rosemarye.

When thrice he o'er the boar's head
    His little wand had drawne,
Quoth he, — "There's never a cuckold's[14] knife
    Can carve this head of brawne." [15] —

_____

[14] *Cuckold.* A man whose wife has been unfaithful; worse, a man whose wife has
borne another man's child. Derives from the cuckoo bird, which lays its eggs in
the nests of other species of birds, who are tricked into raising its young as their
own. Making the sign of the cuckoo — two raised fingers in imitation of the
bird's head feathers — behind a man's head was a signal that he had been thus
deceived.
[15] *Brawne.* The fleshy, edible parts.

<174>

Then some their whittles[16] rubb'd
    On whetstone, and on hone:
Some threwe them under the table,
    And swore that they had none.

Sir Cradock had a little knife
    Of steel and iron made;
And in an instant through the skull
    He thrust the shining blade.

He thrust the shining blade
    Full easily and fast:
And every knight in Arthur's court
    A morsel had to taste.

The boy brought forth a horne,[17]
    All golden was the rim:
Said he, — "No cuckolde ever can
    Set mouth unto the brim.

"No cuckold can this little horne
    Lift fairly to his head;
But or on this, or that side,
    He shall the liquor shed." —

Some shed it on their shoulder,
    Some shed it on their thigh;
And hee that could not hit his mouth,
    Was sure to hit his eye.

Thus he that was a cuckold,
Was known of every man:
But Cradock lifted easily,
And wan the golden can.

---

16 *Whittles.* Knives.
17 *Horne.* A drinking vessel made from or in the shape of an animal horn.

<175>

Thus boar's head, horn, and mantle,
    Were this fair couple's meed:
And all such constant lovers,
    God send them well to speed.

Then down in rage came Guenever,
    And thus could spightful say,
— "Sir Cradock's wife most wrongfully
    Hath borne the prize away.

"See yonder shameless woman,
    That makes herselfe so clean:
Yet from her pillow taken
    Thrice five gallants have been.

"Priests, clarkes, and wedded men
    Have her lewd pillow prest:
Yet she the wonderous prize forsooth
    Must beare from all the rest." —

Then bespake the little boy,
    Who had the same in hold:
— "Chastize thy wife, King Arthur,
    Of speech she is too bold:

"Of speech she is too bold,
    Of carriage all too free;
Sir King, she hath within thy hall
    A cuckold made of thee.

"All frolick light and wanton
    She hath her carriage borne:
And given thee for a kingly crown
    To wear a cuckold's horne."

<176>

THE BOY AND THE MANTLE

ANON., Adapted by BISHOP THOMAS PERCY

In the third day of May,
To Carleile did come
A kind curteous child,
That cold much of wisdome.

A kirtle and a mantle
This child had uppon,
With brouches and ringes
Full richelye bedone.

He had a sute of silke
About his middle drawne;
Without he cold of curtesye,
He thought itt much shame.

— "God speed thee, King Arthur,
Sitting at thy meate:
And the goodly Queene Guénever
I cannott her forgett.

"I tell you, lords, in this hall,
I hett you all to heede,
Except you be the more surer,
Is you for to dread." —

He plucked out of his poterner,
And longer wold not dwell;
He pulled forth a pretty mantle,
Betweene two nut-shells.

— "Have thou here, King Arthur,
Have thou heere of mee;
Give itt to thy comely queene,
Shapen as itt is alreadye.

<177>

"Itt shall never become that wiffe,
That hath once done amisse:" —
Then every knight in the kings court
Began to care for his.

Forth came dame Guénever;
To the mantle shee her hied;
The ladye shee was newfangle,
But yett shee was affrayd.

When shee had taken the mantle,
She stoode as shee had beene madd:
It was from the top to the toe
As sheeres had itt shread.

One while was it gule,
Another while was itt greene;
Another while was it wadded;
Ill itt did her beseeme.

Another while was it blacke,
And bore the worst hue:
"By my troth,"quoth King Arthur,
"I thinke thou be not true."

Shee threw downe the mantle,
That bright was of blee;
Fast, with a rudd redd,
To her chamber can shee flee.

She curst the weaver and the walker
That clothe that had wrought,
And bade a vengeance on his crowne
That hither hath itt brought.

"I had rather be in a wood,
Under a greene tree,
Then in King Arthurs court
Shamed for to bee."

<178>

Kay called forth his ladye,
And bade her come neere;
Saies, "Madam, an[18] thou be guiltye,
I pray thee hold thee there."

Forth came his ladye,
Shortlye and anon;
Boldlye to the mantle
Then is shee gone.

When she had tane the mantle,
And cast it her about,
Then was shee bare
Before all the rout.

Then every knight,
That was in the kings court,
Talked, laughed, and showted
Full oft att that sport.

She threw downe the mantle,
That bright was of blee;
Fast, with a red rudd,
To her chamber can shee flee.

Forth came an old knight
Pattering ore a creede,
And he proferred to this little boy
Twenty markes to his meede,

And all the time of the Christmasse,
Willinglye to ffeede;
For why this mantle might
Doe his wiffe some need.

---

[18] *An*, If.

<179>

When she had tane the mantle,
Of cloth that was made,
Shee had no more left on her,
But a tassell and a threed:
Then every knight in the kings court
Bade evill might shee speed.

Shee threw downe the mantle,
That bright was of blee;
And fast, with a redd rudd,
To her chamber can shee flee.

Craddocke called forth his ladye,
And bade her come in;
Saith, "Winne this mantle, ladye,
With a litle dinne.

"Winne this mantle, ladye,
And it shal be thine,
If thou never did amisse
Since thou wast mine."

Forth came Craddockes ladye,
Shortlye and anon;
But boldlye to the mantle
Then is shee gone.

When she had tane the mantle,
And cast it her about,
Upp att her great toe
It began to crinkle and crowt:
Shee said, "Bowe downe, mantle,
And shame me not for nought.

<180>

"Once I did amisse,
I tell you certainlye,
When I kist Craddockes mouth
Under a greene tree;
When I kist Craddockes mouth
Before he marryed mee."

When shee had her shreeven,
And her sines shee had tolde,
The mantle stoode about her
Right as shee wold,

Seemelye of coulour,
Glittering like gold:
Then every knight in Arthurs court
Did her behold.

Then spake dame Guénever
To Arthur our king;
"She hath tane yonder mantle
Not with right, but with wronge.

"See you not yonder woman,
That maketh her self soe cleane?
I have seene tane out of her bedd
Of men fiveteene;

"Priests, clarkes, and wedded men
From her, bedeene:
Yett shee taketh the mantle,
And maketh her self cleane."

Then spake the little boy,
That kept the mantle in hold;
Sayes, "King, chasten thy wiffe,
Of her words shee is to bold:

<181>

"Shee is a bitch and a witch,
And a whore bold:
King, in thine owne hall
Thou art a cuckold."

The little boy stoode
Looking out a dore;
And there as he was lookinge
He was ware of a wyld bore.
He was ware of a wyld bore,
Wold have werryed a man:
He pulld forth a wood kniffe,
Fast thither that he ran:
He brought in the bores head,
And quitted him like a man.

He brought in the bores head,
And was wonderous bold:
He said there was never a cuckolds kniffe
Carve itt that cold.

Some rubbed their knives
Uppon a whetstone:
Some threw them under the table,
And said they had none.

King Arthur and the child
Stood looking upon them;
All their knives edges
Turned backe againe.

Craddocke had a little knive
Of iron and of steele;
He britled the bores head
Wonderous weele,
That every knight in the kings court
Had a morssell.

<182>

The little boy had a horne,
Of red gold that ronge:
He said there was "Noe cuckolde
Shall drinke of my horne,
But he shold it sheede,
Either behind or beforne."

Some shedd on their shoulder,
And some on their knee;
He that cold not hitt his mouthe,
Put it in his eye:
And he that was a cuckold
Every man might him see.

Craddocke wan the horne,
And the bores head:
His ladie wan the mantle
Unto her meede.
Everye such a lovely ladye
God send her well to speede.

<183>

Saint Patrick's Purgatory

[ROBERT SOUTHEY][1]

In the *Reliques of Ancient Poetry*, is the following —

"Owaine Myles is a Ballad, giving an account of the wonders of St. Patricks Purgatory. This is a translation into verse of the story related in Mat. Paris's[2] *Hist, sub Ann. 1152.*" The version which is here offered to the Public is evidently modern: I am ignorant of the Author. I think the 19th stanza, in particular, has a great degree of merit. —MGL

— "Now enter in! — the Prior cried,
—"And God, Sir Ouvain, be your guide!
  Your name shall live in story:
Many there are who rich this shore,
But few who venture to explore
  St. Patrick's Purgatory." —

---

[1] This poem's authorship was unattributed in Lewis' *Tales of Wonder*. In his 1838 collected poems, Southey acknowledged authorship:
"This ballad was published (1801) in "Tales of Wonder" by Mr. Lewis, who found it among the wefts and strays of the press. He never knew that it was mine; but, after his death, I bestowed some pains in recomposing it, because he had thought it worth preserving.
   It is founded upon the abridged extract which M. LeGrand has given in his Fabliaux of a metrical legend, by Marie de France" —RS.
   Marie de France (late 12th century CE) based her text on the *Tractatus de Purgatorio Sancti Patrici*, attributed to a monk named Henry of Saltrey, circa 1180-84. This would suggest that the version in Roger of Wendover's chronicle was a paraphrase of an already-existing text. Indeed, there are more than 30 versions of this story in different languages, and more than 150 extant Latin copies. Since the narrative is dated according to the reign of [Irish] King Stephen (1135-1154 CE), any chronicler repeating the legend would date it accordingly. The writing of Roger of Wendover's chronicle commenced around 1195, indicating that the *Tractatus* (1180-1184) is the older text. The story passed into numerous languages, and was in fact, the best-known Latin account of Purgatory. Dante read it, and some of its gruesome details doubtless inspired him —BR.
[2] The chronicle previously attributed to Matthew Paris is now known to be principally by Roger of Wendover.

<184>

Ouvain preparing for the entry to Purgatory in *Le voyage du puys sainct Patrix auquel lieu on voit les peines de Purgatoire et aussi les joyes de Paradis* by Claude Noury, Lyon 1506.

Adown the deep and dark descent
With cautious step Sir Ouvain went,
    And many a pray'r he pour'd;
No helm had he, nor guardian crest,
No hauberk mail'd the warrior's breast,
    Nor grasp'd he shield or sword.

<185>

The earth was moist beneath his tread,
The damps fell heavy on his head,
   The air was piercing chill;
And sudden shudd'rings o'er him came,
And he could feel through all his frame
   An icy tremor thrill.

At length a dim and doubtful light
Dawn'd welcome on th' advent'rer's sight;
   Th' advent'rer hasten'd on.
And now the warrior's steps attain.
To where a high and stately fane
With gem-born radiance shone.

— "Come, enter here!" — the Warden cried,
"And God, oh Pilgrim, be your guide,
   Since you have reach'd this bourne!
Enter, and take assistance due —
'Twill then be time to welcome you,
   If ever you return."

Sir Ouvain pass'd the open gate,
The Warden him conducted straight
   To where a coffin lay:
The train around in silence stand,
With fun'ral torches in their hands,
That gave a gloomy day.

"Few pilgrims ever reach this bourne,
Stranger! but fewer still return:
   Receive assistance due!
Stranger, a dreadful hour is near:
Cast off all mortal feelings here,
   This coffin is for you.

<186>

"Lie here, while we with pious breath
Shall o'er you chaunt the dirge of death, —
    Best aid that we can give:
The rites that wait the Christian dead
Shall never o'er your corpse be said —
    Receive them while you live." —

Sir Ouvain in a shroud was drest,
He held the cross upon his breast,
    And down he laid his head;
The funeral train enclos'd him round,
And sung with deep and solemn sound
    The service of the dead.

— "Now, go your way," the Warden cried,
"And God, oh Pilgrim, be your guide!
    Commend you to the Lord!" —
Adown the deep and dark descent,
With cautious step, the warrior went,
    And many a pray'r he pour'd.

Now deeper grew the dark descent,
With timid step Sir Ouvain went —
    'Twas silence all around;
Save his own echoes through the cell,
And the thick damps that frequent fell,
    With dull and heavy sound.

But colder now he felt the cell,
Those heavy damps no longer fell,
    Thin grew the piercing air:
And on the advent'rer's aching sight
Far rose a pale and feeble light,
    Th' advent'rer hasten'd there.

<187>

And now at length emerg'd to light,
A frozen desart met his sight,
   A desert waste and wide;
Where rocks of ice piled mountain high,
That tower'd into the sunless sky,
   Appear'd on every side.

There many a wretch, with deadly fear,
Ribb'd in the ice, he saw appear
   Alive in this their tomb;
Sir Ouvain's blood stood, still with dread.
And then a voice in thunder said:
   — "Retire, or share their doom!" —

Awhile his heart forgot to beat,
Then on he urg'd his falt' ring feet,
   And sought for strength in pray'r;
Sudden, a pow'r, whose unseen hand
No might of mortal could withstand,
   Upgrasp'd him by the hair;

And through the sky resistless swung,
And full against an ice-rock flung;
   The ice encas'd him in:
Thus by the arm of Daemon thrown,
He felt the crash of every bone,
   And still he lived within.

— "Now, mercy Christ!" the warrior cried,
Instant the rocks of ice divide,
   And ev'ry pain was gone;
He felt new life in ev'ry limb,
And rais'd to heav'n the grateful hymn,
   And fearless hasten'd on.

New fears, new dangers doom'd to meet,
For now a close and piercing heat
   Relax'd each loosen'd limb;
The sweat roll'd out from every part,
In short quick beatings toil'd his heart,
   His throbbing eyes grew dim.

For through the wide and wasted land
A stream of fire, through banks of sand,
   Its burning billows spread;
The vapours, tremulously light,
Hung quiv'ring o'er the glowing white,
   The air he breath'd was red.

Beyond a stately well arose, —
He saw its crystal sides disclose
   Green fields and shady trees,
And running waters cool and clear,
Whose murmurs reach'd his tortur'd ear,
   Born[e] on the fiery breeze.

A voice in thunder cried — "Retire!" —
He look'd, and lo, a form of fire!
   — "Return"— the Daemon said.
His soul grew sick with deep alarm,
The Fiend reach'd out his burning arm,
   And touch'd Sir Ouvain's head.

Sir Ouvain shrieked for then he felt
His eye-balls burn, his marrow melt,
   His brain as liquid lead:
And from his heart the boiling blood
Roll'd fast an agonizing flood
   Through limbs like iron red.

<189>

Oldest printed map of Ireland: the island upside-down, with a gigantic image of Saint Patrick's Purgatory. Betelius, 1560 CE. (British Museum)

The anguish brought a brief despair,
Then mindful of the aid of pray'r,
    He call'd on Christ again;
Instant the gales of Eden came,
At once they quench'd th' infernal flame,
    And heal'd each scorching vein.

To him, relieved from all his woes,
The adamantine gates unclose,
    Free entrance there was giv'n;
And songs of triumph met his ear,
Enrapt Sir Ouvain seem'd to hear
    The harmonies of heav'n.

— "Welcome to this, the bless'd retreat,
Thou who hast pass'd, with fearless feet,
    St. Patrick's Purgatory;
For after death these seats divine,
Reward eternal shall be thine,
    And thine eternal glory," —

Inebriate with the deep delight,
Dim grew Sir Ouvain's swimming sight,
    His senses died away;
To life again revived, before
The entrance of the cave once more
    He saw the light of day.

<191>

Saint Patrick describing the outline of the cave of Purgatory with the Staff of Jesus. From Peter De Navalibus, *Catalogue of Saints*.

SAINT PATRICK'S PURGATORY (REVISED)

ROBERT SOUTHEY

1.
"Enter, Sir Knight," the Warden cried,
"And trust in Heaven whate'er betide,
    Since you have reach'd this bourn;
But first receive refreshment due,
'T will then be time to welcome you
    If ever you return."

2.
Three sops were brought of bread and wine:
Well might Sir Owen then divine
    The mystic warning given,
That he against our ghostly Foe
Must soon to mortal combat go,
    And put his trust in Heaven.

<192>

3.

Sir Owen pass'd the convent gate;
The Warden him conducted straight
    To where a coffin lay:
The Monks around in silence stand,
Each with a funeral torch in hand,
    Whose light bedimm'd the day.

4.

"Few Pilgrims ever reach this bourn,"
They said, "but fewer still return;
    Yet, let what will ensue,
Our duties are prescribed and clear:
Put off all mortal weakness here;
    This coffin is for you.

5.

"Lie there, while we with pious breath,
Raise over you the dirge of death;
    This comfort we can give:
Belike no living hands may pay
This office to your lifeless clay;
    Receive it while you live!"

6.

Sir Owen in a shroud was dressed;
They placed a cross upon his breast,
    And down he laid his head:
Around him stood the funeral train,
And sung with slow and solemn strain,
    The Service of the Dead.

7.

Then to the entrance of the Cave
They led the Christian warrior brave:
    Some fear he well might feel,
For none of all the Monks could tell
The terrors of that mystic cell,
    Its secrets none reveal.

<193>

8.

"Now enter here," the Warden cried,
"And God, Sir Owen, be your guide!
    Your name shall live in story:
For of the few who reach this shore,
Still fewer venture to explore
    St. Patrick's Purgatory."

9.

Adown the Cavern's long descent,
Feeling his way Sir Owen went,
    With cautious feet and slow, —
Unarm'd; for neither sword nor spear,
Nor shield of proof, avail'd him here
    Against our ghostly Foe.

10.

The ground was moist beneath his tread;
Large drops fell heavy on his head;
    The air was damp and chill;
And sudden shudderings o'er him came,
And he could feel through all his frame
    An icy sharpness thrill.

11.

Now steeper grew the dark descent;
In fervent prayer the Pilgrim went;
    'T was silence all around,
Save his own echo from the cell,
And the large drops that frequent fell
    With dull and heavy sound.

12.

But colder now he felt the cell;
Those heavy drops no longer fell;
    Thin grew the piercing air;
And now upon his aching sight,
There dawn'd far off a feeble light:
    In hope he hasten'd there.

<194>

13.

Emerging now once more to day
A frozen waste before him lay,[3]
   A desert wild and wide,
Where ice-rocks, in a sunless sky,
On ice-rocks piled, and mountains high,
   Were heap'd on every side.

14.

Impending as about to fall
They seem'd, and had that sight been all,
   Enough that sight had been
To make the stoutest courage quail;
For what could courage there avail
   Against what then was seen?

15.

He saw, as on in faith he passed,
Where many a frozen wretch was fast
   Within the ice-clefts pent,
Yet living still, and doom'd to bear
In absolute and dumb despair
   Their endless punishment.

16.

A Voice then spake within his ear,
And fill'd his inmost soul with fear, —
   "O mortal Man," it said,
"Adventurers like thyself were these!"
He seem'd to feel his life-blood freeze,
   And yet subdued his dread.

---

[3] Southey's elaborate description of a frozen waste is his own invention, the only parallel in Roger of Wendover's text being "a cold and stinking river." This "Arctic sublime" will be familiar to readers of both Byron and Shelley, who apostrophized Swiss glaciers (and where Mary Shelley set the great creator-monster confrontation in *Frankenstein*). *Frankenstein's* framing narratives are set in the Arctic wastes. Marie de France's 'Second Torment' includes a wasteland with a "cold and light wind" ("La out un freit vent e seri") (l. 921) but all is fiery until the immersion in the "cold and putrid river" ("un fleuve freit e puant') ll.1247-55.

<195>

17.
"O mortal Man," the Voice pursued,
"Be wise in time! for thine own good
    Alone I counsel thee:
Take pity on thyself; retrace
Thy steps, and fly this dolorous place
    While yet thy feet are free.

18.
"I warn thee once! I warn thee twice!
Behold! that mass of mountain-ice
    Is trembling o'er thy head!
One warning is allow'd thee more;
O mortal Man, that warning o'er,
    And thou art worse than dead!"

19.
Not without fear, Sir Owen still
Held on, with strength of righteous will,
    In faith and fervent prayer;
When at the word, "I warn thee thrice!"
Down came the mass of mountain ice,
    And overwhelm'd him there.

20.
Crush'd though it seem'd in every bone,
And sense for suffering left alone,
    A living hope remain'd:
In whom he had believed, he knew,
And thence the holy courage grew
    That still his soul sustain'd.

21.
For he, as he beheld it fall,
Fail'd not in faith on Christ to call, —
    "Lord, thou canst save!" he cried:
Oh heavenly help vouchsafed in need,
When perfect faith is found indeed!
    The rocks of ice divide.

<196>

22.

Like dust before the storm-wind's sway
The shivered fragments rolled away,
    And left the passage free:
New strength he feels; all pain is gone;
New life Sir Owen breathes, and on
    He goes rejoicingly.

23.

Yet other trials he must meet,
For soon a close and piercing heat
    Relax'd each loosen'd limb;
The sweat stream'd out from every part;
In short quick beatings toiled his heart;
    His throbbing eyes grew dim.

24.

Along the wide and wasted land,
A stream of fire, through banks of sand,
    Its molten billows spread;
Thin vapours, tremulously light,
Hung quivering o'er the glowing white;
    The air he breathed was red.

25.

A Paradise beyond was seen,
Of shady groves and gardens green,
    Fair flowers and fruitful trees,
And flowing fountains, cool and clear,
Whose gurgling music reached his ear
    Borne on the burning breeze.

26.

How should he pass that molten flood?
While gazing wistfully he stood,
    A Fiend, as in a dream,
"Thus!" answered the unuttered thought,
Stretched forth a mighty arm, and caught,
    And cast him in the stream.

<197>

27.

Sir Owen groaned; for then he felt
His eyeballs burn, his marrow melt,
    His brain like liquid lead,
And from his heart the boiling blood
Its agonizing course pursued
    Through limbs like iron red.

28.

Yet, giving way to no despair,
But mindful of the aid of prayer,
    "Lord, Thou canst save!" he said;
And then a breath from Eden came;
With life and healing through his frame
    The blissful influence spread.

29.

No Fiends may now his way oppose;
The gates of Paradise unclose;
    Free entrance there is given;
And songs of triumph meet his ear:
Enrapt, Sir Owen seems to hear
    The harmonies of Heaven.

30.

"Come, Pilgrim! take thy foretaste meet,
Thou who hast trod with fearless feet
    St. Patrick's Purgatory;
For, after death, these seats divine,
Reward eternal, shall be thine,
    And thine eternal glory."

31.

Inebriate with the deep delight,
Dim grew the Pilgrim's swimming sight;
    His senses died away;
And, when to life he woke, before
The Cavern-mouth he saw once more
    The light of earthly day.

<198>

A. D. 1153 — SAINT PATRICK'S PURGATORY

FROM ROGER OF WENDOVER'S *FLOWERS OF HISTORY*

A knight named Owen, who had for many years served under King Stephen, obtained the king's licence, and went to visit his parents in Ireland his native country. After spending some time there, he began to call to mind his wicked life, which had been employed from his cradle in plunder and violence. He particularly repented of the violation of churches, and invasion of ecclesiastical property, besides other enormous sins of which he had been guilty. In this state of penitence he went to a bishop of that country, who, having heard his confession, rebuked him severely, asserting that he had committed a great offence against God's mercy, and the knight began to think how he should show due contrition for his misdeeds. The bishop wished to impose on him some just penance, to which the knight replied, "If, as you say, I have so seriously offended my Maker, I will submit to a penance more than usually severe, and, for the remission of my sins, enter the purgatory of St. Patrick." The following is the account which the ancient Irish histories give us of this purgatory and its origin.

Of the nature of the purgatory aforesaid.

Whilst the great Patrick was preaching the work of God in Ireland, and gaining much reputation by the miracles which he there performed, he sought to reclaim from the works of the devil the bestial people of that country, by fear of the torments of hell and desire of the happiness of heaven; but they told him plainly that they would not be converted to Christ, unless they first saw with their eyes the things which he told them. Whilst therefore St. Patrick, with fasting, watching, and prayer, entreated

<199>

God for the salvation of that people, the Son of God appearing to him led him into a desert-place, where he showed him a cave round and dark within, and said to him, "Whosoever in true penitence and constancy of faith shall enter this cave for the space of a day and a night, shall be purified therein from all the sins which he has committed against God during all his life, and shall also there not only behold the torments of the wicked, but, if he shall persevere steadfastly in the love of God, be a witness also of the joys of the blessed." The Lord then disappeared, and St. Patrick, joyful both at having seen Christ and at the discovery of the cave, trusted at last that he should be able to convert the wretched people of Ireland to the true faith of Christ. He immediately, therefore, constructed an oratory on that spot, and, enclosing the cave which is in the burial-ground in front of the church, placed a door there, that no one might enter it without his leave. He next appointed there a society of regular canons, and gave the key to the prior, with orders that whoever came to the prior with a licence from the bishop of that district, should be allowed to enter the purgatory. Many persons availed themselves of this privilege whilst St. Patrick was still alive, and when they came out, they testified that they had seen the torments of the wicked, as well as the great and unspeakable happiness of the good.

How Owen by the licence of the bishop entered the purgatory.

The aforesaid knight, therefore, persevered in demanding necessary licence, and the bishop, seeing him inflexible, gave, him a letter to the prior, requesting him to act in the usual way. The prior, having read the letter, conducted the knight into the church, where he remained in prayer during fifteen days. At the end of this time, the prior first celebrated mass, and administered to him the holy communion; he then led him to the door of the cave, which being opened, he sprinkled him with holy water, and said, "You will enter here in the name of Jesus Christ, and will walk through the cave until you come out upon an open plain, where you will find a hall skillfully constructed; enter it, and God will send you guides who will tell you what you are to do." The man entered with boldness upon this conflict with the demons, and commending himself to the prayers of all, and signing his forehead with the mark of the holy cross, he bravely passed the gate, and the prior, shutting the door after him, returned with the procession into the church.

<200>

How the knight reached the aforesaid hall, and entered into it.

The knight passed courageously along the cave, until he was in total darkness: at last the light again broke upon him, and he found himself in the plain where was the hall that he had been told of; the light was no more than the twilight of evening, and the hall was not enclosed by walls, but by pillars, like a monastic cloister. He entered it, and sat down looking about him on all sides, and admiring the beauty of the building. When he had sat there a short time, fifteen men in white garments, looking like ecclesiastics, and lately shaven, entered the hall, and sat down, saluting him in the name of the Lord. All then kept silence, except one, who, said, "Blessed be Almighty God, who has inspired you with this good resolution to enter this purgatory for the remission of your sins; unless, however, you carry yourself manfully, you will perish, body and soul together. For when we shall leave this building, it will be filled with a multitude of unclean spirits, who will torment you greatly, and threaten to torment you more so. They will promise to conduct you to the gate by which you entered, if by chance they can deceive you, so that you may go out again; but if you suffer yourself to be overcome by their torments or terrified by their threats, or deceived by their promises, and so yield to them assent, you will perish both in soul and body: if, however, you be firm in faith, repose all your hope in the Lord, and yield neither to their torments, their threats, or their promises, but despise them with all your heart, you will be purified from all your sins, and will behold the torments of the wicked and the repose of the good. As long as these demons torment you, call on the name of the Lord Jesus Christ, and, by invoking his name, you shall immediately be released from all their torments. We can now remain here with you no longer, but we commend you to Almighty God."

How the demons grievously afflicted the knight.

The knight, therefore, was left alone, and prepared his mind for this new kind of conflict. He had no sooner wrought up his soul to courage, than a noise was heard around the building, as if all the men in the world, with the animals and beasts, were making it, and after this noise came a terrible apparition of ugly demons, of which an immense multitude rushed into the hall, and in derision addressed the knight: "Other men," said they, "who serve us, are content to wait till they are dead, before they come, but you honour this company of your masters so much that you come to us, soul and body, whilst you are still alive; are you come to receive punishment for your sins? You will have nothing but affliction and sorrow among us; but as you are so zealous a servant to us, if you wish to return through

<201>

the door by which you came in, we will conduct you thither unharmed, that you may again enjoy yourself in the world, and all its pleasures." Thus spoke the demons, wishing to deceive him either by threats or blandishments, but Christ's soldier was neither terrified by their threats nor seduced by their blandishments: he turned a deaf ear to them, and contemptuously answered them not a word. The demons, indignant at being treated with contempt, kindled a large fire in the hall, and, seizing the knight by his arms and legs, threw him into the midst of it, dragging him with iron hooks backwards and forwards through the fire. When he first felt the torture, he called on the name of Jesus Christ, saying, "Jesus Christ, have mercy upon him!" At this name the fire was put out, so that not a spark remained, and the knight, perceiving this, no longer feared them, because he saw that they were vanquished by the name of Christ.

Of the second place of punishment into which the knight was led.

The demons now left the hall, and dragged the knight after them through a wilderness black and dark, towards the place where the sun rises in summer, and he began now to hear lamentations, as if of all the people in the world. At length he was dragged by the demons into a long and wide plain, filled with woe and calamities, and so long that it was impossible to see across it. It was full of persons of both sexes and of every age, naked, and lying with their bellies to the ground, for their bodies and limbs were horribly fastened to the ground with hot nails of iron driven into the earth. Sometimes in the anguish of their sufferings they gnawed the dust, crying and lamenting, "Spare us, oh, spare us; have mercy, have mercy upon us!" though there was no one there to have mercy or to spare them. The demons coursed over these wretched beings, striking them with heavy blows, as they passed, and said to the knight, "These torments which you behold you shall also yourself suffer, unless you consent to be conducted to the door by which you entered; for, if you please, you shall be conducted thither in safety." But the knight, calling to mind how God had released him before, turned a deaf ear to all they said. They then threw him on the ground, and tried to nail him down like the others; but, when he invoked the name of Jesus Christ, they were unable to do him further injury in that place, and dragged him away into another open plain. Here he perceived this difference between them and the first, that whereas in the former place they had their bellies to the ground, all here were lying on their backs. Fiery dragons were sitting on some of them, and gnawing them with iron teeth, to their inexpressible anguish; others were the victims of fiery

<202>

serpents, which, coiling round their necks, arms, and bodies, fixed iron fangs into their hearts. Toads, also, of immense size and terrific to behold, sat upon the breasts of some, and tried to tear out their hearts with their ugly beaks: demons also coursed along over them, lashing them as they passed, and never let them rest a moment from their sufferings. Thence the demons dragged the knight into another plain of punishment, where there was so large a multitude that it seemed to surpass the population of the whole world. Some were suspended over fires of brimstone by iron chains fastened to their feet and legs, with their heads downward; others hung by the hands and arms, and some by the hair of their heads. Some were hung over the flames by hot iron hooks passed through their eyes and nostrils, others by their ears and mouths, others by their breasts and secret members, and amid all their groans and lamentations the lash of the demons never for a moment ceased. Here also, as in the other place of punishment, the enemy sought to torment the knight, but he invoked the name of Jesus, and was safe.

Of the red-hot wheel of iron.

From this place of punishment the demons dragged the knight to a hot iron wheel, the spokes and tires of which were fixed with red-hot nails, to which were suspended men who were grievously burned by the flame of the brimstone-fire which rose from the ground. The demons impelled this wheel with iron bars so rapidly, that it was impossible to distinguish one man from another; for on account of the rapidity of the motion, they all looked one mass of fire. Others endured equal torments, being fixed to spits, and basted by the demons with liquid metal; whilst others were baked in ovens or fried in frying-pans. The knight saw, moreover, as his conductors dragged him away, a house containing numerous large cauldrons, which were full of liquid pitch, sulphur, and melted metals, wherein were human beings of both sexes, and of all ranks and ages; some wholly immersed, some up to their eyes, others to their lips and necks, others to their breasts, and others again only to their knees and legs. Some had only one hand or foot, others had both immersed; all were howling and crying piteously for the greatness of their sufferings. When the demons tried to plunge the knight into the cauldrons with the rest, he invoked the name of Christ, and that saved him.

<203>

Of the strong wind and the stinking river.

The demons now hurried the knight to the top of a lofty mountain, and showed him a large number of people of both sexes and of different ages. All were sitting naked, bent down upon their toes turned towards the north, and apparently awaiting in terror the approach of death. Suddenly a violent whirlwind from the north swept them away, and the knight with them, and carried them, weeping and lamenting, to another part of the mountain, into a cold and stinking river; and when they endeavoured to rise out of its chilling waters, the demons coursed over the surface and again sank them into its depths: the knight, however, invoked the name of Christ, and immediately found himself on the other bank. The demons then dragged him towards the south, and showed him a noisome flame, which arose with a stinking smell out of a well, over which were naked men, apparently red-hot, who were shot forth into the air like sparks, and again, when the flame subsided, fell into the pit beneath. The demons said to the knight, "That fiery well is the entrance to hell, where we live; and since you have served us so diligently heretofore, you shall remain here with us for ever. If you enter this pit, you will perish body and soul together; but, if you will listen to us even now, and return to the door by which you came in, you shall pass unharmed:" but the knight trusting in the help of God, who had so often delivered him, turned a deaf ear to all their exhortations. The demons then, in indignation, rushed into the fiery pit, and dragged the knight with them: the deeper he went, the wider it became, and the more terrible were the punishments which he beheld. In that pit, also, the knight perceived such woe and misery, that for some time he forgot Him who had supported him; but at last, by God's grace, he invoked the name of Jesus, and immediately was driven by the flames into the open air above, where he stood some time amazed and thunderstruck. But, lo, some new demons sallying from the pit's mouth said to him, "Ho, you, who stand there, our comrades told you that this was the mouth of hell; but it is not so: we are in the habit of telling falsehoods; that if we cannot deceive by the truth, we may do so by what is false. This is not hell, but we will now lead you thither."

Of the bridge which was narrow, high, and slippery.

These new enemies dragged the knight with a terrible clamour to a broad and stinking river, covered with flame and fire of brimstone, and full of demons, who told him that under that river was hell. A bridge reached across it, having as it seemed three impossibilities connected with it. In the first place it was so slippery, that even if it had been broad, hardly

<204>

any one could have had a firm footing upon it; but. in the second place, it was so narrow, that no one could walk or even stand upon it; and thirdly, it was so high above the river that it was dizzying to look down. "You must cross that bridge," said the demons, "and the wind which blew you into the other river will blow you into this. You will then be caught by our comrades who are in the river, and be sunk into the pit of hell;" but the knight, invoking the name of Jesus Christ, bravely set foot upon the bridge; the farther he went, the wider he found it, until it was as wide as a high road. The demons, seeing the knight walk so freely across the bridge, shook the air with their horrid cries, which alarmed the knight more than all the torments he had before endured from them: others of his enemies, under the bridge, threw red-hot hooks of iron at him, but they could not touch him, and thus he crossed the bridge in safety, for he rapt with nothing that could prevent him.

How the knight was released from the annoyances of the demons.

The brave knight, now released from the persecutions of these unclean spirits, saw before him a high wall of wonderful workmanship, having in it one gate, which was shut: this gate was adorned with precious stones, and shone brilliantly. When the knight approached it, the gate opened, and so sweet a smell came forth, that he resumed his courage, and was revived from all the torments which he had suffered. A procession such as has never been seen in this world came forth to meet him, with crosses, tapers, banners, and branches of golden palms; followed by a multitude of men and women of every rank; archbishops, bishops, abbots, monks, priests, and ministers of every ecclesiastical degree, all clad in sacred garments, suited to their ranks. They received the knight with pleasing salutations, and with concerts of unequalled harmony led him within the gate in triumph. When the concert was ended, two archbishops, conversing with him, blessed the Lord for having embued his soul with courage to resist the torments which he had passed through and suffered. As they conducted him through that region, they pointed out to him the most delightful meadows, adorned with different flowers and fruits, of many kinds of herbs and trees, on the sweet odours of which he fancied he could live for ever. Darkness is never felt in that region, for it is illuminated by a celestial brilliancy that never fails. He saw there such a multitude of men and women, that he supposed all the rest of the world could hardly have held them; choir succeeded to choir, and all in sweet harmonious concert lauded the Creator of all things. Some approached crowned like kings, others were clothed in golden garments, some with robes of different colours, according to what had been their habits when they were in this

<205>

world. Some of them rejoiced in their own happiness, others at the freedom and happiness of the rest; all, when they looked on the knight, thanked God for his arrival, and congratulated him that he had escaped from the regions of death. No one there felt heat or cold, nor did he there behold anything which could create offence or injury.

How the knight was conducted to the heavenly paradise, where he saw the joys of the blessed.

Then the holy pontiffs, who had shown the knight this delightful country, said to him, "Since by the mercy of God you have come uninjured among us, you must hear from us an account of all that you have seen. This region is the terrestrial paradise from which man was first expelled for his sins, and plunged into that miserable condition in which men die in the world. All of us who are here were born in the flesh, and in original sin, and by faith in the Lord Jesus Christ, which we received in our baptism, we returned to this paradise; but since we all committed actual sins without number after we were baptized, it was only by being purged of our sins, and receiving punishment for them, that we were able to reach this place. For the penance which we undertook before our death, or at the hour of death, but did not complete on earth, must still be discharged by suffering in the places of punishment which you have seen, according to the nature and magnitude of the sin. All of us who are here have been in those places of punishment for our sins, and all whom you there saw suffering punishment, except those who are within the mouth of the infernal pit, will come to this place of rest and at last be saved. For some of them come here every day, purified from their sins, and we go to meet them and bring them in, as we did you; neither does any of us know how long he will remain here. But by masses and psalms, by the alms and prayers of the universal church, as well as the special aid of their own friends, the torments of those who are in purgatory may be much lessened, or they may even receive a lighter kind of punishment in exchange for those to which they were first doomed, until in the end they are released entirely. Thus, as you behold, we here enjoy much tranquility, though not yet worthy to enter into the full happiness of heaven. Each of us, hereafter, when the time which God has fixed arrives, shall pass into the heavenly kingdom, according as God shall provide."

<206>

How the knight was refreshed by a heavenly vision, and strengthened with spiritual food.

The reverend prelates now led the knight to the sloping side of a mountain, and bade him look upwards; which when he had done, they asked him of what colour heaven was in respect of the place on which he stood. He replied that it was like the colour of gold that is red-hot in the furnace. "This," said they, "which you now see, is the entrance to heaven and the celestial paradise; when any one goes from us he ascends this way to heaven: as long as we remain here God daily feeds us upon heavenly food, the nature of which we will now communicate by letting you taste thereof." The words were hardly spoken, when a ray of light, descending from heaven, covered the whole country, and the flame, settling in rays upon the heads of each, entered into the bodies of all. The knight felt such a delicious sweetness pervade his heart and whole body, that he hardly knew whether he was alive or dead, but this feeling was over in a moment. He would gladly have remained for ever in this place, if he could have enjoyed these delights, but he was in the next place told of other things not so pleasant. "Since you have now set eyes," said the holy prelates, "on the happiness of the blessed, according to your wish, and have also in part beheld the torments of the wicked, you must now return by the same way as you came; and if, (which God forbid!) when you return to the world, you lead a wicked life, you have here seen what torments await you. If, however, you lead a good and religious life, you may rely upon coming to us again, when your spirit is released from the body. You need not fear the torments of the demons on your way back, for they will not be able to come near you, nor can their torments which you have seen hurt you." The knight replied with tears: "I am not able to return from this place; for I fear lest the frailty of human nature lead me to err, and I may be prevented from returning." "No," said they, "these things are not as you wish, but according to the will of Him who made both us and you." The knight was then, with sorrow and mourning, re-conducted to the gate, which, after he had reluctantly passed through it, was shut behind him.

How the knight, after his return to the world, devoted himself to the Jerusalem pilgrimage.

The knight Owen returned by the same way as he went, to the hall before mentioned, but the demons, whom he saw in his return, fled from him in alarm, and the torments, through which he had passed, were unable to hurt him. Immediately, when he had entered the hall, the fifteen men, before described, glorified God for having given him such fortitude under

<207>

the torments, "You must now go up hence with speed; for the day is already dawning in your country; and if the prior does not find you, when he opens the door, he will think you are lost, and shutting the door will return into the church." The knight then received their blessing, and hastening away, met the prior at the moment that he opened the door, and was conducted by him, with praises and thanksgivings to Christ, into the church, where he remained fifteen days in prayer. After this, he took the sign of the cross, and set out to the Holy Land, seeking in holy meditation the sepulchre of our Lord and the other sacred places. From thence, when he had discharged his vow, he returned home, and prayed his lord, king Stephen, that he might be allowed to pass the remainder of his life in the service of religion, and become a soldier in the armies of the King of kings. It happened at this time, that Gervais, abbot of Louth, had obtained from King Stephen a grant of land on which to build an abbey in Ireland, and he sent one of his monks named Gilbert to the king, to take possession of the land and to build on it the abbey. But Gilbert, coming before the king, complained that he did not know the language of that country; to which the king replied that he would, with God's help, soon find him an able interpreter; and, calling Owen before him, he bade him go with Gilbert and remain in Ireland. This was agreeable to Owen, who gladly went with Gilbert and served him faithfully, but he would not assume the habit of a monk, because he chose rather to be a servant than a master. They crossed over into Ireland, and built an abbey, wherein the knight Owen acted as the monk's interpreter and faithful servant in all he did. Whenever they were alone together, the monk asked him minutely concerning purgatory and the marvelous modes of punishment which he had there seen and felt, but the knight, who never could hear about purgatory without weeping bitterly, told his friend for his edification and under the seal of secrecy, all that he had seen and experienced, and affirmed that he had seen it all with his own eyes. By the care and diligence of this monk, all that the knight had seen was reduced into writing, together with the narratives of the bishops and other ecclesiastics of that country, who for truth's sake gave their testimony to the facts.

—Translated from the Latin by J.A. Giles (1849)

<208>

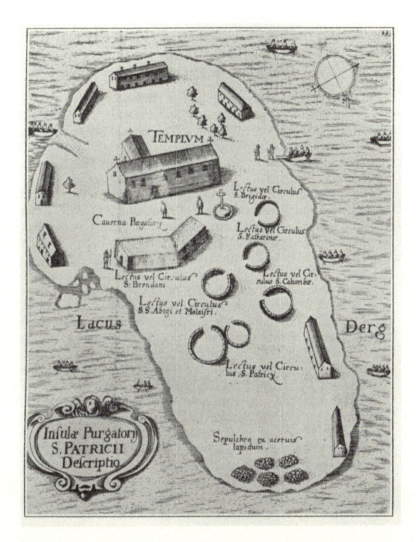

Station Island and St. Patrick's Purgatory, from the 1666 edition of Thomas Carve's *Lyra Seu Anacephalos Hiberniae.* The circular, low-walled structures are the "beds" *(lectus,* pl. *lecti)* of the Saints. If the original of this printed map was drawn prior to the 1632 demolition, some of the shoreline buildings, with thatched roofs, were the "Irish houses" torn down by Bishop Clogher's men.

THE DESTRUCTION OF ST. PATRICK'S
PURGATORY

The monastery and "cave" depicted in "Saint Patrick's Purgatory" were real, situated on what is now called "Station Island" in the middle of Lough Derg, a lake in Donegal County. The demand for penitence and self-mortification had become so great that the cave was made to house as many as nine penitents at a time, instead of the solitary victim depicted in the *Tractatus*.

News reached Pope Alexander VI (the Borgia Pope) of the popularity of Saint Patrick's Purgatory as a place of pilgrimage, and the fees extracted at each level of the local church bureaucracy from penitents who wished to submit themselves to the terrors of its cave. The Pope ordered the Purgatory destroyed in 1497, with this result:

> This recommendation was officially carried out around the time of the Feast of St. Patrick in 1497 with the monk of Eymstadt, the Primate of Ireland, the Bishop of Clogher (whose diocese included Lough Dergh), and the Guardian of the Franciscan abbey in Donegal looking on. Oddly however, the cave that was dug up appears to have been a substitute; it was excavated on Saints' Island [a different island altogether!] by the Augustinian canons, perhaps for their own convenience in dealing with the crowds that came to Lough Dergh on pilgramage each year. Whatever the case, this first act of suppression had negligible impact on pilgrimage to Saint Patrick's Purgatory. Alexander VI's act of suppression was formally revoked in 1522 at the urging of the primate of Armagh.[4]

---

[4] Curley, Michael J. "Introduction." *Saint Patrick's Purgatory*, p 18. The ongoing controversy over whether the "cave" on Saints' Island was the *original* Purgatory is repeated in Father Dominic Brullaughan's 1735 *De Purgatorio Sancti Patritii*, who asserts that the Augustinian priests on Saints' Island were annoyed by the exceeding number of pilgrims, and hence constructed the second, smaller Purgatory on Station Island, whose conditions were "more suitable for mortification, prayer and penance." This Father, writing a century after the pilgrimages were supposedly suppressed, notes: "It is wonderful (as I have often seen) that men of eighty years and even blind men (using the eyes of others) are led and devoutly perform this station . . .[B]esides the fasts, vigils, long prayers and other austerities, we are bound to remain for twenty-four hours watching without any food (except water) in the Cave." (Leslie, 118-119).

<210>

After this ruse, the pilgrimages continued unabated through the 1600s. When the region became the site of English and Scottish settlements, the Anglican authorities used Saint Patrick's Pilgrimage as an example of barbaric popery, and as evidence of Celtic degeneracy.

The following description of the rituals enforced on the penitents by the priests and monks at the Purgatory suffices to give the reader the essence of the ritual:

Messingham[5] and several other ecclesiastical writers of the Roman church give very full accounts of the ceremonies performed by the pilgrims, in the earlier part of the seventeenth century. ... A pilgrim — when admitted as such by the spiritual father, as Messingham phrases it that is, probably, when he had paid his initiation fee — which, in Lord Dillon's time, was eight pence — took off his shoes, and walked, bare-footed, seven times round the inside, and seven times round the outside of the church. Going then to the saint's beds, he walked seven times round the exterior, and crawled, on his bare knees, the same number of times round the interior of each bed. This being done, he next went to the lake, and placed his bruised and weary feet on the flat stone named Lackevany, from which he felt so much relief as to be soon able to resume his circumambulations. This round of penance was termed a "station;" and during its performance a whole rosary of *paters* and *aves* had to be repeated, the lips and feet keeping proper time, so that neither should be in advance of the other; and for seven days, three times per day, morning, noon, and evening, a station had to be performed. At night the wearied penitents slept on hay or straw, wrapt in their mantles and truises, without either bed or bed-clothes. On the eighth day a double duty had to be performed, three stations for that day, and three for the following, when the pilgrim would be in purgatorial durance. During these eight days, he ate a little bread or oatmeal, once only in each twenty-four hours, but partook freely of the water of the lake, which had a strong mineral flavour — *"ac si a vena metallica fluerat."*

Early on the ninth morning, the nine pilgrims, intending to enter the Purgatory, were assembled, and addressed by the spiritual father, who warned them of the dreadful peril they were about to incur, in language calculated to arouse the most stupid, soften the most hardened, and terrify the most audacious. And it was particularly impressed upon their minds that, if any one of them fell asleep, the whole number would be immediately seized and carried off by the ever-watchful enemy of mankind — that this had already happened twice, and that saintly prophecy had revealed it was to happen a third

---

[5] Thomas Messingham authored two St. Patrick-related texts: *Officia S. Patricii* (Paris, 1620) and *Florilegium Insulae Sanctorum* (Paris, 1624).

<211>

time. Then, after they had confessed and received the sacrament, a funeral procession was formed, and the nine, preceded by the banner of the cross (*praeunte vexillo crucis*), and followed by a crowd of mourners, went towards the Purgatory, as if they were going to death and the other world; in an agony of sighs and groans they begged for forgiveness of all they had offended, and freely forgave all who had offended them; and thus, in tears and lamentations, they entered the cave, and the door being shut, those who had attended the funeral returned to their avocations.

Without any other refreshment than a little water, which was occasionally handed in through the crevice, the nine pilgrims passed twenty-four hours in the wretched hole. Then they were revisited by the spiritual father, who released and led them to the lake, where they washed themselves; and lastly, they went to the church, and thanked God that their pilgrimage was accomplished. And the poor creatures had reason to be thankful, for, as Messingham says: — "If it be in summer, who does not know how painful it must be, to be shut up so long in a place so confined and dark, exposed to the heat of the sun from the outside, and the stifling breaths of so many crowded together within. If in winter, how difficult to bear the immersion in the lake; and, whatever season it may be, how painful is the walking bare-footed, and kneeling in penitential cells, the fasting, want of sleep, *et cetera*."[6]

The English repression went beyond denunciation to outright action in 1632, as recounted in the following documents.

BY THE LORDS JUSTICES AND COUNCELL.
ADAM LOFTUS CANC. R . CORKE.

Forasmuch as the frequent and publicke resort of people in great numbers to that place or Island called S. Patrike's Purgatory, there performing superstitious *ceremonies, pilgrimages, and offerings*, is so extreamely abusive and superstitious, as is not fit to be endured. We, therefore, taking the same into our due consideration, and foreseeing that albeit there may be a seeming cessation there for a time from those abuses and superstitions, in regard they observe the State to resent the same: Yet many times the seduced people will secretly finde opportunitie to resort thither, and so by stealthe continue those superstitious abuses, while the place standeth as it now doth. We have therefore adjudged it the best and fittest meanes to prevent and wholly take away the continuance of that abuse hereafter, that the place be defaced and utterly demolished. And therefore we doe hereby order and resolve

---
6 Pinkerton, 72-73.

<212>

that letters shall be dispatched from this Board unto the Reverend Father in God, the Lord Bishop of Clogher, Sir John Dunbarre, High Sheriffe of the County of Fermanagh, Edward Tarleton, Esquier, High Sheriff of the Countie of Donnegall, Edward Archdale, and Leonard Blennerhassett, Esquier, and Archibald Areskon, clearke, or any three or more of them, whereof the said Lord Bishop, or Sir John Dunbarre, or Edward Tarleton, to be always one.

Requiring and authorising them, or any three or more of them as aforesaid, by or before the third day of December next, to cause the chappel and all the Irish houses now scituate in that Island which is called S. Patricke's Purgatory, all the buildings, pavements, walls, works, foundations, *Circles, Caves, Cels, and Vaults* thereof, of lime or stone, or otherwise, to be broken downe, defaced, and utterly demolished. And that also called S. Patricke's *Bed*, as also that rocke or stone standing in the water there having a clift in it, which (as is vainely said) S. Patricke made kneeling at his prayers: And also that stone covered there with water which hath the print of a man's foot, and which (as the seduced people do believe) S. Patricke made with standing thereupon; and likewise all other things there, whereunto those superstitious people have used to goe in pilgrimage: And that they cause all the stones to be throwne into the Lough or water wherein the Island standeth, saving onely such of the stones of the said chappel as James MeeGrath, Esquier, the proprietor of the land, will forthwith carry cleere out of the island, and make use of in some other place.

We doe also order that the said James MacGrath shall forthwith enter into bond to the Clerk of the Councell for his Majestie's use, in the summe of one thousand pounds English, with condition to beare all the charges necessary, for the performing of all that by this order is required to be done, and to be personally present at the seeing of it done, and not to suffer any interruption or impediment to be given there unto. And that such of the stones of the chappel as the said James shall carry out, shall not at any time hereafter during his life be returned to that Island. And that he shall from time to time take order, that no person or persons be admitted at any time hereafter during his life with his permission or knowledge, or privily to go in to that Island or place called S. Patrickes Purgatory, to the end to say Masse there, or to performe any *pilgrimage, offeringes*, or any other superstitious *ceremonies* there. And that he shall suffer no Boate to bee kept there to pass to or from the said Island.

And that during his life there shall not be any conventions there of Jesuits, Fryars, Priests, Nuns, or any other superstitious Orders of the popish pretended Cleargie, that the said MacGrath shall be able

<213>

to prevent; which Bond being so entered into, the Sargeant at Armes, in whose custodie the said MacGrath now remayneth, is upon Certificate hereof from the Clerke of the Councell to release the said MacGrath, he paying his fees.

For which a copy of this Order, attested by the Clerke of the Councill, shall be his warrant. — Dated the 13 of Sept., 1632.[7]

James Spottiswood, the Bishop of Clogher, made his report to the Lord Primate, Bishop Ussher, and since it has a full description of the Purgatory as found (and destroyed), it is worth reproducing here in full.

MOST REVEREND AND MOST HONOURED LORD.

Your Grace like enough may be desirous to know what is done touching the demolition of S. Patricke's Purgatory, required by the Lords Justices and Councell to be done by me, and some other joynt Commissioners with me. May it please your Grace, then, the next day after I tooke my leave of yourself at Ardmagh, I sent the Coppy of the Lords Justices and Councell's Letter, with the Order and Commission, to every one of my fellow Commissioners, and appointed our Randevouze at the towne next Lough-derge, the 25 day of this instant October.

From them I received answer, that they might well come alone, but could get none to accompany them, or any labourer or tooles upon any tearmes; and that an hundred men were not able to execute the Commission in a fortnight: notwithstanding whereof, I required them againe to keep the day, and assured them, however, that I my selfe would be present; and accordingly I came to the place appointed the 24 day, with some twenty able men in my company well armed; and brought with us all sorts of tooles fitting for the service.

If I had not come so appointed, we had returned without effecting anything: for the High Sheriffe of Donnegall camie not at the day. The Highe Sheriffe of Farmanagh, on the other side, came no better appointed than the one serving man; and showed himself altogether unwilling, and refused to enter the Island. I had many discouragements myselfe. For first I was forced on a rainy day, on a bleake place without any shelter to horse or man, three houres before we could have the Boate. The winde in the meantime did rise, and there was none could take in hand to guide, the Boate through dangerous rockes lying betweene the maine and the Island. Againe we were certified that we might be hardly put to it for faullt of victuals, if we tooke thenm not in with ourselves; for the windes would sometimes blowe ten dayes together so strong that no Boate could venture out or in: notwithstand-

_____
[7] Pinkerton, 67-68.

<214>

ing all which discouragements, I adventured to goe in without victuals, and stayd in the Island till the service was done.

The first thing I searched diligently after was the *Cave*, wherein I remembered your Grace enjoyned me to digge to the very foundations, and leave no corner unsought, and so I did; I caused to dig about it on all sides, till I came to the Rocke, but found no appearance of any secret passage, eyther to the Chappell or to the Lough: neyther would the nature of the ground suffer it; in a word this Cave was a poore beggerly hole, made with some stones, layd together with men's hands without any great art: and after covered with earth, such as husbandmen make to keepe a few hogs from the raine.

When I could finde nothing there, I undermined the Chappell, which was well covered with shingles, and brought all downe together. Then wee brake downe the Circles and Saint's Beds, which were like so many Cole-pits, and so pulled downe some great Irish houses. Thus, when I had defaced all, saving one Irish house, I came out of the Island myselfe, and left one halfe of my men behind to pull that down also as soon as they should see me landed, not sooner; lest if by a storme we were driven backe, we might want a place to shelter us.

The countrie people expected that S. Patricke would have wrought some miracle; but thankes be to God none of my companye received any other harme than the bad wayes, broken cawsies, and the dangers going in a little Boate: Yet our comfort is, we effected that for which we came thither, which was more than was expected could be done in so short a time, which hath wonderfully displeased them who were bewitched with these fooleries.[8]

But that I doe not stand much upon, in regard I have obeyed the Command of the State, and punctually also done what your Grace did enjoyne: whose directions I shall be ever ready to followe, and shall ever remaine

Your Grace's most affectionate in all duty,

Clogher, Oct. 31, Ann 1632.   JAMES CLOGHER[9]

---

[8] Clogher makes no mention of the priests and penitents found on the island. Sir William Stuart's letter to the Privy Council provides more details: "[The] Abbot, Priests and Friers which were in the Island had gotten knowledge of your Lordship's directions: whereupon in the night time they stole out of the island in a boat, which at the least would carry forty persons." Stuart and his men then took it upon themselves to raid another nearby island (almost certainly Saints' Island) "Where I found 431 persons doing such fooleries as is not to be imagined could be done among Christians. All the aforesaid number of persons I have caused to put safe to shore: which was done without any kind of violence: for seeing the Priests and Friers had left the island and carried with them all manner Provision and goods that therein was, the people were willing and desirous to be put on shore" (Leslie 77).
[9] Pinkerton, 68-69.

<215>

Thus, Anglican fury struck out at Irish superstition. All in vain, it turned out. In 1701, Queen Anne ordered a ten shilling fine or a public whipping for anyone found on the island in Lough Dergh. The cave was restored in 1727. Above-ground "caves," rather more like beehives or coke-ovens, were constructed, to accommodate more penitents in less horrifying conditions, and the pilgrims kept coming.

At last count, Station Island, sans Purgatory, receives 30,000 pilgrims a year.

<216>

The Cinder King

The following was sent me anonymously; the reader will of course observe that it is a burlesque imitation of the ballads of "The Erl-King," and "The Cloud-King."

"Who is it that sits in the kitchen, and weeps,
While tick goes the clock, and the tabby-cat sleeps;
That watches the grate, without ceasing, to spy
Whether purses or coffins will out of it fly?" —

'Tis Betty; who saw the false tailor, Bob Scott,
Lead a bride to the altar; which bride she was not:
'Tis Betty; determined love from her to fling,
And woo, for his riches, the dark Cinder-King.

Now spent tallow-candle-grease fattened the soil,
And the blue-burning lamp had half wasted its oil,
And the black-beetle boldly came crawling from far,
And the red coals were sinking beneath the third bar;

When, "one" struck the clock — and instead of the bird
Who used to sing cuckoo whene'er the clock stirred,
Out burst a grim raven, and uttered "caw! caw!"
While puss, though she woke, durst not put forth a claw.

Then the jack fell a-going as if one should sup,
Then the earth rocked as though it would swallow one up;
With fuel from hell, a strange coal-skuttle came,
And a self-handled poker made fearful the flame.

A cinder shot from it, of size to amaze,
With a bounce, such as Betty ne'er heard in her days,
Thrice, serpent-like, hissed, as its heat fled away,
And lo! something dark in a vast coffin lay.

<217>

— "Come, Betty!" quoth croaking that nondescript thing,
"Come, bless the fond arms of your true Cinder-King!
Three more kings, my brothers, are waiting to greet ye,
Who — don't take it ill! — must at four o'clock eat ye.

"My darling! it must be so, do make up your mind;
We element brothers, united, and kind,
Have a feast and a wedding, each night of our lives,
So constantly sup on each other's new wives." —

In vain squalled the cook-maid, and prayed not to wed;
Cinder crunched in her mouth, cinder rained on her head,
She sank in the coffin with cinders strewn o'er,
And coffin nor Betty saw man any more.

<218>

The Bleeding Nun

I am not at liberty to publish the name of the author of this Ballad: it is founded on the fourth chapter of the Romance of "Ambrosia, or the Monk."[1]

Where yon proud turrets crown the rock,
    See'st thou a warrior stand?
He sighs to hear the castle clock
    Say midnight is at hand.

It strikes, and now his lady fair
    Comes tripping from her hall,
Her heart is rent by deep despair,
    And tears in torrents fall.

— "Ah! woe is me, my love," she cried,
    "What anguish wrings my heart:
Ah! woe is me," she said, and sighed,
    "We must for ever part.

"Know, ere three days are past and flown,
    (Tears choke the piteous tale!)
A parent's vow, till now unknown,
    Devotes me to the veil." —

---

[1] The poem is a freestanding adaptation of an episode in Lewis's own novel, *The Monk*, written between 1795 and 1796. The Bleeding Nun story in prose was also extracted and published separately as *Raymond and Agnes*.
By the fourth edition, in 1798, Lewis had expunged and euphemised many of the more appalling details of his original. *The Monk* was not republished in all its original luridness until Louis F. Peck's Grove Press edition of 1952; in 1972, Oxford University Press issued a version based on Lewis's original manuscript. In the interim, the subplot of the Bleeding Nun continued to escape from the confines of Lewis's novel.
In 1854, librettist Eugène Scribe and composer Charles Gounod premiered the Monk-inspired opera, *La Nonne Saglante*, in Paris. In 1855, Edward Loder composed an English-language opera titled *Raymond and Agnes*, with a libretto by Edward Fitzball. Earlier, France's greatest Romantic composer, Hector Berlioz, completed two acts of an opera based on Scribe's libretto, but abandoned the project as a result of Parisian opera politics. The Berlioz partial work remains unperformed, a pity since it would be intriguing to hear what the composer of *The Damnation of Faust* would make of this material.

<219>

The Bleeding Nun appears to Raymond.

Agnes with her Child in the Dungeon.

— "Not so, my Agnes!" Raymond cried,
　　"For leave thee will I never;
Thou art mine, and I am thine,
　　Body and soul for ever!

"Then quit thy cruel father's bower,
　　And fly, my love, with me." —
— "Ah! how can I escape his power,
　　Or who can set me free?

"I cannot leap yon wall so high,
　　Nor swim the fosse[2] with thee;
I can but wring my hands, and sigh
　　That none can set me free." —

— "Now list, my lady, list, my love,
　　I pray thee list to me,
For I can all your fears remove,
　　And I can set you free.

---

[2] *Fosse.* Moat.

<220>

"Oft have you heard old Ellinore,
　　Your nurse, with horror tell,
How, robed in white, and stained with gore,
　　Appears a spectre fell.[3]

"And each fifth year, at dead of night,
　　Stalks through the castle gate,
Which, by an ancient solemn rite,
　　For her must open wait.

"Soon as to some far distant land,
　　Retires to-morrow's sun,
With torch and dagger in her hand,
　　Appears the Bleeding Nun.

"Now you shall play the Bleeding Nun,
　　Arrayed in robes so white,
And at the solemn hour of one,
　　Stalk forth to meet your knight.

"Our steeds shall bear us far away,
　　Beyond your father's power,
And Agnes, long ere break of day,
　　Shall rest in Raymond's bower." —

— "My heart consents, it must be done,
　　Father, 'tis your decree;
And I will play the Bleeding Nun,
　　And fly, my love, with thee.

"For I am thine," fair Agnes cried,
　　"And leave thee will I never;
I am thine, and thou art mine,
　　Body and soul for ever!" —

---

[3] *Fell.* Fierce or dreadful.

<221>

Fair Agnes sat within her bower,
    Arrayed in robes so white,
And waited the long wished-for hour,
    When she should meet her knight.

And Raymond, as the clock struck one,
    Before the castle stood;
And soon came forth his lovely Nun,
    Her white robes stained in blood.

He bore her in his arms away,
    And placed her on her steed;
And to the maid he thus did say,
    As on they rode with speed:

— "O Agnes! Agnes! thou art mine,
    And leave thee will I never;
I am thine, and thou art mine,
    Body and soul for ever!" —

— "O Raymond! Raymond, I am thine,
    And leave thee will I never;
I am thine, and thou art mine,
    Body and soul for ever!" —

At length, — "We're safe!" the warrior cried;
    "Sweet love, abate thy speed;" —
But madly still she onwards hied
    Nor seem'd his call to heed.

Through wood and wild, they speed their way,
    Then sweep along the plain,
And almost at the break of day,
    The Danube's banks they gain.

<222>

— "Now stop ye, Raymond, stop ye here,
 And view the farther side;
Dismount, and say, Sir Knight, do'st fear
 With me to stem the tide?" —

Now on the utmost brink they stand,
 And gaze upon the flood,
She seized Don Raymond by the hand,
 Her grasp it froze his blood.

A whirling blast from off the stream
 Threw back the maiden's veil;
Don Raymond gave a hideous scream,
 And felt his spirits fail.

Then down his limbs, in strange affright,
 Cold dews to pour begun;
No Agnes met his shudd'ring sight,
 — "God! 'Tis the Bleeding Nun!" —

A form of more than mortal size,
 All ghastly, pale, and dead,
Fixed on the knight her livid eyes,
 And thus the Spectre said:

— "O Raymond! Raymond! I am thine,
 And leave thee will I never;
I am thine, and thou art mine,
 Body and soul for ever!" —

Don Raymond shrieks, he faints; the blood
 Ran cold in every vein,
He sank into the roaring flood,
 And never rose again!

<223>

The Maid of the Moor;
or, The Water fiends[1]

G[EORGE] COLMAN, JUN.[2]

On a wild moor, all brown and bleak,
　　Where broods the heath-frequenting grouse,
There stood a tenement antique,
　　Lord Hoppergollop's country house.

Here silence reigned with lips of glue,
　　An undisturbed maintained her law;
Save when the owl cried — "whoo! whoo! whoo!"
　　Or the hoarse crow croaked — "caw! caw! caw!"

---

[1] Lewis had an epigraph to this poem reading, "This Tale, which is unavoidably misplaced, should have formed No. XXXVI." The poem appeared in the collection, *My Nightgown and Slippers, or Tales in Verse* (1797), pp. 12-20. Colman adopts a cheery air about his Gothic production, as evidenced from his preface: "Let me, however, give you a brief account of these Trifles.
The Maid of the Moor, The Newcastle Apothecary, and *Lodgings for Single Gentlemen,* are slip-shod Tales, written for an Entertainment which I proposed to offer to the Publick, at the Haymarket Theatre, during Lent; and two of them were intended to be *spoken,* (read them, therefore, with a view to recitation) and the third to be sung, as light matter, calculated to relieve the gravity of a didactick performance.
The whole performance (for reasons unnecessary to mention, here) was relinquished: —
But, as it is my custom to avoid the accumulation of my own papers, in my Bureau, I hold it more advisable to print my three Stories (light as they are) than to burn them.
. . . [I]f *The Maid of the Moor* acts as an antidote, with one Boarding-school Miss, to the poison, so plentifully distributed, in the shape of Novels, Romances, Legendary Tales, &c. &c. I may say, with Philosophers, that the most insignificant things are of some utility.
[2] George Colman the Younger (1762-1836) was a humorist in verse and a prolific playwright, specializing in comedies. In *My Nightgown and Slippers,* Colman mocks the Gothic in novels, and, by implication, in the theater. He doubtless regarded Lewis as a theatrical rival and an upstart. Colman's vituperations of critics were included in his book, *Broad Grins.* He inherited from his father the position of manager of the Haymarket Theater, and earned the enmity of many London playwrights when he become the official censor for plays, a power he did not hesitate to wield to enforce his taste.

<224>

Neglected mansion! for 'tis said,
    Whene'er the snow came feathering down,
Four barbed steeds, from the Bull's Head,
    Carried thy master up to town.

Weak Hoppergollop! Lords may moan,
    Who stake in London their estate,
On two small rattling bits of bone,
    On little figure, or on great.

Swift whirl the wheels, — he's gone; a Rose
    Remains behind, whose virgin look,
Unseen, must blush in wint'ry snows;
    Sweet beauteous blossom! 'twas the Cook!

A bolder, far, than my weak note,
    Maid of the Moor! thy charms demand:
Eels might be proud to lose their coat,
    If skinned by Molly Dumpling's hand.

Long had the fair one sat alone,
    Had none remained save only she;
She by herself had been, if one
    Had not been left, for company.

'Twas a tall youth, whose cheek's clear hue
    Was tinged with health and manly toil;
Cabbage he sowed, and when it grew,
    He always cut it off to boil.

Oft would he cry, — "Delve, delve the hole!
    And prune the tree, and trim the root!
And stick the wig upon the pole,
    To scare the sparrows from the fruit!" —

<225>

A small mute favourite by day
　　Followed his steps; where'er he wheels
His barrow round the garden gay,
　　A bobtail cur is at his heels.

Ah, man! the brute creation see,
　　Thy constancy oft need to spur!
While lessons of fidelity
　　Are found in every bobtail cur.

Hard toiled the youth, so fresh and strong,
　　While Bobtail in his face would look,
And marked his master troll the song,
　　— "Sweet Molly Dumpling! O thou Cook!" —

For thus he sung: while Cupid smiled,
　　Pleased that the Gard'ner owned his dart;
Which pruned his passions, running wild,
　　And grafted true love on his heart.

Maid of the Moor, his love return!
　　True love ne'er tints the cheek with shame;
When gard'ners hearts, like hotbeds burn,
　　A cook may surely feed the flame.

Ah! not averse from love was she;
　　Though pure as heaven's snowy flake:
Both loved; and though a Gard'ner he,
　　He knew not what it was to rake.

Cold blows the blast, the night's obscure:
　　The mansion's crazy wainscots crack;
The sun had sunk, and all the moor,
　　Like eve'ry other moor, was black.

<226>

Alone, pale, trembling, near the fire,
　　The lovely Molly Dumpling sat;
Much did she fear, and much admire,
　　What Thomas, gard'ner, could be at.

Listening, her hand supports her chin,
　　But, ah! no foot is heard to stir;
He comes not from the garden in,
　　Nor he, nor little bobtail cur.

They cannot come, sweet maid, to thee;
　　Flesh, both of cur and man, is grass:
And what's impossible can't be,
　　And never, never, comes to pass!

She paces through the hall antique,
　　To call her Thomas, from his toil;
Opes the huge door: the hinges creak,
　　Because the hinges wanted oil.

Thrice on the threshold of the hall,
　　She "Thomas" cried with many a sob;
And thrice on Bobtail did she call,
　　Exclaiming sweetly—"Bob! Bob! Bob!"

Vain maid! a gard'ner's corpse, 'tis said,
　　In answers can but ill succeed;
And dogs that hear when they are dead,
　　Are very cunning dogs indeed!

Back through the hall she bent her way,
　　All, all was solitude around;
The candle shed a feeble ray,
　　Though a large mould of four to the pound.

<227>

Full closely to the fire she drew,
    Adown her cheek a salt tear stole;
When, lo! a coffin out there flew,
    And in her apron burnt a hole.

Spiders their busy death-watch ticked;
    A certain sign that fate will frown;
The clumsy kitchen clock, too, chicked,
    A certain sign it was not down.

More strong, and strong, her terrors rose,
    Her shadow did the maid appall;
She trembled at her lovely nose,
    It looked so long against the wall.

Up to her chamber damp and cold,
    She climbed Lord Hoppergollop's stair,
Three stories high, long, dull, and old,
    As great lords' stories often are.

All nature now appeared to pause;
    And — "O'er the one half world seemed dead;"
No "curtained sleep,"[3] had she; because
    She had no curtains to her bed.

Listening she lay; with iron din
    The clock struck twelve, the door flew wide,
When Thomas grimly glided in,
    With little Bobtail by his side.

Tall like the poplar was his size,
    Green, green his waistcoat was, as leeks;
Red, red as beetroot, were his eyes,
    And pale as turnips were his cheeks!

---

[3] "Now o'er the one half-world/Nature seems dead, and wicked dreams
abuse/The curtain'd sleep; witchcraft celebrates/Pale Hecate's offerings" *Macbeth*
II.1

<228>

Soon as the spectre she espied,
    The fear-struck damsel, faintly said,
— "What would my Thomas?" — He replied,
    — "O Molly Dumpling, I am dead!

"All in the flower of youth I fell,
    Cut off with healthful blossom crowned;
I was not ill, but in a well
    I tumbled backwards, and was drowned.

"Four fathom deep thy love doth lie,
    His faithful dog his fate doth share;
We're fiends; this is not he and I,
    We are not here, for we are there.

"Yes! two foul water-fiends are we;
    Maid of the Moor, attend us now!
Thy hour's at hand, we come for thee!"
    The little fiend-cur said, — "Bow! wow!"—

— "To wind her in her cold, cold grave,
    A Holland sheet[4] a maiden likes,
A sheet of water thou shalt have;
    Such sheets there are in Holland dykes." —

The fiends approach; the maid did shrink,
    Swift through the night's foul air they spin,
They took her to the green well's brink,
    And, with a souse[5] they plumped her in.

So true the fair, so true the youth,
    Maids, to this day, their story tell,
And hence the proverb rose, that truth
    Lies in the bottom of a well.

---

[4] *Holland sheet.* Linen.
[5] *Souse.* A sudden plunge.

<229>

The Laidley[1] Worm[2]
of Spindlestone Heughs

[ROBERT LAMBE][3]

I have seen another version of this story, with some variations, under the title of Kempion;[4] *the one, which I here insert, in my opinion, is by far the best of the two. It is taken from the 3d volume of Evans'* Old Ballads.
— MGL

The King is gone from Bamborough castle:[5]
   Long may the Princess mourn,
Long may she stand on the castle wall,
   Looking for his return.

She has knotted the keys upon a string,
   And with her she has them ta'en;
She has cast them o'er her left shoulder,
   And to the gate she is gane.

---

[1] This is a northern corruption for loathly, i.e., loathsome — RL.
[2] *Worm.* Serpent or dragon; in this instance, certainly the latter —BR.
[3] Robert Lambe (1712- 1769), another bachelor-vicar-antiquarian, claimed to have recovered fragments of variant versions of "The Laidley Worm," the original of which he attributed as "a song above 500 hundred years old, made by the old mountain-bard, Duncan Frasier, living on Cheviot, A.D. 1270." Duncan Frasier is now believed to be an Ossianic fabrication of the Rev. Lambe. Percy, apparently not deceived, did not include the work in his collection, so it fell to Evans to collect and preserve it for future readers in his ballad collection. The poem's first appearance was in Hutchinson's *A View of Northumberland,* Vol II., 1778, pp. 162-64 —BR.
[4] *Kempion.* Kemp Owyne is Child Ballad No. 34.
[5] Bamburgh Castle is on the coast of Northumberland. Bamborough was once the capital of the Anglian kingdom of Bernicia. The castle was the home base of Henry VI during the Wars of the Roses. An interesting anthology titled *Metrical Legends of Northumberland* (1834) includes "The Laidley Worm," exactly as found in *Tales of Wonder.* That volume's editor, James Service, accepts the poem as authentic and attempts, not very convincingly, to read it allegorically or historically as a representation of the triumph of Christianity over paganism — BR.

<230>

Childe Wynd thrice kisses the Laidly Worm & rescues his Sister the Princess Margaret.

John D. Batten (1890), from *English Fairy Tales*, J. Jacobs, ed.

She tripped out, she tripped in,
    She tript into the yard;
But it was more for the King's sake,
    Than for the Queen's regard.

<231>

It fell out on a day, the King
    Brought the Queen with him home;
And all the lords in our country
    To welcome them did come.

— "Oh! welcome father," the lady cries,
    Unto your halls and bowers;
And so are you, my step-mother,
    For all that is here is yours." —

A lord said, wond'ring while she spake,
    — "This Princess of the north,
Surpasses all of female kind,
    In beauty and in worth." —

The envious Queen replied, — "At least
    You might have excepted me;
In a few hours I will her bring
    Down to a low degree.

"I will liken her to a laidley worm,
    That warps about the stone,
And not, till Childy[6] Wynd[7] comes back,
    Shall she again be won." —

The Princess stood at her bower door,
    Laughing: who could her blame?
But e'er the next day's sun went down,
    A long worm she became.

For seven miles east, and seven miles west,
    And seven miles north and south,
No blade of grass or corn could grow,
    So venomous was her mouth.

---

[6] *Childy.* Childe, archaic word for "Knight."
[7] There is now a street called the Wynd, at Bamborough — RL.

<232>

The milk of seven stately cows,
    (It was costly her to keep,)
Was brought her daily, which she drank
    Before she went to sleep.

At this day may be seen the cave,
    Which held her folded up,
And the stone trough, the very same,
    Out of which she did sup.

Word went east, and word went west,
    Arid word is gone over the sea,
That a laidley worm in Spindleston Heughs
    Would ruin the north country.

Word went east, and word went west,
    And over the sea did go;
The Child of Wynd got wit of it,
    Which filled his heart with woe.

He called straight his merry men all,
    They thirty were and three;
— "I wish I were at Spindleston,
    This desperate worm to see.

"We have no time now here to waste,
    Hence quickly let us sail;
My only sister Margaret
    Something I fear doth ail." —

They built a ship without delay,
    With masts of the rown tree,[8]
With fluttering sails of silk so fine,
    And set her on the sea.

---

[8] *Rown*. Mountain Ash — MGL. Also known as the Rowan or Witch Tree —BR.

<233>

They went aboard: the wind with speed
    Blew them along the deep;
At length they spied an huge square tower
    On a rock high and steep.

The sea was smooth, the weather clear;
    When they approached nigher,
King Ida's[9] castle they well knew,
    And the banks of Bamboroughshire.

The Queen look'd out at bower window,
    To see what she could see;
There she espied a gallant ship
    Sailing upon the sea.

When she beheld the silken sails
    Full glancing in the sun,
To sink the ship she sent away
    Her witch-wives every one.[10]

Their spells were vain. The hags return'd
    To the Queen in sorrowful mood,
Crying, that witches have no power
    Where there is rown-tree wood

Her last effort she sent a boat,
    Which in the haven lay,
With armed men to board the ship;
    But they were driven away.

The worm leapt up, the worm leapt down,
    She plaited round the stone;
And as the ship came to the land,
    She bang'd it off again.

---

[9] *King Ida,* (died c. 559 CE), the first king of the Anglian kingdom of Bernicia, which he ruled from around 547 CE.
[10] Witches were credited with the power to summon winds and storms.

<234>

The Child then ran out of her reach,
    The ship on Budle[11] sand,
And, jumping into the shallow sea,
    Securely got to land.

And now he drew his bonny brown sword,
    And laid it on her head,
And swore if she did hasten to him,
    That he would strike her dead.

— "O! quit thy sword, and bend thy bow,
    And give me kisses three;
For though I am a pois'nous worm,
    No hurt will I do to thee.

"Oh! quit thy sword and bend thy bow,
    And give me kisses three;
If I am not won e'er the sun go down,
    Won I shall never be."

He quitted his sword, he bent his bow,
    He gave her kisses three;
She crept into a hole a worm,
    But stept out a lady.

No cloathing had this lady fine
    To keep her from the cold;
He took his mantle from him about,
    And round her did it fold.

---

11 *Budle*. Northumberland historian Hutchinson associates this place-name with pagan archaeology: "Near *Budle*, at a place called Spindleston, is a Danish camp, circular in form and fortified with a triple ditch and vallium." He then inserts Lamb's poem, which he says "seems to be of a historic nature, but wrapped up in such dark allegory, the humor of those times, as to render it unintelligible in this age. The fortifications are Danish, and it is probable that the ballad relates to the conflicts of that people, with the garrison of Bambrough" (153 and fn).

<235>

He has his mantle from him about
    And it he wrapt her in;
And they are up to Bamborough castle
    As fast as they can win.

His absence and her serpent shape
    The King had long deplor'd,
He now rejoic'd to see them both
    Again to him restor'd.

The Queen they wanted, whom they found,
    All pale and sore afraid;
Because she knew her power must yield
    To Childy Wynd's; who said,

— "Woe be to thee, thou wicked witch,
    An ill death may'st thou dee;[12]
As thou my sister hast likened,
    So likened shalt thou be.

"I will turn thee into a toad,
    That on the ground doth wend;
And won and won shalt thou never be,
    Till this world hath an end."

Now on the sands near Ida's tower,
    She crawls a loathsome toad;
And venom spits on every maid
    She meets upon the road.

The virgins all of Bamborough town
    Will swear that they have seen
This spiteful toad of monstrous size,
    Whilst walking they have been.

---

[12] *Dee.* Die.

<236>

All folks believe, within the shire,
    This story to be true;
And they all run to Spindleston,
    The cave and trough to view.

This fact now Duncan Frasier
    Of Cheviot sings in rhime;
Lest Bamboroughshire men should forget,
    Some part of it in time.

<237>

Mary's Dream

[JOHN LOWE][1]

The moon had climb'd the highest hill,
    Which rises o'er the source of Dee,
And from the eastern summit shed,
    Her silver light on tower and tree:
When Mary laid her down to sleep,
    Her thoughts on Sandy, far at sea,
When soft and low a voice was heard
    Say, — "Mary, weep no more for me."—

She from her pillow gently raised
    Her head, to ask, who there might be;
She saw young Sandy shiv'ring stand,
    With visage pale and hollow eye;
— "O! Mary dear, cold is my clay,
    It lies beneath a stormy sea;
Far, far from thee, I sleep in death,
    So Mary, weep no more for me.

---

[1] This poem, not a traditional ballad, is included, unattributed, in the Appendix to Volume II of the 1776 edition of Herd's *Ancient and Modern Scottish Songs,* its earliest appearance in print I have found. The poem is by John Lowe (1750-1798), a Scottish divinity student who worked as a tutor for a family in Airds, the locale described in the poem. According to Chambers' *Biographical Dictionary of Eminent Scotsmen,* the poem "was written at the Airds, in reference to the death of a gentleman named Miller, a surgeon at sea, who was attached to the sister of his own mistress [i.e., fiancee], and perished in the manner described in the poem" (III, 495). Lowe left Scotland in 1773, still unmarried but engaged to another woman, and emigrated to America. After 20 years there, he married an American lady, a disastrous union, and, as the Chambers editors tell it, "His wife proved totally unworthy of his affections, and by driving him for relief to the bottle, caused his death under the most miserable circumstances in 1798. . . . The wretched woman to whom he had been united made no inquiries after her husband for more than a month afterwards, when she sent for his horse, which had been previously sold to defray the expenses of the funeral" (496). Lowe's slender poetic reputation rests on this single poem.

<238>

"Three stormy nights, and stormy days,
　　We toss'd upon the raging main;
And long we strove our bark to save,
　　But all our striving was in vain:
E'en then when horror chill'd my blood,
　　My heart was fill'd with love for thee;
The storm is past, and I at rest,
　　So Mary, weep no more for me.

"O Maiden dear, thyself prepare,
　　We soon shall meet upon that shore,
Where love is free from doubt and care,
　　And thou and I shall part no more."
Loud crow'd the cock, the shadow fled,
　　No more of Sandy could she see,
But soft the passing spirit said,
　　— "Sweet Mary, weep no more for me."

<239>

Clerk Colvin

[SCOTTISH BALLAD][1]

Clerk Colvin and his lady gay,
    They walked in yonder garden sheen:
The girdle round her middle jimp[2]
    Had cost Clerk Colvin crowns fifteen.

— "Oh, hearken well, my wedded lord,
    Oh, hearken well to what I say;
When ye gae[3] by the wells of Stane,
    Beware, ye touch nae well-faced may."[4]

— "Oh! haud[5] your tounge, my lady gay,
    And haud, my lady gay, your din:
Did I never yet see a fair woman,
    But wi' her body I wad sin?"

Then he's rode on frae his lady fair,
    Nought reeking what that lady said,
And he's rode by the wells[6] of Stane,
    Where washing was a bonnie maid.

---

[1] Anna Gordon Brown of Falkland was a major source for Percy and the early collectors of traditional ballads. It is only fair to credit her here: first, since Percy and others relied on her as a primary source of the tradition; second, because it is now known that Mrs. Brown not only remembered but *embellished*, sometimes adding supernatural elements to ballads that may not have possessed them originally. The 1769 printing of the ballad in Herd's *Ancient and Modern Scots Songs* is most likely where Lewis may have found it. The ballad is Child Ballad No. 42b —BR.

[2] *Jimps.* Stays.

[3] *Gae.* Go.

[4] *May.* Maiden.

[5] *Haud.* Hold.

[6] *Wells.* In this case, springs and pools of water, not subterranean wells —BR.

<240>

Arthur Rackham's illustration for "Clerk Colvin."

— "Wash on! wash on! my bonnie may!
    Sae clean ye wash your sark[7] of silk." —
—"And weel fa you,[8] fair gentle knight,
    Whose skin is whiter far than milk!" —

He has ta'en her by the lily hand,
    He has ta'en her by the grass-green sleeve,
And thrice has pried her bonnie mou,[9]
    Nor of his lady speered he leave.[10]

Soon as his mouth her lip had press'd,
    His heart was fill'd with doubt and dread;
— "Ohan![11] and alas!" Clerk Colvin says,
"Ohan, and alas! What pains my head?" —

— "Sir Knight, now take your little penknife,
    And frae my sark ye's cut a gare;[12]
Row[13] that around your face so pale,
    And o' the pain ye'll feel na mair."[14] —

Syne[15] out has ta'en his little penknife,
    And frae her sark he cut a gare,
He rowed it around his face so pale,
    But the pain increased still mair and mair.

Then out, and spake the knight again,
    — "Alas! more sairly throbs my head!" —
And merrily did the mermaid laugh,
    — "'Twill ever be wae,[16] till ye be dead!" —

---

7 *Sark.* Shift.
8 *Weel fa you.* Good luck to you.
9 *Pried her mou.* Kissed her mouth.
10 *Speered he leave.* Asked her leave.
11 *Ohan.* "Ohon" in other versions of the ballad. Possibly a polite "O Lord!" exclamation, from *Johanan,* "God is merciful" —BR.
12 *Gare.* A piece. From "gore," meaning a small, triangular piece of cloth. Another version says "share" —BR.
13 *Row.* Rap.
14 *Na mair.* No more.
15 *Syne.* Then.
16 *Be wae.* Be painful.

<242>

He has drawn out his trusty blade,
    All for to kill her where she stood,
But she was changed to monstrous fish,
    And quickly sprang into the flood.[17]

He has mounted on his berry-brown steed,
    And dowie,[18] dowie, on he rides,
Till he has reached Dunallan's towers,
    And there his mother dear resides.

— "Oh! mother, mother, make my bed,
    And lay me down, my fair la-dye;
And brother dear, unbend my bow,
    'Twill never more be bent by me!"

His mother, she has made his bed,[19]
    She has laid him down, his fair la-dye;
His brother has unbent his bow,
    And death has closed Clerk Colvin's eë![20]

There is a great resemblance between this old Scotch Ballad and the Danish tradition of "The Erl-King's Daughter." —MGL.

---

[17] Lewis has improved upon the original stanza (see Child Ballads 42a), which reads
Then out he drew his trusty blade,
And thought wi' it to be her dead,
But she's become a fish again,
And merrily sprang into the fleed.

The other variant (b) is equally awkward, as a "far off" distance is unlikely in a small pool:
Out then he drew his shining blade,
Thinking to stick her where she stood,
But she was vanish'd to a fish,
And swam far off, a fair mermaid.

[18] *Dowie.* Swiftly.
[19] This last stanza is Lewis's invention —BR.
[20] *Eë.* Eye.

<243>

Willy's Lady

[M.G. LEWIS, FROM A SCOTTISH BALLAD][1]

Willy's gone over the salt sea foam,
He has married a wife, and brought her home;
He wooed her for her yellow hair,
But his mither wrought her mickle care;
And mickle dolour[2] suffers she,
For lighter[3] she can never be;
But in her bour[4] she sits wi' pain,
And Willy mourns over her in vain.

Then to his mither he speaks his mind,
That vile rank witch of foulest kind;
He says, —"My ladye has a cup,
With gold and silver all set up,
The handles are of the ivory bones,
And all set round wi' sparkling stones;
This gudely gift she'll give to thee,
If of her young bairn[5] she may lighter be."

---

[1] Walter Scott provided Lewis a copy of this ballad in June 1798 along with three others, noting "You will easily distinguish whether any of these may with propriety enter your collection as specimens of the ancient Scottish marvellous Ballad. ... I really burn to see the Tales of [T]error." (Letter reprinted in *The Lady's Magazine and Museum*, Jan. 1837, p. 490). The ballad was first written down from the dictation of Mrs. Anna Brown of Falkland, in 1783, and appears as Child Ballad No. 6. The version presented here by Scott and Lewis is modernized. The Scottish dialect is mixed with newer language, and the rhyme is regularized (in the original, some of the couplets do not rhyme at all). The final lines betray Lewis's taste for the grisly bits. In the *Minstrelsy of the Scottish Border* (1808), Scott reprints the original and notes, "Mr Lewis, in his *Tales of Wonder*, has presented the public with a copy of this ballad, with additions and alterations." (*Minstrelsy*, Vol. II.) Scott subtitles the original as "Never Before Published" and cites Mrs. Brown as the source.

[2] *Mickle dolour.* Much sadness.

[3] *Lighter.* To be delivered of a child, to give birth.

[4] *Bour.* Bower.

[5] *Bairn.* Child.

<244>

— "Of her young bairn shall she never be lighter,
Nor in her bour to shine the brighter,
But she shall die, and turn to clay,
And you shall wed another may."[6] —

— "Another may I'll never wed,
Another may I'll never bed!" —
Then sorely did that lady sigh,
— "I wish my hour of death were nigh!

"Yet speak ye again to your mither your mind,
That foul rank witch of cruel kind,
And say your ladye has a steed,
The like of him's not in the land of Leed;
Of that horse's mane at every tress,
There's a silver bell and a golden jess;[7]
This gudely gift I'll give her with glee,
If of my young bairn I may lighter be." —

— "Of her young bairn shall she never be lighter,
Nor in her bour to shine the brighter;
But she shall die, and turn to clay,
And you shall wed another may." —
— "Another may I'll never wed,
Another may I'll never bed!" —
Then evermore sighed that lady bright,
— "I wish my day had reached its night."

<hr>

[6] *May.* Maiden.
[7] *Jess.* A hawk's bell.

<245>

With that arose the Billy Blynde,[8]
And in good time spake he his mind,
— "Yet gae ye to the market-place,
And there buy ye a loaf of wace,[9]
Shape it bairnly-like, to view,
Stick in't twa glassy een[10] of blue,
Then bid the witch the christening to,
And notice well what she shall do."—

The Willy has bought a loaf of wace,
And framed it to a bairn-like face,
And says to his mither, with seeming joy,
— "My ladye is lighter of a young boy;
And he'll in St. Mary's be christened to-night,
And you to the christ'ning I come to invite." —

Syne has he stopped a little to see,
When this she heard, what say might she.

— "Oh, who has the nine witch knots untied,
That were among the locks of your bride;
Or who has ta'en out the comb of care,
Which fastened that ladye's yellow hair?
And who has ta'en down the bush of woodbine,[11]
That hung between her bour and mine?
And who has killed the master-kid,
That ran below that ladye's bed?
And who has her left shoe-string undone,
And let that ladye be light of her son?" —

---

[8] *Billy Blynde*. A familiar spirit, or good genius —MGL.
[9] *Wace*. Wax —MGL.
[10] *Een*. Eyes.
[11] *Woodbine*. Honeysuckle, some varieties of which have a poisonous berry.

<246>

Then Willy the nine witch knots untied,
That were among the locks of his bride;
And he has ta'en out the comb of care,
Which fastened his lady's yellow hair,
And he has ta'en down the woodbine flowers,
Which the witch had hung between the bowers;
And he has slain the master-kid,
Which ran below that ladye's bed;
And he has the left shoe-string undone,
And letten his ladye be light of her son;
But when she heard that his ladye was light,
That foul rank witch, she burst for spite![12]

---

[12] There is no exploding witch at the end of the original ballad, which ends
simply: "And now he's gotten a bonny young son,/ And mickle grace be him
upon." Child notes the similarity of this narrative to several Danish originals,
and stories of mothers-in-law preventing a birth, and being tricked by the false
birth announcement, are known in myth and folklore —BR.

<247>

Courteous King Jamie

[M.G. LEWIS, FROM A SCOTTISH BALLAD][1]

Courteous King Jamie is gone to the wood,
    The fattest buck to find;
He chased the deer, and he chased the roe,
    Till his friends were left behind.

He hunted over moss and moor,
    And over hill and down,
Till he came to a ruined hunting hall
    Was seven miles from a town.

He entered up the hunting hall,
    To make him goodly cheer,
Full of all the herds in the good green wood,
    He had slain the fairest deer.

He sat him down, with food and rest
    His courage to restore;
When a rising wind was heard to sigh,
    And an earthquake rocked the floor.

And darkness covered the hunting hall,
    Where he sat all at his meat;
The grey dogs howling left their food,
    And crept to Jamie's feet.

---

[1] The source for this ballad is another manuscript/recitation from Mrs. Brown, captured in a manuscript by William Tytler. The original is preserved as Child Ballad No. 32, "King Henry." Sir Walter Scott included the original in his *Minstrelsy of the Scottish Border*, Vol II, p. 132. In his emphasis on the knightly virtue of "courtesy," Lewis manages to increase the poem's *reductio ad absurdum* of manners and morals, the more so since King Jamie's "hospitality" is not extended in his own house, but in an uninhabited building where both king and witch are guests. Perhaps the extreme moral of this is that a knight is obligated to grant a lady's wishes no matter how hideous her demeanor, or alarming her manners at table.

<248>

And louder howled the rising storm,
    And burst the fastened door,
And in there came a grizly Ghost,
    Loud stamping on the floor.

Her head touched the roof-tree of the house,
    Her waist a child could span;
I wot, the look of her hollow eye
    Would have scared the bravest man.

Her locks were like snakes, and her teeth like stakes,
    And her breath had a brimstone smell:
I nothing know that she seemed to be,
    But the Devil just come from Hell!

— "Some meat! some meat! King Jamie,
    Some meat now give to me;" —
— "And to what meat in this house, lady,
    Shall ye not welcome be?" —
— "Oh! ye must kill your berry-brown steed,
    And serve him up to me!" —

King Jamie has killed his berry-brown steed,
    Though it caused him mickle[2] care;
The Ghost eat him up both flesh and bone,
    And left nothing but hoofs and hair.

— "More meat! more meat! King Jamie,
    More meat now give to me;" —
— "And to what meat in this house, lady,
    Shall ye not welcome be?" —
— "Oh! ye must kill your good greyhounds,
    They'll taste most daintily." —

---

[2] *Mickle.* Much.

<249>

King Jamie has killed his good greyhounds,
    Though it made his heart to fail;
The Ghost eat them all up one by one,
    And left nothing but ears and tail.

— "A bed! a bed! King Jamie,
    Now make a bed for me!" —
— "And to what bed in this house, lady,
    Shall ye not welcome be?" —
— "Oh! ye must pull the heather so green,
    And make a soft bed for me." —

King Jamie has pulled the heather so green,
    And made for the Ghost a bed,
And over the heather, with courtesy rare,
    His plaid hath he daintily spread.

— "Now swear! now swear! King Jamie,
    To take me for your bride;" —
— "Now heaven forbid!" King Jamie said,
    "That ever the like betide,
That the Devil so foul, just come from Hell,
    Should stretch him by my side." —

— "Now fye! now fye! King Jamie,
    I swear by the holy tree,
I am no devil, or evil thing,
    However foul I be.

"Then yield! then yield! King Jamie,
    And take my bridegroom's place,
For shame shall light on the dastard knight,
    Who refuses a lady's grace."—

<250>

Then quoth King Jamie, with a groan,
    For his heart was big with care,
— "It shall never be said that King Jamie
    Denied a lady's prayer." —

So he laid him by the foul thing's side,
    And piteously he moaned;
She pressed his hand, and he shuddered!
    She kissed his lips, and he groaned!

When day was come, and night was gone,
    And the sun shone through the hall;
The fairest lady that ever was seen,
    Lay between him and the wall.

— "Oh! well is me!" King Jamie cried,
    "How long will your beauty stay?" —
Then out and spake that lady fair,
    — "E'en till my dying day.

"For I was witched to a ghastly shape,
    All by my step-dame's skill;
Till I could light on a courteous knight,
    Who would let me have all my will."

I have altered and added so much to this ballad, that I might almost claim it for my own. It bears a great resemblance to the tale of "The Marriage of Sir Gawain" (in Percy's *Reliques of Ancient English Poetry*). But the stories are related in a manner so totally different, that I did not think the resemblance so strong as to destroy the interest of "King Jamie's Adventure." —MGL

<251>

Tam Lin

[SCOTTISH BALLAD][1]

Perhaps some information may be collected from the following extract from the Records of Justiciary in Scotland, respecting the popular superstition on which this Ballad is founded. I have made some considerable alterations in the tale itself. —

> Alison Pearson, of Byre Hill, confest that she had haunted, and repaired with the 'gude neighbors' (i.e., Fairies) and the Queen of Elfland, divers years by past, and that she had friends in that court whilk were of her own blude. Item, that it was the 'gude neighbors' that cured her of her disease, when she was twelve years old, and that she saw them making their salves, with pans and fyres; that they gathered the herbs before the sun was up; and that Mr. William Sympson was with him, who was her cousin. When he was about eight years of age, he was taken away to Egypt, by an Egyptian, who was a giant, and with him he remained twelve years, and then came home. He was a young man, not six years older than herself, and it was he who taught her what herbs were fit to cure every disease, and particularly taught her to make a posset, which she gave to the Bishop of St. Andrews, when sick; and Mr. William Sympson told her that he had been carried away by the 'gude neighbors,' and bade her sign herself, that she might not be taken away for 'the tiend of them who are taken to hell every year.'

The sole evidence against this poor creature was her own confession, on the strength of which she was burned alive, in 1588. — MGL.[2]

---

[1] Robert Burns supplied this traditional ballad, known as far back as 1549, to James Johnson for Volume V of his song collection, *The Scottish Musical Museum* (1793). This text is in the Child Ballad collection as No. 39A, one of fourteen different variants.

[2] Lewis's epigraph here is misleading, suggesting that he has somehow based the poem on the witch-trial case, instead of merely making his own paraphrase of a well-known ballad, that had also been adapted by Walter Scott. Lewis intends only to show the reference in witch-lore of the tiend/tithe of stolen children offered by the fairies to the Devil. Child Ballad 39A is appended after Lewis's version so the reader can compare Lewis's Anglicised text to the original.

<252>

— "Oh! I forbid you, maidens all,
   That wear gold in your hair,
To come or go by Kerton Hall,
   For young Tam Lin is there!

"To the maid who goes by Kerton Hall,
   Some foul trick still is played;
She loses her ring, or her mantle of green,
   Or returns not thence a maid."—

Janet has belted her kirtle of green,
   A little above her knee,
And she's away to Kerton Hall,
   As fast as go can she.

And when she came to Kerton Hall,
   Tam Lin was at the well;
There she found his milk-white steed,
   But he was away himsel.

And near her was a bonny bush
   Of roses, red and white,
And tempting did those roses seem,
   And no one was in sight.

She pulled a white, she pulled a red,
   And asked no owner's leave;
When lo! from the bush sprang young Tam Lin,
   And caught her by the sleeve.

— "Now, Janet, say, who gave to thee,
   Yon roses in thy hand,
And why comest thou to Kerton Hall,
   Against my strict command?

<253>

"Who stole a rose from young Tam Lin,
    Its price hath ever paid;
And the maid who came to Kerton Hall,
    Never yet returned a maid." —

He fixed on her his witching eye
    He muttered elfin charms;
Her head grew light, her heart beat quick,
    And she sank into his arms.

Janet has kilted her kirtle of green,
    A little above her knee,
And she's away to her father's tower,
    As fast as go can she.

<254>

Four-and-twenty ladies fair,
    Were seen to play at ball,
And out then came fair Janet once,
    The flower among them all.

Four-and-twenty ladies fair,
    To play at chess were seen,
And out fair Janet came, her face
    As any grass was green.

Out then spake an old grey knight,
    As he lay on the castle wall,
And says, "Alas! fair Janet, for thee,
    Shall we now be blamed all." —

— "Now hold your tongue, ye old grey knight,
    An ill death may ye see!
Father my bairn whoever will,
    I'll father none on thee!" —

Out then spake her father dear,
    And he spake so meek and mild;
— "And ever, alas! sweet Janet," he says,
    "I think thou art with child!" —

"If that I be with child, father,
    Myself must bear the blame;
There's never a laird about your hall,
    Shall bear my leman's[3] name.

---

[3] *Leman.* Lover.

<255>

"But if my love were an earthly knight,
    As he's an elfin grey,
For never a laird in the land, would I
    My true love give away.

"The steed my true love rides upon,
    Is lighter than the wind;
With silver he is shod before,
    With burning gold behind." —

Janet has kilted her kirtle of green,
    A little above her knee,
And she's away to Kerton Hall,
    As fast as go can she.

And first she pulled a white rose,
    And next she pulled a red,
And then from the bush sprang young Tam Lin,
    And thus to her he said:

<256>

— "Now, Janet, say, who gave to thee
    Yon rose in thy hand?
And why comest thou to Kerton Hall
    Against my strict command?" — 4

"Oh! tell me, tell me, Tam Lin!" she says,
    "For His sake who died on tree,
If ever in holy chapel ye were,
    Or Christendom did see?"

— "My grandsire he was Roxburgh's earl,
    And loved me passing well;
Seven years, alas! are nearly gone,
    In hunting since I fell.

---

4 This is the most expurgated variant of the ballad. In the oldest version, Janet is
warned that pulling the roses will kill the baby she is carrying. In the variant
Child Ballad 39D, she is warned about plucking a *different* flower that would kill
the baby:"So do not pluck that flower, lady, /That has these pimples gray;/ They
would destroy the bonny babe/ That we've got in our play." Tam Lin's
intervention stops this process and gives her the opportunity to ascertain
whether he is human, and whether he is a suitable candidate for a husband.

Indeed, the variant Child Ballad No. 39F changes the flower to an abortifacient
herb and provides the missing details, changing the locale of the second
encounter to a churchyard:

Up starts Lady Margaret's mother,
An angry woman was she:
There grows ane herb in yon kirk-yard
That will scathe the babe away."

She took her petticoats by the band,
Her mantle owre her arm,
And she's gane to yon kirk-yard
As fast as she could run.

She scarcely pulled an herb, an herb,
She scarse pulled two or three,
    Till up starts there Thomas
Upon this Lady Margret's knee.

"How dare ye pull a rose?' he says,
"How dare ye break the tree?
How dare ye pull this herb," he says,
    To scathe my babe away?"

<257>

"The Queen of Fairies long had watched,
    To work her wayward will,
She seized, and bore me straight away,
    To dwell in yon green hill.

"And pleasant is the fairy land,
    But doleful 'tis to tell,
That once in every seven years,
    We pay a tiend[5] to hell;
And I'm so fair, and full of flesh,
    I fear, 'twill be mysel!

"But the night is Hallowe'en, lady,
    The morn is Hallow-day:[6]
So win me, win me, if you will,
    For if you will, you may.

"Just at the murk and midnight hour,
    The fairy-folk will ride,
And they, who would their true loves know,
    At Miles Cross[7] must abide." —

— "But how shall I thee ken, Tam Lin,
    Or how my true love know,
Among so many stranger knights,
    With that rabble rout who go?"

"Oh! first let pass the black, lady,
    And then let pass the brown;
But quickly run to the milk-white steed,
    And draw its rider down.

---

[5] *Tiend.* A tithe. Traditionally, Christians were expected to donate a tithe (one tenth) of their income to the Church.
[6] *Hallow-Day.* November 1, All-Saint's Day.
[7] *Miles Cross.* Crossroads often figure in supernatural tales all the way back to Greek Hecate legends. Unhallowed dead were sometimes buried there, and many witches' spells involved ingredients gathered in graveyards or at crossroads. Some were also hazardous places where bandits might lurk nearby.

<258>

"For I shall ride on the milk-white steed,
　　And be nearest to the town;
Because I was an earthly knight,
　　They give me that renown.

"My right hand will be gloved, lady,
　　My left hand will be bare;
Cockt up shall be my bonnet blue,
　　Combed down my yellow hair;
And by these signs I give to thee,
　　Thou'lt know that I am there.

"They'll turn me into a snake in your arms,
　　But hold me fast the rather;
Grasp me well, and fear me not,
　　That snake is your child's father.

"They'll turn me into a bear so grim,
　　And into a tiger wild!
But hold me fast, and fear me not,
　　As you do love your child.

"And last, they'll turn me, in your arms,
　　To a bar of burning steel;
Then throw me into the stream with speed,
　　And thou no hurt shalt feel.

"But there, in place of the burning bar,
　　A naked knight thou'lt see,
Then cover me with thy cloak of green,
　　And I'll thy true love be." —

Eerie, eerie, was the way,
　　The night was dark and dread,
When Janet in her mantle green,
　　Alone to Miles Cross sped.

<259>

About the dead of night she heard
    The fairy-bridles ring;
The lady was as glad at that,
    As any earthly thing.

First she let the black pass by,
    And next she let the brown,
But quickly ran to the milk-white steed,
    And drew its rider down.

So well did she her task perform,
    That she her love did win,
And blithe as birds in spring, she cast
    Her mantle round Tam Lin.

Out then spake the Queen o' Fairies,
    Out of a bush o' broom,[8]
— "She that has gotten young Tam Lin,
    Has gotten a stately groom."

Out then spake the Queen o' Fairies,
    And an angry queen was she:
"Shame betide her ill-fared face,
    And an ill death may she see;
For she's ta'en away the bonniest knight,
    In all my companie!

"But had I guessed, Tam Lin," she said,
    "What to-night is come to pass,
I had scratched out thy two blue een,[9]
    And put in two een of glass!"

---

[8] *Broom.* In this case, most likely gorse (*Ulex*), a thorny evergreen shrub common to Northern Europe and Great Britain.
[9] *Een.* Eyes.

<260>

TAM LIN
Scottish Ballad, transmitted by Robert Burns

O I forbid you, maidens a',[10]
That wear gowd on your hair,
To come or gae by Carterhaugh,
For young Tam Lin is there.

There's nane that gaes by Carterhaugh
But they leave him a wad,[11]
Either their rings, or green mantles,
Or else their maidenhead.

Janet has kilted her green kirtle
A little aboon[12] her knee,
And she has broded her yellow hair
A little aboon her bree,
And she's awa to Carterhaugh
As fast as she can hie.

When she came to Carterhaugh
Tam Lin was at the well,
And there she fand his steed standing,
But away was himsel.

She had na pu'd a double rose,
A rose but only twa,
Till upon then started young Tam Lin,
Says, Lady, thou's pu nae mae.

Why pu's thou the rose, Janet,
And why breaks thou the wand?[13]
Or why comes thou to Carterhaugh
Withoutten my command?

---

[10] *A'.* All.
[11] *Wad.* Wage or portion.
[12] *Aboun.* Above.
[13] *Wand.* Stem.

<261>

"Carterhaugh, it is my own,
My daddy gave it me,
I'll come and gang by Carterhaugh,
And ask nae leave at thee."

Janet has kilted her green kirtle
A little aboon her knee,
And she has broded her yellow hair
A little aboon her bree,[14]
And she is to her father's ha,[15]
As fast as she can hie.

Four and twenty ladies fair
Were playing at the ba, [16]
And out then came the fair Janet,
The flower among them a'.

Four and twenty ladies fair
Were playing at the chess,
And out then came the fair Janet,
As green as onie glass.[17]

Out then spake an auld grey knight,
Lay o'er the castle wa,
And says, "Alas, fair Janet, for thee,
But we'll be blamed a'." —

— "Haud your tongue, ye auld fac'd knight,
Some ill death may ye die!
Father my bairn on whom I will,
I'll father none on thee." —

---

[14] *Bree*. Brow.
[15] *Ha*. Hall.
[16] *Playing at the ba*. Playing a ball game.
[17] *Onie glass*. Probably green onyx.

<262>

Out then spak her father dear,
And he spak meek and mild,
"And ever alas, sweet Janet," he says,
"I think thou gaest wi child." —

— "If that I gae wi child, father,
Mysel maun bear the blame,
There's neer a laird about your ha,
Shall get the bairn's name.

"If my love were an earthly knight,
As he's an elfin grey,
I wad na gie my ain true-love
For nae lord that ye hae.

"The steed that my true love rides on
Is lighter than the wind,
Wi siller he is shod before,
Wi burning gowd behind."

Janet has kilted her green kirtle
A little aboon her knee,
And she has broded her yellow hair
A little aboon her bree,
And she's awa to Carterhaugh
As fast as she can hie.

When she came to Carterhaugh,
Tam Lin was at the well,
And there she fand his steed standing,
But away was himsel.

She had na pu'd a double rose,
A rose but only twa,
Till up then started young Tam Lin,
Says, "Lady, thou pu's nae mae.

<263>

"Why pu's thou the rose, Janet,
Amang the groves sae green,
And a' to kill the bonny babe
That we gat us between?" —

— "O tell me, tell me, Tam Lin," she says,
"For's sake that died on tree,
If eer ye was in holy chapel,
Or christendom did see?" —

— "Roxbrugh he was my grandfather,
Took me with him to bide
And ance it fell upon a day
That wae did me betide.

"And ance it fell upon a day
A cauld day and a snell,[18]
When we were frae the hunting come,
That frae my horse I fell,
The Queen o' Fairies she caught me,
In yon green hill to dwell.

"And pleasant is the fairy land,
But, an eerie tale to tell,
Ay at the end of seven years,
We pay a tiend to hell,
I am sae fair and fu o flesh,
I'm feard it be mysel.

"But the night is Halloween, lady,
The morn is Hallowday,[19]
Then win me, win me, an ye will,
For weel I wat ye may.

---

[18] *Snell.* Bitter, severe.
[19] *Hallowday.* All Saint's Day, November 1.

<264>

"Just at the mirk[20] and midnight hour
The fairy folk will ride,
And they that wad their true-love win,
At Miles Cross they maun bide." —

— "But how shall I thee ken, Tam Lin,
Or how my true-love know,
Amang sa mony unco[21] knights,
The like I never saw?" —

— "O first let pass the black, lady,
And syne[22] let pass the brown,
But quickly run to the milk-white steed,
Pu ye his rider down.

"For I'll ride on the milk-white steed,
And ay nearest the town,
Because I was an earthly knight
They gie me that renown.

"My right hand will be gloved, lady,
My left hand will be bare,
Cockt up shall my bonnet be,
And kaimed down shall my hair,
And thae's the takens[23] I gie thee,
Nae doubt I will be there.

"They'll turn me in your arms, lady,
Into an esk and adder,
But hold me fast, and fear me not,
I am your bairn's father.

_____

[20] *Mirk*. From "mirk night," the darkest part of the night.
[21] *Unco*. Strange.
[22] *Syne*. Then.
[23] *Takens*. Tokens, clues.

<265>

They'll turn me to a bear sae grim,
And then a lion bold,
But hold me fast, and fear me not,
And ye shall love your child.

"Again they'll turn me in your arms
To a red het gand of airn,[24]
But hold me fast, and fear me not,
I'll do you nae harm.

"And last they'll turn me in your arms
Into the burning gleed,[25]
Then throw me into well water,
O throw me in with speed.

"And then I'll be your ain true-love,
I'll turn a naked knight,
Then cover me wi your green mantle,
And hide me out o' sight." —

Gloomy, gloomy was the night,
And eerie was the way,
As fair Jenny in her green mantle
To Miles Cross she did gae.

At the mirk and midnight hour
She heard the bridles sing,
She was as glad at that
As any earthly thing.

First she let the black pass by,
And syne she let the brown,
But quickly she ran to the milk-white steed,
And pu'd the rider down.

---

[24] *Red her gand of airn.* Red-hot bar of iron.
[25] *Burning gleed.* A live coal.

<266>

Sae weel she minded what he did say,
And young Tam Lin did win,
Syne covered him wi her green mantle,
As blythe's a bird in spring

Out then spak the Queen o' Fairies,
Out of a bush o broom,
"Them that has gotten young Tam Lin
Has gotten a stately-groom."

Out then spak the Queen o' Fairies,
And an angry woman was she,
— "Shame betide her ill-far'd face,
And an ill death may she die,
For she's taen awa the bonniest knight
In a' my companie.

"But had I kend,[26] Tam Lin," said she,
"What now this night I see,
I wad hae taen out thy twa grey een,[27]
And put in twa een o' tree."[28]

---

[26] *Kend.* Foreseen.
[27] *Een.* Eyes.
[28] *Een o' tree.* Eyes of wood.

<267>

Lenora

German. [WILLIAM TAYLOR OF NORWICH,
      after GOTTFRIED AUGUSTUS BÜRGER]

This version of Bürger's well-known Ballad[1] was published in the
Monthly Magazine, and I consider it as a masterpiece of translation;
indeed, as far as my opinion goes, the English Ballad is, in point of
merit, far superior, both in spirit and in harmony, to the German,
which is written in a stanza, producing an effect very unsatisfactory
to the ear; that my readers may judge of this for themselves, I shall
here add a stanza similar to that in which Bürger's "Lenora" is
written: I rather imagine that the effect made by it upon others is
the same with that which is produced upon me, since among the
numerous translators of this Ballad not one has adopted the metre of
the original.

> [Lenora wakes at dawn of day,
> Tears down her fair cheeks trickle:
> "Oh! why, my William, dost thou stay,
> And art thou dead or fickle?"
> With Frederick's host young William went,
> But since the fight of Prague he sent
> No word to tell his speeding,
> And soothe her bosom bleeding.]

I cannot but think that the above metre will be universally
disapproved of, when compared with that adopted in the following
Ballad. —MGL[2]

---

[1] It can safely be said that Bürger's "Lenore" was the most famous ballad poem
in Europe in the late 1790s. Lewis had rejected Scott's "William and Helen," a
Lenore paraphrase, because many of its Scottish rhymes were not rhymes to the
English ear, in favor of the well-known translation by Taylor. Seven different
translations of this poem appeared in 1796, and it took scholars a hundred years
to sort out who did it first. The earliest-written, and best, is that of William
Taylor of Norwich, composed in 1790 and, although widely circulated in
manuscript, not printed until its appearance in the *Monthly Magazine* in March,
1796, which set off a fire-storm of rival versions. Lewis himself may have known
the German original, and his own poem "Alonzo the Brave," which appeared in
The Monk, clearly imitates the theme of "Lenore," although the lady, in Lewis's
poem, is unfaithful to her lover and the skeleton-abduction is thus read as a
punishment. Taylor changes the heroine's name to "Lenora," possibly for
metrical reasons.
[2] Most of Lewis's epigraph is taken verbatim from the *Monthly Magazine.*

<268>

William Taylor of Norwich (1765–1836), prolific literary critic, helped propel German Romanticism into the British consciousness. A lifelong bachelor, he was a freethinker (nicknamed "godless Billy"), and a supporter of the French Revolution, counting Lafayette and Thomas Paine as friends. Although he published more than 1700 articles, several anthologies, and a study of German poetry, his irreligion and dissipation were frowned upon. As the *Dictionary of National Biography* puts it, "He was accused of initiating young men into habits of conviviality . . . He was known to argue for an hour in proof that Adam was a negro; no one venturing to reply, he spent the next hour in answering himself and proving that Adam was white. . . A revolting paradox as to our Lord's parentage was maintained by him in an anonymous 'Letter concerning the Two First Chapters of Luke' (1810). His religious philosophy appears . . . in the 'Monthly Magazine,' 1811; he describes it as 'Philonic pantheism.'"

At break of day, with frightful dreams
    Lenora struggled sore:
— "My William, art thou slaine," said she,
    "Or dost thou love no more?" —

He went abroade with Richard's host,[3]
    The Paynim foes to quell;
But he no word to her had writt,
    An[4] he were sick or well.

With sowne[5] of trump and beat of drum,
    His fellow soldyers come;
Their helmes bedeckt with oaken boughs,
    They seeke their long'd-for home.

And ev'ry roade, and ev'ry lane,
    Was full of old and young,
To gaze at the rejoicing band,
    To hail with gladsome toung.

"Thank God!" their wives and children saide;
    "Welcome!" the brides did say:
But greete or kiss Lenora gave
    To none upon that daye.

She askte of all the passing traine,
    For him she wisht to see:
But none of all the passing traine
    Could tell if lived he.

---

[3] *Richard's host.* The Crusade of English king Richard I began in 1190 CE. Taylor changes the locale of the German poem, which was set in Prague during the Seven Years' War (1756-1763). While the original was set in recent history, Taylor's medieval setting compelled him to employ archaic words and diction. Taylor's poem casts a long shadow, and Coleridge's "Rime of the Ancient Mariner" shows its stylistic influence. Taylor was also the first translator to employ an English ballad style in translating this poem.
[4] *An.* If.
[5] *Sowne.* Sound.

<270>

And when the soldyers all were bye,
    She tore her raven haire,
And cast herself upon the growne
    In furious despaire.

Her mother ran and lyfte her up,
    And clasped in her arme,
— "My child, my child, what dost thou ail?
    God shield thy life from harm!" —

—"O mother, mother! William's gone!
    What's all besyde to me?
There is no mercye, sure, above!
    All, all were spared but hee!" —

— "Kneel downe, thy pasternoster saye,
    'Twill calm thy troubled spright:
The Lord is wyse, the Lord is good;
    What hee hath done is right." —

— "O mother, mother! say not so;
    Most cruel is my fate:
I prayde, and prayde, but watte avayled?
    'Tis now, alas! too late!" —

— "Our Heavenly Father, if we praye,
    Will help a suff'ring childe:
Go take the holy sacrament,
    So shall thy grief grow milde." —

— "O mother, what I feel within,
    No sacrament can staye,
No sacrament can teche the dead
    To bear the sight of daye." —

<271>

— "May be, among the heathen folk
    Thy William false doth prove,
And puts away his faith and troth
    And takes another love.

"Then wherefore sorrow for his loss?
    Thy moans are all in vaine;
And when his soul and body parte,
    His falsehode brings him paine." —

— "O mother, mother! gone is gone,
    My hope is all forlorn;
The grave mie onlye safeguarde is,
    O, had I ne'er been born!

"Go out, go out, my lampe of life,
    In grislie darkness die:
There is no mercye, sure, above!
    For ever let me lie." —

— "Almighty God! O do not judge
    My poor unhappy childe;
She knows not what her lips pronounce,
    Her anguish makes her wilde.

"My girl, forget thine earthly woe,
    And think on God and bliss;
For so, at least, shall not thy soule
    Its heavenly bridegroom miss." —

"O mother, mother! what is blisse,
    And what the infernal[6] celle?
With him 'tis heaven anywhere,
    Without my William, helle.

---

[6] *Infernal celle.* Taylor's original reads "fiendis," possibly for "fiendish." Because of a typographical error, this appeared as "fiend is" in the *Monthly Magazine.* Lewis substituted "infernal."

<272>

"Go out, go out, my lamp of life,
    In endless darkness die:
Without him I must loathe the earth,
    Without him scorn the skye." —

And so despaire did rave and rage
    Athwarte her boiling veins;
Against the providence of God
    She hurdle her impious strains.

She beat her breaste, and wrung her hands,
    And rollde her tearless eye,
From rise of morne, till the pale stars
    Again did freeke⁷ the skye.

When harke! abroade she hearde the trampe
    Of nimble-hoofed steed;
She hearde a knighte with clank alighte,
    And climb the staire in speede.

And soon she herde a tinkling hande,
    That twirled at the pin;
And through her door, that opened not,
    These words were breathed in.

— "What! what ho! thy dore undoe;
    Art watching or asleepe?
My love, dost yet remember mee,
    And dost thou laugh, or weep?" —

— "Ah! William here so late at night!
    Oh! I have watchte and waked,
Whence dost thou come? for thy return
    My herte has sorely aked." —

---

⁷ *Freeke.* Freak, to fleck or streak randomly. A word invented by Milton.

<273>

— "At midnight only we may ride;
  I come o'er land and sea;
I mounted late, but soone I go,
  Aryse, and come with me." —

— "O William, enter first my bowre,
  And give me one embrace:
The blasts athwarte the hawthorne hiss;
  Awayte a little space." —

— "Though blasts athwarte the hawthorne hiss,
  I may not harbour here;
My spurre is sharpe, my courser pawes,
  My houre of flighte is nere.

"All as thou lyest upon thy couch,
  Aryse, and mount behinde;
To-night we'll ride a thousand miles,
  The bridal bed to finde." —

— "How, ride to-night a thousand miles?
  Thy love thou dost bemocke:
Eleven is the stroke that still
  Rings on within the clocke." —

— "Looke up, the moone is bright and we
  Outstride the earthlie men:
I'll take thee to the bridal bed,
  And night shall end but then." —

— "And where is, then, thy house and home,
  And where thy bridal bed?" —
"'Tis narrow, silent, chilly, dark;
  Far hence I rest my head." —

<274>

— "And is there any room for mee,
    Wherein that I may creepe?" —
— "There's room enough for thee and mee,
    Wherein that we may sleepe.[8]

"All as thou lyest upon thy couch,
    Aryse, no longer stop;
The wedding guests thy coming waite,
    The chamber door is ope." —

All in her sarke,[9] as there she lay,
    Upon his horse she sprung,
And with her lily hands so pale
    About her William clung.

And hurry-skurry forth they goe,
    Unheeding wet or drye;
And horse and rider snort and blow,
    And sparkling pebbles flye.

How swift the flood, the mead, the wood,
    Aright, aleft, are gone;
The bridges thunder as they pass,
    But earthlie sowne is none.

Tramp, tramp, across the land they speed,
    Splash, splash, across the sea:
— "Hurrah! the dead can ride apace;[10]
    Dost feare to ride with mee?"

---

[8] This stanza, and the stanza preceding, reveal Bürger's source: the English
ballad "Sweet William's Ghost." The German poet had read Percy's *Reliques* and
other English ballad collections, and routinely relocated his adaptations of
English poems to Continental settings.
[9] *Sarke*. Shift or night-gown.
[10] This line is better known as "The dead travel fast." The passages from this line
forward, with their rapid pace, repetition, and archaizing, are likely to have been
a direct inspiration to Coleridge for his "Rime of the Ancient Mariner."

<275>

"The moon is brighte, and blue the nyghte,
   Dost quake the blast to stem?
Dost shudder, mayde, to seeke the dead?" —
   — "No, no, but what of them?

"How glumlie sownes yon dirgye song,
   Night-ravens flappe the wing;
What knell doth slowlie toll ding-dong?
   The psalmes of death who sing?

"It creeps, the swarthie funeral traine,
   The corse is on the biere;
Like croke of todes from lonely moores,
   The chaunt doth meet the eere." —

<276>

Gottfried August Bürger (1747-1794). His fame in the supernatural genre
rested on "Lenore" and "Der Wild Jäger," but he is also credited with
creating the entire genre of the Romantic German ballad which would
enrich not only poetry but also art song. He also translated, from the
English original, the fantastic adventures of Baron Münchhausen. He had
an unpaid University position at Göttingen, suffered from disastrous
marriages, and died in poverty. He did not live long enough to see the
extent of the world-wide fame of "Lenore," which inspired dozens of
printed editions, many of them illustrated almost stanza by stanza.
"Lenore" was also adapted into a melodrama for recitation and piano by
Franz Liszt and into a full-length symphony by Joachim Raff. Above: the
Bürger memorial sculpture in Göttingen.

<277>

— "Go, bear her corse when midnight's past,
　　With song, and tear, and wayle;
I've gott my wife, I take her home,
　　My howre of wedlocke hayl.

"Lead forth, O clarke, the chaunting quire,
　　To swell our nuptial song;
Come, prieste, and read the blessing soone,
　　For bed, for bed we long." —

They heede his calle, and hushte the sowne,
　　The biere was seen no more;
And followde him o'er[11] feeld and flood
　　Yet faster than before.

Halloo! halloo! away they goe,
　　Unheeding wet or drye;
And horse and rider snort and blowe,
　　And sparkling pebbles flye.

How swifte the hill, how swifte the dale,
　　Aright, aleft, are gone;
By hedge and tree, by thorpe[12] and towne,
　　They gallop, gallop on.

Tramp, tramp, across the land they speede,
　　Splash, splash, across the sea;
— "Hurrah! the dead can ride apace;
　　Dost fear to ride with me?

"Look up, look up, an airy crewe
　　In roundel daunces reele;
The moone is bryghte, and blue the nyghte,
　　May'st dimlie see them wheele.

---

[11] *O'er.* Taylor writes this as "ore," a confusing archaism which I have modernized.
[12] *Thorpe.* Thorp, a village, hamlet or homestead.

"Come to, come to, ye ghostlie crew,
    Come to, and follow me,
And daunce for us the wedding daunce,
    When we in bed shall be." —

And brush, brush, brush, the ghostlie crew
    Come wheeling o'er their heads,
All rustling like the withered leaves
    That wyde the whirlwind spreads.

Halloo! halloo! away they goe,
    Unheeding wet or drye,
And horse and rider snorte and blowe,
    And sparkling pebbles flye.

And all that in the moonshyne lay,
    Behynde them fled afar;
And backward scudded overhead,
    The skye and every star.

Tramp, tramp, across the land they speede,
    Splash, splash, across the sea:
— "Hurrah! the dead can ride apace;
    Dost fear to ride with me?

"I weene the cock prepares to crowe,
    The sand will soone be runne;
I snuff the earlye morning aire,
    Downe, downe! our work is done.

"The dead, the dead can ryde apace,
    Oure wed bed here is fit;
Oure race is ridde, oure journey oer,
    Our endless union knit." —

<279>

And lo! an yren-grated grate
    Soon biggens to their viewe;
He cracked his whype, the clangynge boltes,
    The doores asunder flewe.

They pass, and 'twas on grave they trode,
    "'Tis hither we are bounde;"
And many a tombstone ghostlie white,
    Lay in the moonshyne round.

And when he from his steede alytte,
    His armour, green with rust,
Which damps of charnel vaults had bred,
    Straight fell away to dust.[13]

His head became a naked skull,
    Nor haire nor eyne had hee;
His body grew a skeleton,
    Whilome so blythe of blee.[14]

And at his dry and boney heele
    No spur was left to be;
And in his witherde hand you might
    The scythe and hour-glass see.

And lo! his steede did thin to smoke,
    And charnel fires outbreathe;
And paled, and bleached, then vanished quite,
    The mayde from underneathe.

And hollow howlings hung in aire,
    And shrieks from vaults arose;
Then knew the mayde she might no more
    Her living eyes unclose.

---

[13] Lewis altered Taylor's original in this stanza, which reads: "His armour, black as cinder/ Did moulder, moulder all awaye,/ As were it made of tinder."
[14] *Whilome so blythe of blee.* Roughly, "that had once been so wholesome in appearance."

<280>

But onwarde to the judgment seat,
    Through myste and moonlight dreare:
The ghostlie crewe, their flyghte persewe,
    And hollowe inn her eare:

— "Be patient, though thyne herte should breke,
    Arrayne not heaven's decree;
Thou nowe art of thie bodie refte,
    Thie soule forgiven bee!" —

<281>

Bibliography

Allen, John Barrow. *Parnell's Hermit, with Life, Explanatory Notes, Hints for Analysis of Sentences, etc.* 1874. London: Longmans, Green, and Co.

Alliborne, S. Austin. *A Critical Dictionary of English Literature and British and American Authors.* 1858. Philadelphia: J.B. Lippincott.

Anon. *The Anglo-Saxon Chronicle.*

Anon. *A Collection of Old Ballads* [Corrected from the best and most Ancient Copies Extant. With Introductions, Historical, Critical or Humorous]. 1723. London: J. Roberts. [Authorship attrib. to Ambrose Philips (1674-1749).]

Anon. *A Collection of Old Ballads* [Corrected from the best and most Ancient Copies Extant. With Introductions, Historical, Critical or Humorous]. Vol II. 1723. London: J. Roberts. [Authorship attrib. to Ambrose Philips (1674-1749).]

Anon. *A Collection of Old Ballads* [Corrected from the best and most Ancient Copies Extant. With Introductions, Historical, Critical or Humorous]. Vol III. 1725. London: J. Roberts. [Authorship attrib. to Ambrose Phlilips (1674-1749).]

Anon. *Poems of the Elder Edda.* Patricia Terry, trans. (1969) 1990. Philadelphia: University of Pennsylvania Press. [Includes a fine modern translation of "The Waking of Angantyr."]

Axon, William E.A. *The Literary History of Parnell's 'Hermit'.* 1881. London: Taylor and Francis.

Baring-Gould, Sabine. *Curious Myths of the Middle Ages.* Vol 2. 1868. London: Rivingtons. [Discusses "Porsenna, King of Russia" and also has an entire chapter on the legends of Bishop Hatto.]

Barnouw, A.J. *The Making of Modern Holland: A Short History.* 1944. W.W.. Norton & Company.

Bartholin, Thomas [the Younger]. *Antiqvitatum danicarum de causis contemptae a danis adhuc gentilibus mortis libri tres.* (Danish Antiquities on the Causes of the Contempt of Death Felt by The Danish Peoples, in Three Books). 1689. Copenhagen. [With texts in Icelandic and Latin, one source of "King Hakon's Death Song." The original of "The Fatal Sisters," in Icelandic and Latin are on pp. 617-19.]

Brewer, Ebenezer Cobham. *Dictionary of Phrase and Fable.* (1870). Revised by Ivor H. Evans. 1970. London: Cassell & Co.

Brullaughan, Domonick. *Opusculum de Purgatorio Sancti Patritii, Hybernae Patroni. (A Little Work on the Purgatory of St. Patrick, Patron*

<282>

Saint of Ireland) 1735. Louvain: F. Vande Velde. (British Museum, Grenville 4340).

de Bry, Johannes Theodorus. *Florilegium Renovatum et Auctum*. 1641: Frankfurt-am-Main. (Source for illustration of the mandrake root, *Mandragora faemina*.)

Burns, Robert. *The Letters of Robert Burns*. J Logie Robertson, ed. 1887. London: Walter Scott.

————. *Poems, Chiefly in the Scottish Dialect*. Vol. II. 1800. London: Cadell & Davies. [See pp. 195-208 for "Tam O'Shanter."]

Chambers, Robert, ed. *A Biographical Dictionary of Eminent Scotsmen*. Vol III. 1855. Glasgow: Blackie & Son.

Child, Francis James, ed. *The English and Scottish Popular Ballads*. Part I. 1882. Boston: Houghton, Mifflin & Co.

————. *The English and Scottish Popular Ballads*. Part IV. 1886. Boston: Houghton, Mifflin & Co.

————. *The English and Scottish Popular Ballads*. Part V. 1888. Boston: Houghton, Mifflin & Co.

————. *The English and Scottish Popular Ballads*. Part VIII. 1892. Boston: Houghton, Mifflin & Co.

————. *The English and Scottish Popular Ballads*. Part X. 1898. Boston: Houghton, Mifflin & Co.

Collison-Morley, Lacy. *Greek and Roman Ghost Stories*. 1912. Oxford: B.H. Blackwell.

Colman, George, the Younger. *My Night-Gown and Slippers; Tales in Verse*. 1797. London: "Printed for T. Cadell, Jun. and W. Davies."

Costello, Dudley. *A Tour Through the Valley of the Meuse: With the Legends of the Walloon Country and the Ardennes*. Second edition. 1846. London: Chapman and Hall.

Courtney, W.P. "Thomas Lisle." *Notes and Queries*. 10th Series: Nov. 21 1908, 403-04. [Biographical information about Thomas Lisle].

Dasent, George Webbe. *The Story of Burnt Njal, or Life in Iceland at the End of the Tenth Century, From the Icelandic of the Njals Saga*. Volume 2. 1861. Edinburgh: Edmonston and Douglas. [Victorian translation including the poem and framing narrative of "The Fatal Sisters."]

Davenport, R.A. *A Dictionary of Biography*. 1831. London: Thomas Tegg.

Davenport, R.A. "Life of Mickle," in *The British Poets. LXVI: Mickle and Smollett*. 1822. Chiswick: C. Whittingham.

DeLattre, Floris. *English Fairy Poetry: From the Origins to the Seventeenth Century*. 1912. London: Henry Frowde.

Dickinson, A.E.F. "Berlioz's 'Bleeding Nun'." *The Musical Times*. 107:1481 (Jul 1966) pp. 584-588.

<283>

Dodsley, J., ed. *A Collection of Poems in Six Volumes by Several Hands*. Vol 6. 1770. London: Printed for J. Dodsley. [Includes Lisle's "Porsenna, King of Russia" and lines by Pope about Lisle's grotto.]

Dryden, John. *The Sixth Part of Miscellany Poems*. 1716. London: "Printed for Jacob Tonson at Shakespear's Head." [Includes a translation of "The Incantation of Hervor," untitled, with a Latin introductory paragraph, on pp. 387-91. The translator is unattributed, although the poem is in the midst of a group of poems by Richard Corbet, (1582-1635). It seems to have been a random editorial insertion among Corbet's poems. Andrew Wawn states that this is a reprint of Hickes' translation of 1703-05.]

————. *The Works of John Dryden, In Verse and Prose*. Vol. I. 1837. New York: Harper & Brothers.

Edwards, George Wharton. *The Forest of Arden With Some of Its Legends*. 1914 New York: Frederick A. Stokes Company.

Emerson, Oliver Farrar. "The Earliest English Translations of Bürger's Lenore: A Study in English and German Romanticism." *Western Reserve University Bulletins*. xviii:3 May 1915. [Traces the complicated history of the seven different translations of "Lenora" published in 1796.]

Evans, Thomas. *Old Ballads, Historical and Narrative, With Some of Modern Date*. Second edition. 1784. London: T. Evans.

Evans, Thomas, and R.H. Evans. *Old Ballads, Historical and Narrative, With Some of Modern Date*. [A New Edition, Revised and Considerably Enlarged from Public and Private Collections, By His Son]. 1810. London: R.H. Evans

Farley, Frank Edgar. *Scandinavian Influences in the English Romantic Movement*. Studies and Notes in Philology and Literature IX. 1903. Boston: Ginn & Company.

————. "Three 'Lapland Songs'" *PMLA*. 21:1 (1906) 1-39.

Fiske, Christabel Forsythe. *The Tales of Terror*. 1899. Washington, D.C.: The Neale Company.

Fowler, David C. *A Literary History of the Popular Ballad*. 1968. Durham, NC: Duke University Press.

Garlington, Aubrey S. " 'Gothic' Literature and Dramatic Music in England 1781-1802." *Journal of the American Musicological Society*. 15:1 (Spring 1962) 48-64.

Garnett, R. *The Age of Dryden*. 1895. London: George Bell and Sons.

Geyl, P. *The Revolt of the Netherlands (1555-1609)*. 1932. London: Williams & Norgate Ltd.

Gilfillan, George, ed. The *Poetical Works of Johnson, Parnell, Gray, and Smollet, With Memoirs, Critical Dissertations, and Explanatory Notes*. 1855. Edinburgh: James Nichol.

<284>

von Goethe, Johann Wolfgang. *The Poems of Goethe: Translated in the Original Metres*. Edgar Alfred Bowring, trans. 1853. London: J.W. Parker.

———. *The Poems of Goethe*. F.H. Hedge and Leopold Noa, eds. 1882. Boston: S.E. Cassino. [Translation of Goethe by 12 translators, including Bowring, Carlyle, and Longfellow].

Goldsmith, Oliver. The *Miscellaneous Works of Oliver Goldsmith*. Volume 1. James Prior, ed. 1837. London: John Murray. [Includes the essay, "Beauties of English Poetry," commenting on Parnell's poetry.]

Gordon, Alexander. "Taylor, William (1765-1836)." *Dictionary of National Biography*. (1885-1900) Vol. 55. Available online at en.wikisource.org/wiki/Taylor,_William_(1765-1836)_(DNB00)

Le Grand d'Aussy, Pierre Jean Baptiste. *Fabliaux or Tales, Abridged from French Manuscripts of the XIIth and XIIIth Centuries*. G.L. Way, trans. 3 vols. 1815. London: J. Rodwell.

Gray, Thomas. *The Poetical Works of Thomas Gray, With the Life of the Author*. 1782. Edinburgh: "At the Apollo Press." "The Fatal Sisters," pp. 64-8. "The Descent of Odin," pp. 68-72.

———. *The Poetical Works of Thomas Gray*. 1799. London: "Printed for J. Scratcherd." [Includes a literal translation of the original of "The Descent of Odin," showing Gray's omission of the first five stanzas.]

Grose, Francis. *The Antiquities of Scotland: The First Volume*. 1797. London: Hooper & Wigstead. [First printing of Burns' "Tam O'Shanter."]

Gruntvig, Svend. *Danmarks Gamle Folkviser*. (1853).

Guthke, Karl S. "Some Unidentified Early English Translations from Herder's *Volkslieder*." *Modern Language Notes*, 73:1 (Jan 1958) 52-56.

Haller, William. *The Early Life of Robert Southey: 1774-1803*. 1917. New York: Columbia University Press.

Hartman, Geoffrey H. "Wordsworth and Goethe in Literary History." *New Literary History*. 6:2 (Winter 1975) 393-413.

Harvey, Wallace. *Chronicles of Saint Mungo, or, Antiquities and Traditions of Glasgow*. 1843. Glasgow: John Smith & Son.

Herd, David. *The Ancient and Modern Scots Songs, Heroic Ballads, &c.* 1769. Edinburgh: Martin & Wotherspoon. [Expanded to two volumes in 1776. Source for "Clerk Colvill" and "Fair Margaret and Sweet Willliam." Volume II of the 1776 edition includes "Mary's Dream."]

von Herder, Johann Gottfried. *Volkslieder*. (1778-79) 1840. Leipzig: Genhart & Reisland.

———. *Volkslieder*. Part II. (1779) 1911. Munich: Georg Müller.

<285>

Heywood, Thomas. *Gynaikeion, or Nine Books of Various History Concerning Women*. 1624. London: Adam Islip.

Heywood, Thomas. *Hierarchies of the Blessed Angels*. 1635. London: Adam Islip.

Hickes, George. *Linguarum Veterum Septentrionalium Thesaurus Grammatico-Criticus et Archaeologicus*. 1703-1705. Oxford. [6 parts, in 2 vols. I have not seen this volume, and happily cite Andrew Wawn's summary of its contents: "details of saga manuscripts, summaries of saga stories, a supplemented version of Runólfur Jónsson's 1651 Grammar, runic transcriptions and interpretations, and numismatic information." (*Vikings*, 19) "The Incantation of Hervor" appears here in Icelandic and in an English translation, "the first ever published in Britain of a complete Old Icelandic poem" (Wawn, *ibid*, 21)]

Hutchinson, William. *A View of Northumberland, with an Excursion to The Abbey of Mailross in Scotland*. Vol. II. (1776) 1778. Newcastle: Vesey & Whitfield. [First publication of Robert Lambe's "The Laidley Worm of Spindelston Heughs."]

Irwin, Joseph James. *M.G. "Monk" Lewis*. 1976. Boston: Twayne Publishers.

Israel, Jonathan. *The Dutch Republic: Its Rise, Greatness and Fall 1477-1806*. 1995. Oxford: Clarendon Press.

Johnson, James. *The Scottish Musical Museum; Consisting of Upwards of Six Hundred Songs*. Volume V. (1793) 1839. Edinburgh: Wiliam Blackwood & Sons. [Probable source for the version of "Tam Lin" adapted by Lewis.]

Jones, Henry. *Saint Patricks Purgatory, Containing the Description, Originall, Progresse and Demolition of That Superstitious Place*. 1647. London. [Now attributed to Bishop James Spottiswoode.]

Kahlert, Karl Friedrich, and Peter Teuthold. *The Necromancer: Or, The Tale of the Black Forest, Founded on Facts. Translated from the German of Lawrence Flammenberg* (pseud.). 1794. London: Printed for William Lane at the Minerva Press.

Lewes, G.H. *The Life and Works of Goethe: With Sketches of His Age and Contemporaries*. Vol 1. 1856. Boston: Ticknor and Fields.

Lewis, Matthew Gregory. "Giles Jollup the Grave, and Brown Sally Green." *The Spirit of the Public Journals for 1798*. 1:321. 1799 London: James Ridgway.

———. *The Isle of Devils: A Historical Tale, Funnded* [sic] *on an Anecdote in the Annals of Portugal*. 1827. Kingston, Jamaica.

———. *The Monk*. Louis F. Peck, ed. (1796) 1952. New York: Grove Press. [Original text restored, with variant readings.]

<286>

————. *Raymond and Agnes; or, The Bleeding Nun.* The Romancist and Novelist's Library. 1841. London: J. Clements.

————. *Tales of Terror and Wonder.* Henry Morley, ed. 1887. New York: G. Routledge & Sons. [includes the spurious *Tales of Terror.*]

————. *Tales of Wonder.* 1801. London: J. Bell

————. *Tales of Wonder.* 1805. Dublin: P. Wogan.

————. *Tales of Wonder.* 1805. Vienna: R. Sammer. [A three-volume edition with many additional poems, including more selections from Percy's *Reliques.* The edition is badly typeset and has a fragment of "Porsenna, King of Russia" in the middle of another poem in Volume III. It is doubtful that Lewis had anything to do with this production.]

————. *Tales of Wonder.* Douglass H, Thomson, ed. 2010. Ontario: Broadview Editions. [A must-read for Lewis scholars. Includes poems I-XXXII, and LVI to LX of *Tales of Wonder,* seven poems from *Tales of Terror,* and extensive notes and excerpts on the critical reception of Lewis's work. Provocative discussion of Lewis, his sources, the confusing print history of *Tales of Wonder,* and the critical issues surrounding parody in these texts.]

Leyden, John. *The Poetical Remains of the Late Dr. John Leyden.* 1819 London: Longman, Hurst, Rees, Orme and Brown.

————. *Scotish* (sic) *Descriptive Poems; with some Illustrations of Scotish* (sic) *Literary Antiquities.* 1803. Edinburgh: Mundell & Son.

Lindsay, Lady. *The Apostle of the Ardennes.* 1899. London: Kegan, Paul, Trench, Trübner & Co., Ltd.

Lockhart, John Gibson. *The Life of Sir Walter Scott.* Vol II. (1837) Abbotsford Edition (Edinburgh Univ. Press). n.d. Boston: Dana Estes & Co. [Details on Scott's correspondence and meetings with Lewis in 1798-99.]

Lynch, Bohun. *A History of Caricature.* 1926. London: Faber and Gwyer.

MacDonald, D.L. *Monk Lewis: A Critical Biography.* 2000. Toronto: Univ. of Toronto Press.

MacQuoid, Katherine S. *In the Ardennes.* 1881. London: Chatto & Windus, Picadilly.

Magnus, Olaus. *Historia de Gentibus Septentrionalibus.* 1555. Rome. [One source for the story of the "Old Woman of Berkeley," including an illustration of her carried off on horseback by the Devil.]

Mallet, David. *Ballads and Songs.* With notes and a Memoir of the Author by Frederick Dinsdale. 1857. London: Bell and Daldy.

Mallet, Paul-Henri. *Introduction à l'Histoire de Dannemarc.* 1755. Copenhagen. [Translated into English in 1770 by Thomas Percy, with many added notes, as *Northern Antiquities.*]

<287>

Malory, Sir Thomas. *Le Morte d'Arthur, or The Hole Book of Kynge Arthur and of His Noble Knyghtes of The Rounde Table*. Stephen A. Shepherd, ed. 2004 New York: W.W. Norton.

Marie de France. *L'Espurgatoire Seint Patriz: An Old French Poem of the Twelfth Century*. Thomas Atkinson Jenkins, ed. 1894. Philadelphia: Press of Alfred J. Ferris. [Complete text of Marie de France's poetic setting of "St. Patrick's Purgatory."]

————. *Saint Patrick's Purgatory*. Michael J. Curley, trans. and ed. 1993. Binghamton: Medieval & Renaissance Texts and Studies Vol. 94. [Side-by-side edition of "Saint Patrick's Purgatory in French and English.]

Mason, Tom. "Dryden's The Cock and the Fox and Chaucer's Nun's Priest's Tale." *Translation and Literature*. 16: Part 1, Spring 2007. pp 1-28.

Mickel, Emanuel J., Jr. *Marie de France*. Twayne's World Authors Series 306: France. 1974. New York: Twayne Publishers Inc.

Mickle, William Julius. *The British Poets*. Vol LXVI: Mickle and Smollett. 1822. Chiswick, C. Whittingham.

Monmouth, Geoffrey. *Historia Regum Britanniae*. (1136).

Nelson, Louise. "The Bokkerijders." Canadian Journal of Netherlandic Studies. 5:2 (1984). [History of the "Goat-Riders."]

Ober, Kenneth H. "Žukovskij's Early Translations of the Ballads of Robert Southey." *The Slavic and East European Journal* 9:2 (Summer 1965) 181-190.

Parnell, Thomas. *Poems on Several Occasions*. Alexander Pope, ed. [Includes "The Life of Dr. Parnell" by Oliver Goldmsith]. 1770. London: T. Davies.

————. *The Poetical Works of Thomas Parnell*. Aldine Edition. [With 1832 "Life of Parnell by John Mitford."] London: Bell and Daldy.

Pausanius. *Description of Greece*. W.H.S. Jones, trans. Vol IV. 1965. Cambridge: Harvard University Press.

Peck, Louis F. *A Life of Matthew Gregory Lewis*. 1961. Cambridge: Harvard University Press.

————. "Southey and Tales of Wonder." *Modern Language Notes*. December 1935. [Asserts that Southey may not have consented to his poems' inclusion in *Tales of Wonder*. Southey's eight poems from the first edition were dropped in the second edition of 1801. Southey's poems do appear in the subsequent 1805 Dublin edition; they are omitted from the 1887 *Tales of Terror* by Morley. Peck appears to mistake Scott's Kelso printing of *An Apology for Tales of Terror* for Lewis's first edition.]

<288>

Percy, Thomas. *Reliques of Ancient English Poetry: Consisting of Old Heroic Ballads, Songs, and Other Pieces of Our Early Poets.* Vol I. Fourth Edition. 1794. London: F. & C. Rivington.

—————. *Reliques of Ancient English Poetry: Consisting of Old Heroic Ballads, Songs, and Other Pieces of Our Early Poets.* Vol III. Third Edition. 1775. London: J. Dodsley.

—————. *Five Pieces of Runic Poetry Translated from the Icelandic Language.* 1763. London: R. & J. Dodsley. [Based upon Verelius and Hickes.]

—————. *Northern Antiquities: Or A Description of the Manners, Customs, Religion and Laws of the Ancient Danes.* [Translated from Paul-Henri Mallet's *l'Introduction a l'Histoire de Dannemarc*, etc.] (1770). 1809. Edinburgh: C. Stewart. [This influential volume was reprinted and expanded in 1847 by I.A. Blackwell, and was reprinted numerous times up to the turn of the 20th century.]

Pinkerton, William. "Saint Patrick's Purgatory. Part IV. Modern History." *Ulster Journal of Archaeology.* First series, Vol. 5 (1857), pp. 61-81. [Includes descriptions of St. Patrick's Purgatory, and the Bishop of Clogher's detailed depiction of its destruction in 1632.]

Railo, Eino. *The Haunted Castle: A Study of the Elements of English Romanticism.* 1927. London: George Routledge & Sons Ltd.

Ramsay, Allan. *The Tea-Table Miscellany: A Collection of Choice Songs, Scots and English.* (1732-37) 13th Edition. 1762. Edinburgh: A. Donaldson.

Riely, John C. "Horace Walpole and 'The Second Hogarth'." *Eighteenth-Century Studies* 9:1 (Autumn 1975) 28-44. [Concerning the life and career of Henry Bunbury.]

Robertson, John G. *A History of German Literature.* 1902. New York: G. P. Putnam's Sons.

Roger of Wendover. *Flowers of History, Comprising the History of England From the Descent of the Saxons to A.D. 1235.* [Formerly attributed to Matthew Paris, a.k.a, Matthew of Westminster.] J.A. Giles, trans. (1567) 1849. London: Henry G. Bohn.

Ross, Margaret Clunies. *The Cambridge Introduction to The Old Norse-Icelandic Saga.* 2010. Cambridge: Cambridge Univ. Press. [A definitive overview of Norse-Icelandic sagas, including a fine chapter on the reception of sagas in the 17th to 19th centuries.]

—————. *The Old Norse Poetic Translations of Thomas Percy.* Series: Making the Middle Ages, Volume 4, Center for Medieval Studies, Univ. Of Sydney, Australia. 2001. Turnhout, Belgium: Brepols Publishers.

<289>

Scheffer, Johannes Gerhard. *The History of Lapland*. 1674 Oxford: "At the Theatre." [Also, a second, expanded English edition in 1704, with Addenda.]

————. *Lapponia, id est, Regionibus Lapponum et Gentis Nova et Verissima Descriptio*. 1673. Frankfurt. [Original Latin version of *The History of Lapland*, with wood engravings illustrating Lapland customs, pagan religious practices and witchcraft.]

Scott, Sir Walter. *An Apology for Tales of Terror*. 1799. Kelso: "Printed at the Mail Office." Online version by Douglass H. Thomson at www.walterscott.lib.ed.ac.uk/works/poetry/apology/home.html

————. "Copy of An Original Letter by the Late Sir Walter Scott, Bart." *The Lady's Magazine and Museum*. Jan 1837:490. [A letter from Scott to Lewis concerning "Willy's Lady" and several other Scottish Ballads.]

————. "Essay on Imitations of the Ancient Ballad," in *The Complete Works of Sir Walter Scott*. Vol 1. 1833: New York: Cooner & Cooke. [Account of Scott's collaboration with Lewis, and of the publisher of *Tales of Wonder*, pp. 188-89].

————. "Evans's Old Ballads," in *The Miscellaneous Works of Sir Walter Scott*, Vol XVII. 1861 Edinburgh: Adam and Charles Black. 119-136.

————. *Minstrelsy of the Scottish Border*. (1802, 3 vols). One-volume edition. 1869. London: Alex Murray & Son. [First publication of the original version of "Willy's Lady," along with a note about Lewis's version of that ballad for *Tales of Wonder*, pp. 369-72.]

————. *The Pirate*. (Waverly Novels, Volume 23). (1821) 1831. Boston: Samuel H. Parker. [Notes in Volume 1 concerning the oral transmission of the original of "The Fatal Sisters" from the *Saga of Burnt Njal*.]

Scribe, Eugene and Germaine Delavigne. *La Nonne Saglante*. Opera libretto, 1854. Anne Williams, trans. Available online at www.rc.umd.edu/praxis/opera/williams/williams_translation.pdf

Service, James. *Metrical Legends of Northumberland: Containing the Traditions of Dunstanborough Castle, and Other Poetical Romances*. 1834. Alnwick: W. Davison. [Includes notes attempting to connect Lambe's "Laidley Worm of Spindleston Heughs" to historical events and to the struggle between Christianity and paganism in Northumberland.]

Shane, Leslie. *Saint Patrick's Purgatory: A Record from History and Literature*. 1932. London: Burns Oates & Washbourne Ltd. [A compilation of documents about Logh Derg, discussion over the controversy of the "original" cave, and details on the reception and transmisson of the text, including its use by Dante.]

<290>

Skilling, John H. "Auld Nick's View of Alloway." [A detailed traveler's guide to the locales of Burns' "Tam O'Shanter."] Accessed from www.allowaychurch.org/htnl/ourparish.html

Southey, Robert. *Metrical Tales and Other Poems.* 1805. London: Longman, Hurst, Rees, and Orme. [Includes poems that had appeared in *Tales of Wonder.*]

————. *The Poetical Works of Robert Southey.* New Edition. 1845. London: Longman, Brown, Green, and Longmans. [Includes the "Ballads and Metrical Tales" and the preface describing the discovery of the Latin text for "The Old Woman of Berkeley."]

Spooner, Shearjashub. *Anecdotes of Painters, Engravers, Sculptors and Architects, and Curiosities of Art.* 3 vols. 1865. New York: J.W. Bouton.

Stempel, Guido H. *A Book of Ballads Old and New.* 1917. New York: Henry Holt & Co.

Stoupe, J.G.A., ed. *A Collection of Poems by Several Hands.* 1779. Paris: J.G.A. Stoupe. [Includes Lisle's "Porsenna, King of Russia" and Parnell's "The Hermit."]

Sturluson, Snorri. *Heimskringla, or The Lives of the Norse Kings.* Trans. by A.H. Smith, trans. Erling Monsen, ed. (1932) 1990. New York: Dover Books. [Includes the full text of "King Hakon's Death Song" The original edition of this book is *Snorre Sturlessøns Norske kongers chronica* (1633, Copenhagen)].

Torfaeus (Þormóður Torfason). *Ancient History of Orkney, Caithness, & The North.* Rev. Alexander Pope, trans. 1861. Wick: Peter Reid.

————. *Orcades, Seu Rerum Orcadensium Historiae.* 1697. Copenhagen. [One of Thomas Gray's sources for "The Fatal Sisters," in Icelandic and Latin, pp. 36-7.]

Turberville, George. *Epitaphes, Epigrams, Songs and Sonnets, with a Discourse of the Friendly Affections of Tymetes to Pyndara His Ladie.* (1567). c. 1908. London: Henry Denham.

Vedel, Anders Sörensen and Peder Syv. *Et Hundrede udvalde Danske Viser, forögede med det andet Hundrede.* 1695. Copenhagen. [This Danish collection of Icelandic poems contains ballads rather than epic sagas, and is based on Vedel's edition titled *It Hundrede vduaalde Danske Vise* (1591, Ribe).]

Verelius, Olaus. *Hervarar Saga ok Heiðreks Konungs.* (The Saga of Hervor and Heidrekr) 1672. Uppsala. [Swedish with Latin footnotes; the first printed text of this saga.]

Virgil. *Eclogues, Georgics,* [and] *Aeneid.* Vol 1. H. Rushton Fairclough, trans. 1965. Cambridge: Harvard University Press.

Wann, Andrew. "The Post-Medieval Reception of Old Norse and Old Icelandic Literature." in *A Companion to Old Norse-Icelandic Literature and Culture.* Rory McTurk, ed. 2005. Malden, MA:

<291>

Blackwell Publishing. pp. 320-337. [Detailed chronology of early
editions and translations of Norse poetry and sagas.]
————— *The Vikings and the Victorians: Inventing the Old North in
Nineteenth-Century Britain.* 2000. Cambridge: D.S. Brewer. [A
magisterial survey of the reception of Norse myth and literature,
including the publishing history of major source books (Hickes,
Percy et al), and the later adoption of Norse themes into poetry and
fiction. An indispensible and exhaustive study.]
Warrack, Alexander, comp. *The Scots Dialect Dictionary.* 1911. London:
W.R. Chambers.
William of Malmesbury. *Chronicle of the Kings of England.* (1127) John
Allen Giles, ed. (1847) 1904. London: George Bell & Sons [A
revision of the 1815 translation by John Sharpe. Alternate source
for the narrative of "The Old Woman of Berkeley."]
Willson, Anthony Beckles. "Alexander Pope's Garden in Twickenham."
Garden History. 26:1 (Summer 1998) 31-59.
Wimberly, Lowry C. *Folklore in the English and Scottish Ballads.* 1928.
New York: Frederick Ungar Publishing Co.
Wright, Herbert G. "Southey's Relations with Finland and
Scandinavia." *The Modern Language Review* 27:2 (April 1932) 149-
167.

<292>

About This Book

This book was completely reset from the original 1801 London edition using Aldine type, a face inspired by the designs of the great Venetian humanist printer and publisher, Aldus Manutius. Titles are set in Morris Troy, a typeface designed by William Morris for the Kelmscott Press.

British and archaic spellings, as found in the 1801 *Tales of Wonder*, have been retained for the most part. Repetitive quotation marks within stanzas have been eliminated for esthetic reasons, instead relying on opening and closing quotes for passages. Long dashes, employed by some poets irregularly to separate dialogue, have been added judiciously to help the reader distinguish change of voice.

This book is also available in a PDF ebook edition.

<293>

CPSIA information can be obtained
at www.ICGtesting.com
Printed in the USA
FSOW03n1215120318
45606FS